SPARKNOTES™

5 Practice Tests for the SAT II Biology

2003 Edition

Editorial Director Justin Kestler

Executive Editor Ben Florman

Managing Editor Vince Janoski

Technical Director Tammy Hepps

Series Editor John Crowther

Editor Laurel Hartley

Contributing Editor Jen Chu

This edition published by Spark Publishing.

Spark Publishing
A Division of SparkNotes LLC
120 Fifth Avenue, 8th Floor
New York, NY 10011

Please submit all comments and questions or report errors to www.sparknotes.com/errors

Library of Congress information available upon request

Printed and bound in Canada

ISBN 1-58663-872-6

Welcome to SparkNotes Test Preparation

IF YOU WANT TO SCORE HIGH ON THE SAT II BIOLOGY, YOU NEED TO KNOW more than just the material—you need to know how to take the test. Practice tests are the most effective method for learning the ins and outs of the test. But practice tests that accurately reflect the actual SAT II Biology have been hard to find—until now. *5 More Practice Tests for the SAT II Biology* is the first book anywhere dedicated to giving you accurate practice tests so you can perfect your test-taking skills. This book contains:

- **Five full-length SAT II Biology tests.** The practice tests in this book are the most accurate, true-to-life tests available. Our experts, who've been teaching the SAT II Biology for years, researched the exam extensively so they could give you tests that reflect exactly what you'll see at the test center. Our tests replicate the format and content of the actual test so closely that nothing will catch you off guard on test day.

- **Clear, helpful explanations for every question—so you can study smarter.** Our explanations do more than tell you the right answer—they identify flaws in your thinking and show you exactly what topics you need to work on. We help you pinpoint your weaknesses, so you can make your studying more efficient by going straight to the stuff you need to review.

- **Specific, proven strategies for the SAT II Biology.** We give you smart, easy strategies on the best ways to guess, pace yourself, and find shortcuts to answers. These strategies help you maximize your score by showing you how to avoid the test's traps and turn the test's format to your own advantage.

Contents

Orientation

Practice Tests

Orientation

Introduction to the SAT II Tests

THE SAT II SUBJECT TESTS are created and administered by the College Board and the Educational Testing Service (ETS), the two organizations responsible for the dreaded SAT I, which most people just call the SAT. The SAT II Subject Tests were created to act as complements to the SAT I. Whereas the SAT I is a three-hour test that assesses your critical-thinking skills by asking math and verbal questions, the SAT II Subject Tests are hour-long affairs that test specific subjects covered in standard American high school classes. There are SAT II Subject Tests on writing, literature, history, math, science, and a host of languages from Korean to Hebrew.

In our opinion, the SAT II Subject Tests are better tests than the SAT I because they cover clearly-defined topics rather than an ambiguous set of critical thinking skills. However, just because the SAT II Subject Tests do a better job of testing your actual knowledge doesn't mean that the tests are necessarily easier or that they demand less study. A "better" test isn't necessarily "better for you" in terms of how easy it will be. But a "better" test will probably reflect your knowledge of that subject better than your SAT I verbal result will reflect your reading abilities.

In comparison to taking the SAT I, there are good things and bad things about taking an SAT II Subject Test.

The Good

- Because SAT II Subject Tests cover actual topics like Biology, Chemistry, and U.S. History , you can very effectively study for them. If you don't know a topic in biology, such as the process of protein synthesis, you can look it up and learn it. The SAT II tests are straightforward tests: if you know your stuff, you will do well on them.

- Often, the classes you've taken in school have already prepared you well for the test. If you took a biology course in high school, then you probably covered most of the topics that are tested on the SAT II Biology test.

- In studying for the SAT II Biology, Chemistry, and U.S. History, you really are learning biology, chemistry, and U.S. history. In other words, you are learning valuable, interesting knowledge. If learning is something you enjoy, you might actually find the process of studying for an SAT II test worthwhile and gratifying. It's hard to say the same about studying for the SAT I.

The Bad

- Because SAT II subject tests quiz you on specific knowledge, "beating" or "outsmarting" an SAT II test is much harder than outsmarting the SAT I. For the SAT I, you can use all sorts of tricks or strategies to figure out an answer. There are far fewer strategies to help you on the SAT II. Don't get us wrong: having test-taking skills *will* help you on an SAT II, but knowing the subject will help you much, much more. In other words, to do well on the SAT II, you can't just rely on your quick thinking and intelligence. You need to study.

Colleges and the SAT II Subject Tests

Why would you take an SAT II Subject Test? Is it to prove to yourself how much you've learned in the year? That seems unlikely. Is it to prove to your teacher how much you've learned? No, you've got finals for that. Is it to win a new car? You wish. No, there's only one reason to take an SAT II Subject Test: colleges want you to, and sometimes they require you to.

Colleges care about SAT II Subject Tests for two related reasons:

1. Your performance on SAT II tests demonstrates your interest, knowledge, and skill in a broad range of topics.

2. Because SAT II tests are standardized, they show your abilities in these topics *in relation to the entire country.* The grades you get in high school don't offer such a measurement to colleges: some high schools are more difficult than others, meaning that students of equal ability might receive

different grades, even in biology classes that have basically the same curriculum. By contrast, SAT II tests provide colleges with a definite yardstick against which they can measure your, and every other applicant's, knowledge and skills.

When it comes down to it, colleges like the SAT II tests because the tests make the colleges' job easier. The tests are tools that allow the colleges to compare students easily.

But because you know how colleges use the SAT II, you can make the tests your tool as well. Since SAT II tests provide an objective standard by which colleges can judge all their applicants, the tests provide you with an ideal opportunity to shine. If you got a 93 in a biology course and some other kid got a 91, colleges won't necessarily know what to make of that difference. But if you get a 720 on the SAT II Biology and that other kid gets a 670, colleges will recognize the difference.

The Importance of SAT II Tests in College Applications

Time for some perspective: SAT II tests are *not* the primary tools that colleges use to decide whether to admit an applicant. High school grades, extracurricular activities, and SAT or ACT scores are all more important to colleges than your scores on SAT II tests. If you take AP tests, those scores will also be more important to colleges than your SAT II scores. But because SAT II tests provide colleges with such a nice and easy measurement tool, they are an important *part* of your application to college. Good SAT II scores can give your application the extra shove that pushes you from the maybe pile into the accepted pile.

College Placement

Occasionally, colleges use SAT II tests to determine placement. For example, if you do very well on the SAT II Biology, you might be exempted from a basic science class. Though colleges do not often use SAT II tests for placement purposes, it's worth finding out whether the colleges to which you are applying do.

Scoring the SAT II Subject Tests

There are three different names for your SAT II score. The "raw score" is a simple score of how you did on the test, like the grade you might receive on a normal test in school. The "percentile score" takes your raw score and compares it to the rest of the raw scores in the country for the same test. Percentile scores let you know how you did on the test in comparison to your peers. The "scaled score," which ranges from 200–800, compares your score to the scores received by all students who have ever taken that subject SAT II.

The Raw Score

You will never see your SAT II raw score because the raw score is not included in the SAT II score report. But you should understand how it is calculated, as this knowledge can affect your strategy on the test.

Your raw score on SAT II tests is based on a few simple rules:

- You earn 1 point for every correct answer

- You lose $1/4$ of a point for each incorrect answer

- You receive 0 points for each question left blank

Calculating the raw score is easy. Simply add up the number of questions answered correctly and the number of questions answered incorrectly. Then multiply the number of wrong answers by $1/4$, and subtract this value from the number of right answers.

$$\text{raw score} = \text{right answers} - (\frac{1}{4} \times \text{wrong answers})$$

In the chapter called "Strategies for the SAT II Biology," we'll discuss how the rules for calculating a raw score should influence your strategies for guessing and leaving questions blank.

The Percentile Score

Your percentile score describes your score in relation to the scores of everyone else who took the same test as you. Another way to think of the score is as a marker of what percentage of test-takers received a lower raw score than you did. For example, if Gregor Mendel took the SAT II Biology Test and got a score that placed him in the ninety-third percentile, that means he scored better on that particular test than did 92 percent of the other students who took the same test. It also means that 7 percent of the students taking that test got the same score or scored better than he did.

The Scaled Score

ETS takes the raw score and uses a formula to turn that raw score into the the scaled score, which ranges between 200 and 800. The scaled score is the one your parents will brag about and your curious classmates will want to know.

The curve to convert raw scores to scaled scores varies from test to test. For example, a raw score of 33 on the Math IC might scale to a 600, while the same 33 on the Math IIC might scale to a 700. In fact, the scaled score can even vary on different editions of the *same* test. A raw score of 33 on the February 2003 Biology test might scale to a 710, while a 33 in June of 2003 might scale to a 690. These differences in scaled scores reflect the differences in difficultly level of the test from edition to edition. The difference in the curve for various versions of the same test will not vary by more than 20 points or so.

Which SAT II Subject Tests to Take

There are three types of SAT II test: those you must take, those you should take, and those you shouldn't take. The SAT II tests you *must* take are those that are required by the colleges you are interested in. The SAT II tests you *should* take are tests that aren't required, but which you'll do well on, thereby impressing the colleges looking at your application. The SAT II tests you *shouldn't* take are those that aren't required and that cover subjects in which you don't feel confident.

Determining Which SAT II Tests are Required

To find out whether the colleges to which you are applying require that you take a particular SAT II test, you'll need to do a bit of research. Call the schools you're interested in, look at their web pages online, or talk to your guidance counselor. Often, colleges request that you take the following SAT II tests:

- The Writing SAT II test

- One of the two Math SAT II tests (either Math IC or Math IIC)

- Another SAT II in some other subject of your choice

The SAT II Biology is not usually required by colleges. But taking it and doing well can show a liberal arts college that you are well rounded, or a science-oriented college that you are serious about science. In general, it is a good idea to take one science-based SAT II, such as Biology, Chemistry, or Physics.

Determining Whether You Should Take an SAT II
Even if it isn't Required

There are two rules of thumb for deciding which additional test to take beyond the Writing and Math tests:

1. **Go with what you know.** If history is your field, a strong score on the American History test will impress admissions officers far more than a bold but mediocre effort on the Physics test.

2. **Try to show breadth.** Scoring well on similar subject tests such as Math, Biology, and Chemistry will not be as impressive as good scores in more diverse subjects, such as Math, Writing, World History, and Biology.

Of course, the bottom line is that you need to get a good score on the tests you do take. Before you decide to take a specific SAT II test, you should know two things:

1. What a good score on that SAT II test is

2. Whether you can get that score

Below, we have included a list of the most commonly taken SAT II tests and the average scaled score on each.

Test	Average Score
Writing	590–600
Literature	590–600
American History	580–590
World History	570–580
Math IC	580–590
Math IIC	655–665
Biology E/M	590–600
Chemistry	605–615
Physics	635–645

For most schools, a score that is 50 points above this average will provide a significant boost to your college application. If you are applying to an elite school, you may need to aim closer to 100 points above the average. A little research in this area can get you a long way: call the schools you're interested in or talk to a guidance counselor.

AP vs. SAT II

As we've said, it's a good idea to take three SAT II tests that cover a range of topics, such as one math SAT II, one humanities SAT II (history or writing), and one science SAT II. However, there's no real reason to take *more* than three SAT II tests. Once you've taken the SAT II tests you need to take, the best way to set yourself apart from other students is to take AP courses and tests.

AP tests are harder than the SAT II tests, and, as a result, they carry quite a bit more distinction. SAT II test give you the opportunity to show colleges that you can learn and do well when you need to. Taking AP tests shows colleges that you are a disciplined, sophisticated student who *wants* to learn as much as possible.

When to Take an SAT II Subject Test

The best time to take an SAT II subject test is right after you've finished a yearlong course in that subject. If, for example, you take biology in tenth grade, then you should take the SAT II Biology near the end of that year, when you've learned all the material and it's still fresh in your mind. (This rule does not apply for the Writing, Literature, and Foreign Language SAT II tests; it's best to take those after you've had as much study in the area as possible.)

Make sure to finish taking all your SAT II Subject Tests by the end of November of your senior year of high school. Unless the colleges to which you are applying use the SAT II for placement purposes, there is no point in taking SAT II tests after November of your senior year, since you won't get your scores back from ETS until after the college application deadline has passed.

ETS usually sets testing dates for SAT II subject tests in October, November, December, January, May, and June. However, not every subject test is administered in each of these months. To check when the test you want to take is being offered, visit the College Board website at www.collegeboard.com, or do some research in your school's guidance office.

Registering for SAT II Tests

To register for the SAT II tests of your choice, you have to fill out some forms and pay a registration fee. We know—it's ridiculous that *you* have to pay for a test that colleges require you to take in order to make *their* jobs easier, but, sadly, there isn't anything we, or you, can do about it. It is acceptable for you to grumble here about the unfairness of the world.

After grumbling, of course, you still have to register. There are two ways to register: online or by mail. To register online, go to www.collegeboard.com. To register by mail, fill out and send in the forms enclosed in the *Registration Bulletin*, which should be available in your high school's guidance office. You can also request a copy of the *Bulletin* by calling the College Board at (609) 771-7600, or writing to:

College Board SAT Program
P.O. Box 6200
Princeton, NJ 08541–6200

You can register to take up to three SAT II tests for any given testing day. Unfortunately, even if you decide to take three tests in one day, you'll still have to pay a separate registration fee for each.

Introduction to the SAT II Biology

THE BEST WAY TO DO WELL ON THE SAT II Biology is to be really good at biology. For that, there is no substitute. But the biology whiz who spends the week before taking the SAT II cramming on the nuances of mitochondrial DNA and the physiological role of the amygdala probably won't fare any better on the test than the average student who reviews this book carefully. Why? Because the SAT II Biology doesn't cover mitochondrial DNA or the amygdala.

This chapter will tell you precisely what the SAT II Biology *will* test you on, how the test breaks down, and what format the questions will take. Take this information to heart and base your study plan around it. There's no use spending hours studying topics you won't be tested on, or spending countless hours studying bacterial diversity while ignoring meiosis, which is covered far more extensively by the test.

The Strange Dual Nature of the SAT II Biology

The official name of the SAT II Biology test is not SAT II Biology. The test is actually called the SAT II Biology E/M. The test has this strange name because it's actually two tests built into one. One test, the Biology E test, emphasizes ecology and evolution. The other test, the Biology M test, emphasizes molecular biology and evolution. On test day, you will take either the Biology E or Biology M test. You can't take both.

The Biology E and Biology M tests aren't completely dissimilar. In fact, the two tests share a core of 60 questions. No matter which test you sign up to take, you will have to answer the 60 core questions. In addition to the core questions, the Biology E/M test contains 20 more questions, split equally between two specialty sections. If you decide to take the Biology E test, then you will only have to answer the ecology and evolution specialty section. If you decide to take Biology M, you need only answer the molecular biology and evolution section. In total, both the SAT II Biology E and Biology M contain 80 questions.

Content of the SAT II Biology

The SAT II Biology is written to test your understanding of the topics of biology taught in a standard American high school biology course, with particular emphasis on either ecology or molecular biology. ETS provides the following breakdown of the test covering five basic categories:

Topic	Number of Questions
Cellular and Molecular Biology	8–11
Ecology	8–11
Classical Genetics	7–9
Organismal Biology	22–26
Evolution and Diversity	7–10

As we said, depending on which specialty section you elect to take, you will also face 20 questions (25 percent of the total questions you will see) on either ecology/evolution or molecular biology/evolution.

The breakdown from ETS is a pretty accurate assessment of what appears on the test. But, frankly, some of its categories are so broad that it isn't all that helpful as a tool to help you focus your study. It may be that you have cell structure down pat, but biochemistry throws you for a loop, and you would like to get a sense of how much of the test is devoted to these two topics. To help you out, we've broken the core of the test down even further, so that you'll know exactly where to expect to feel the squeeze.

Topic	Number of Questions
Cellular and Molecular Biology	**8–12**
The Cell and Cell Structure	4–6
Biochemistry and Organic Chemistry	3–5
Cell Processes	1–3

Topic	Number of Questions
Mendelian and Molecular Genetics	**8–10**
Evolution and Diversity	**8–10**
Evolution	2–4
Diversity	4–6
Organismal Biology	**20–26**
Animal Structure, Function, and Behavior	9–13
Plant Structure and Function	9–13
Ecology	**7–9**

Each question in the practice tests has been categorized according to these categories, so that when you study your practice tests you can very precisely identify your weaknesses.

Format of the SAT II Biology

Whether you take the SAT II Biology E or Biology M, the test will last an hour and consist of 80 questions. These questions will be organized in two main groups. The 60 core questions will come first, followed by a 20 question specialty section. All this information you already know. Now for what you don't know.

The core section of the test (and occasionally the specialty sections) contains two different types of questions. Classification questions make up the first 10–12 questions of the core, while the last 48–50 questions of the core are five-choice multiple-choice questions. What are classification and five-choice multiple-choice questions? Funny you should ask—we were just about to tell you.

Classification Questions

Classification questions are the opposite of your normal multiple-choice question: they give you the answers first and the questions second. A classification question presents you with five possible answer choices, and then a string of three to five questions to which those answer choices apply. The answer choices are usually either graphs or the names of five related laws or concepts. Because they allow for several questions on the same topic, classification questions will ask you to exhibit a fuller understanding of the topic at hand.

The level of difficulty within any set of questions is generally pretty random: you can't expect the first question in a set to be easier than the last. However, each set of classification questions is generally a bit harder than the one that came before. In the core questions, for example, you should expect questions 10–12 to be harder than questions 1–3.

Classification Question Example

Directions: Each set of lettered choices below refers to the numbered questions or statements immediately following it. Select the one lettered choice that best answers each question or best fits each statement, and then fill in the corresponding oval on the answer sheet. A choice may be used once, more than once, or not at all in each set.

Questions 1–3 refer to the following organelles.

(A)   Chloroplast
(B)   Mitochondria
(C)   Nucleus
(D)   Cytoplasm
(E)   Cell Membrane

1.   Location of cellular respiration in prokaryotes

2.   Maintains proper concentrations of substances within the cell

3.   Found in plant cells, but not in animal cells

All classification questions on the SAT II Biology come in a format similar to the one above. You can usually answer classification questions a bit more quickly than the standard five-choice completion questions, since you need to review only one set of answer choices to answer a series of questions. (By the way, the answers to the questions are (C), (E), and (A), respectively.)

Five-Choice Completion Questions

These are the multiple-choice questions we all know and love, and the lifeblood of any multiple-choice exam. You know the drill: they ask a question, and give you five possible answer choices, and you pick the best one.

Directions: Each of the questions or incomplete statements below is followed by five suggested answers or completions. Some questions pertain to a set that refers to a laboratory or experimental situation. For each question, select the one choice that is the best answer to the question and then fill in the corresponding oval on the answer sheet.

As the directions imply, some five-choice completion questions are individual questions in which the five answer choices refer to only one question. But more than half of the five-choice completion questions are group questions, in which a set of questions all refer to the same biological scenario, figure, or experiment.

4.   Giraffes with longer necks can reach more food and are more likely to survive and have offspring. This is an example of

(A)   Lamarck's principle
(B)   natural selection
(C)   adaptive radiation
(D)   convergent evolution
(E)   speciation

A series of about 20 individual multiple-choice questions are found in the core section just after the classification questions. About five individual multiple-choice questions will begin each specialty section. In both the core and the specialty sections, there is a general tendency for the questions to become progressively more difficult. The answer to the example question is (B).

There are actually two types of group questions. Group questions that refer to figures often test your knowledge in a very straightforward manner. For example, the test might contain a figure of a flower, with each part labeled with a number. The questions will ask you to match a function with the correct part of the flower. Group questions that deal with an experiment or scenario are usually more complicated. Some of the questions in the group may test your ability to read the data in the experiment; others may test your understanding of the experiment itself by asking you how the experiment might have been improved, or how the results of the experiment might have changed along with a particular variable.

In both the core and specialty sections, group questions appear after the individual multiple-choice questions. The difficulty of the questions within a group follows no pattern, but each group will generally be more difficult than the last. We provide examples of both kinds of group question below.

Figure-Based Group Questions

Figure-based group questions present you with an image or graphic and ask you to identify the structures or functions being represented. The questions are all five-choice multiple-choice questions. Most of the questions dealing with figures demand only simple recognition and recall. The first two questions in the following sample fit this type: you either know the name for a structure or you don't. Some figure-based questions go further, though, and ask about the major processes associated with the images you're identifying.

Questions 5–7 refer to the diagram below.

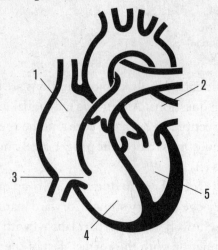

5. Oxygen-rich blood is pumped out to the body by structure

(A) 1
(B) 2
(C) 3
(D) 4
(E) 5

6. Structure 1 is termed the

(A) aorta
(B) right atrium
(C) left atrium
(D) pulmonary artery
(E) right ventricle

7. Which of the following muscle types are involved in circulating the blood?

I. skeletal
II. smooth
III. cardiac

(A) I only
(B) II only
(C) III only
(D) II and III only
(E) I, II, and III

The third question is of this second kind: it requires you to make a leap from recognizing the heart to knowing the general characteristics of the circulatory system. (If you're interested, the answers to questions 5, 6, and 7 are (E), (B), and (E), respectively.)

Before you start answering questions within a figure-based group, try to figure out what is being depicted and remember what biological phenomena are associated with it. For instance, if you recognize a drawing of mitochondria, chances are you'll be asked about cellular respiration. If the drawing specifies a molecule or organism, keep in mind the general characteristics of the class of molecules or organisms it represents. If you're not sure what the image or graphic in the figure-group represents, you can probably pick up hints from the answer choices. Scanning the questions above and seeing the words "atrium," "ventricle," and "circulating the blood" provides pretty strong clues that the image shows a heart. Be careful, though: test writers love to seed misleading answers among the correct ones.

Experiment-Based Group Questions

The SAT II Biology uses group questions based on experiments, biological situations, and data to measure your scientific reasoning and laboratory skills. There is no standard appearance for the experiments; the data can be presented in paragraphs, tables, and/or graphs.

These groups can be the most intimidating part of the SAT II Biology test: they often describe scenarios that are more complex or advanced than what you've been exposed to in biology class or labs. But stay confident: the two main purposes of these group questions are to test how you understand scientific data and how you apply knowledge of biological principles to this data. Any unfamiliar terms or experimental techniques mentioned in the groups usually just mask simple concepts addressed by the individual questions. In fact, some questions might simply ask you to interpret the data. For these questions you won't have to think much about the concept at all.

<u>Questions 8–10</u> refer to the following experiment and results obtained.

Dialysis bags are semipermeable membranes, allowing the transport of small molecules while prohibiting larger ones. In an experiment, students filled dialysis bags with different concentrations of sucrose solution and placed them in a beaker of distilled water. The bags were each weighed before being placed in the beaker. After two minutes, they were removed from the beaker, dried, and weighed again.

Contents in Dialysis Bag	Initial Mass	Final Mass
Distilled Water	25.1 g	25.3 g
0.2 M sucrose	25.9 g	28.4 g
0.4 M sucrose	26.1 g	30.0 g
0.6 M sucrose	26.3 g	30.1 g
0.8 M sucrose	25.9 g	35.6 g
1.0 M sucrose	30.7 g	37.6 g

8.   Which dialysis bag experiences the largest percent change in mass?

(A)   0.2 M sucrose
(B)   0.4 M sucrose
(C)   0.6 M sucrose
(D)   0.8 M sucrose
(E)   1.0 M sucrose

9.   If the 0.6 M sucrose solution bag was left in the beaker for four minutes, all of the following occur EXCEPT

(A)   mass of the dialysis bag increases to more than 30.1 g
(B)   water travels down its concentration gradient
(C)   decrease in the bag's molarity of sucrose
(D)   sucrose leaks into the beaker
(E)   volume of water in the beaker decreases

10.   A glucose molecule is small enough to pass through the bag. If glucose was substituted for sucrose in the dialysis experiment above, by what process does it cross the membrane?

(A)   osmosis
(B)   active transport
(C)   simple diffusion
(D)   facilitated diffusion
(E)   transpiration

For each experiment, identify the following: What is being tested and why? What are the variables, and what factors stay the same? In this example, the mass of the dialysis bags changes with the variable of sucrose concentration. Changes in mass can only come from water entering or leaving the bags, so the question deals with osmosis.

The three sample questions are good examples of the various types of questions the SAT II Biology asks in experiment groups. You don't have to know anything about concentrations, osmosis, or membrane transport to answer the first question in this group; determining percent change in mass demands only simple data interpretation. The second question requires you to extrapolate and make predictions from the data. The third question asks you to make predictions on what would occur if the experiment were slightly modified. This last type of question goes beyond the numbers and requires knowledge of the topic. If you can identify the general biological properties of the experiment in advance, you should have no trouble answering questions of this sort. (Answers to the sample questions: 8 (D), 9 (D), and 10 (C).)

The SAT II Biology may also present data in graph form. For graphs, make sure you know what the axes represent. Think about what relationship exists between these concepts and identify in advance any general trends you can think of. If it helps, sketch out your own tables or notes to sort the data and identify trends or exceptions. For all experiment-based questions, elimination is a helpful tool. You can eliminate answer choices that do not relate to the experiment's variables or what is being tested, or those choices that contradict your knowledge of the biological principles working in the experiment or scenario.

How Your Knowledge of Biology Will Be Tested

The SAT II Biology tests your knowledge of biology in three different ways. Knowing how your knowledge may be tested should help you better prepare yourself for the exam.

Recall Questions.

These questions test your basic knowledge of the fundamental facts and terminology of biology. A typical recall question might ask you to pick out the function of ribosomes, or to name the nitrogenous base that DNA and RNA do not have in common. These questions are straightforward—they're simply a matter of knowing your stuff. Some recall questions might be organized in sets around a figure, as in the example of the questions about the structure of a flower we described earlier.

Interpretation and Application Questions.

These questions test your ability to digest data or biological scenarios and to extrapolate answers from that understanding. These questions often necessitate that you are able to use, in tandem, your knowledge of different topics in biology. An interpretation and application question might present a scenario in which the temperature drops and then ask you to predict how this change will affect the metabolism of a lizard and a dog. To answer this question you have to realize, first, that a question about the change in metabolism due to temperature is asking about warm-blooded and cold-blooded animals. To get the question right, you must first recall that a dog is warm-blooded and a lizard cold-blooded. Then you have to understand how a lowered temperature will affect each type of animal. (As temperatures decrease, the metabolism of a cold-blooded animal will slow down, while the metabolism of the warm-blooded animal will remain constant).

Laboratory Questions.

Laboratory questions describe a situation in a laboratory and often provide you with data. To answer these questions you must be able to read and understand the data, to form hypotheses and conclusions based on the data, and to be able to identify the goals and assumptions underlying the experiment.

You'll find all three types of question all over the test, and at all different levels of difficulty. Ultimately, they all test the very same thing: whether you've grasped the basic principles of biology.

Basic Math and the SAT II Biology

The writers of the SAT II Biology assume that you are able to deal with basic mathematical concepts, such as ratios and proportions. They also assume that you know the metric system. You will not be allowed to use a calculator on the test; this isn't a big deal because you won't have to do any calculations more difficult than multiplication.

Scoring the SAT II Biology

Scoring on the SAT II Biology is very similar to the scoring for all other SAT II tests. For every right answer, you earn 1 point. For every wrong answer, you lose $1/4$ of a point. For each question you leave blank, you earn 0 points. Add all these points up, and you get your raw score. ETS then converts your raw score to a scaled score according to a special curve. On page 21 we've included a raw-score-to-scaled-score conversion chart, so you can translate your raw score on a practice test into scaled scores. But to give you a sense of what sorts of performances convert into what sorts of scores, here's a synopsis. You could score:

- 800 if you answered 79 right and left 1 blank

- 750 if you answered 73 right, 4 wrong, and left 3 blank

- 700 if you answered 67 right, 8 wrong, and left 5 blank

- 650 if you answered 60 right, 12 wrong, and left 8 blank

- 600 if you answered 54 right, 16 wrong, and left 10 blank

This chart should show you that your score doesn't plummet with every question you can't answer confidently. You can do very well on this test without knowing or answering everything. The key to doing well on the SAT II Biology is to follow a strategy that ensures you will see and answer all the questions you can answer, while intelligently guessing on those slightly fuzzier questions. We will talk about these strategies in the next chapter.

Raw Score	Scaled Score	Raw Score	Scaled Score	Raw Score	Scaled Score
80	800	49	600	18	420
79	800	48	590	17	410
78	790	47	590	16	410
77	780	46	580	15	400
76	770	45	580	14	390
75	770	44	570	13	390
74	760	43	560	12	380
73	760	42	560	11	370
72	750	41	550	10	360
71	740	40	550	9	360
70	740	39	540	8	350
69	730	38	540	7	350
68	730	37	530	6	340
67	720	36	520	5	340
66	710	35	520	4	330
65	700	34	510	3	330
64	700	33	500	2	320
63	690	32	500	1	320
62	680	31	490	0	310
61	680	30	490	-1	310
60	670	29	480	-2	300
59	660	28	480	-3	300
58	660	27	470	-4	290
57	650	26	470	-5	280
56	640	25	460	-6	280
55	640	24	450	-7	270
54	630	23	450	-8	270
53	620	22	440	-9	260
52	620	21	440	-10	260
51	610	20	430		
50	600	19	420		

The SAT II Biology

Strategies for the SAT II Biology

A MACHINE, NOT A PERSON, WILL SCORE your SAT II test. The tabulating machine sees only the filled-in ovals on your answer sheet and doesn't care how you came to these answers; it cares only whether your answers are correct. A lucky guess counts in your favor just as much as an answer you give confidently. By the same token, if you accidentally fill in (B) where you meant (C), you won't get any credit for having known what the answer was. Think of the multiple-choice test as a message to you from ETS: "We score your answers—not any of the work behind them."

That may be a dumb way to run a test, but that's the hand that ETS deals you. You might as well take advantage of it. Give them right answers, as many as possible, using whatever means possible. It's obvious that the SAT II Biology test allows you to exhibit your knowledge of biology; but the test gives you the same opportunity to show off your fox-like cunning by figuring out what strategies will allow you to best display that knowledge.

The Strategies

Most of these "strategies" are common sense, and many of them you already know. The funny thing, though, is that in high-pressure situations, common sense often goes out the window. If you review anything in the minutes before taking the test, review these strategies. Of course, that doesn't mean you should skip this section now. It's full of juicy hints, some of which might be new to you.

Be Calm

The best way to do poorly on a test is to psych yourself out. If your mind starts thrashing about wildly, it will have a hard time settling on the right answers. There are a number of preventative measures you can take, beginning weeks, or even months, before you take the test. Buying this book was a good start: it's important to practice taking the test as much as possible before the big day. But you ought to keep a number of other things in mind:

Study in advance

If you've studied at regular intervals leading up to the test, rather than cramming the night before, the information will sit more easily in your mind.

Be well rested

Get a good night's sleep on the two nights leading up to the test. If you're frazzled or wired you're going to have a harder time buckling down and concentrating when it really counts.

Come up for air

Don't assume that the best way to take an hour-long test is to spend the full hour nose to nose with the test questions. If you lift your head occasionally, look about you, and take a deep breath, you'll return to the test with a clearer mind. You'll lose maybe ten seconds of your total test-taking time and will be all the more focused for the other fifty-nine minutes and fifty seconds.

Grid Your Answers Carefully

No kidding. People make mistakes while entering their answers into the grid and it can cost them big-time. This slip up occurs most frequently after you skip a question. If you left question 43 blank, and then unthinkingly put the answer to question 44 into row 43, you could be starting a long, painful chain of wrong answers. Don't do this.

Some test prep books advise that you fill in your answer sheet five questions at a time rather than one at a time. Some suggest that you should fill out each oval as you answer the question. We think you should fill out the answer sheet whatever way feels most natural to you, but make sure you're careful while doing it. In our opinion, the best way to ensure that you're being careful is to talk to yourself. As you figure out an answer in the test booklet and transfer it over to the answer sheet ovals, say to yourself: "Number 23, B. Number 24, E. Number 25, A."

Pace Yourself

At the very least, aim to at least look at every question on the test. You can't afford to lose points because you didn't find the time to look at a question you could have easily answered. You can spend an average of forty-eight seconds on each question, though you'll probably breeze through some in ten seconds and dwell on others for two minutes. Knowing how to pace yourself is a critical skill—these three guidelines should help.

Don't dwell on any one question for too long

If you've spent a couple minutes laboring over the question, you might just want to make a note of it and move on. If you feel the answer is on the tip of your tongue, it might come more easily if you just let it rest and come back to it later. Not only is it demoralizing to spend five minutes on a single question, but it also eats up precious time in which you might have answered a number of easier questions.

Nail the easy questions

As we said in the previous chapter, the test questions get progressively harder as you go along. Nonetheless, there will be some tough ones thrown in right at the start, and you'll be finding gimmes right up until the end. One of the reasons you don't want to dwell too long on tough questions is to ensure that you get a look at all the questions and snatch up the easy ones. Remember: you get as many points for correctly answering an easy question as a difficult one. You get a lot more points for five quickly answered easy questions than one hard-earned victory.

Skip the unfamiliar

If you encounter a question you can't make heads or tails of, just skip it. Don't sweat too hard trying to sort out what's going on. If you have time at the end, you can come back to it and see if you can make an educated guess. Your first priority should be to get all the easy questions, and your second priority should be to work through the questions you can solve with difficulty. Unfamiliar material should be at the bottom of your list of priorities.

Set a Target Score

You can make the job of pacing yourself much easier if you go into the test knowing how many questions you have to answer correctly in order to earn the score you want. What score do you want to get? Obviously, you should strive for the best score possible, but be realistic: consider how much you know about biology and how well you do, generally, on these sorts of tests. You should also do a little research and find out what counts as a good score to the colleges to which you're applying: is it a 600? 680? Talk to the admissions offices of the colleges you might want to attend, do a little research in college guidebooks, or talk to your guidance counselor. Find out the average scores of students admitted to the schools of your choice, and set your target score above it (you want to be above average, right?). Then take a look at the chart we showed you before. You can score:

- 800 if you answered 79 right and left 1 blank

- 750 if you answered 73 right, 4 wrong, and left 3 blank

- 700 if you answered 67 right, 8 wrong, and left 5 blank

- 650 if you answered 60 right, 12 wrong, and left 8 blank

- 600 if you answered 54 right, 16 wrong, and left 10 blank

Suppose the average score on the SAT II Biology for the school you're interested in is 650. Set your target at about 700. To get that score, you need to get 67 questions right, while leaving yourself room to get 8 wrong and leave 5 blank. In other words, you can leave a number of tough questions blank, get a bunch more wrong, and still earn the score you want. As long as you have some idea of how many questions you need to answer, bearing in mind that you'll likely get some questions wrong, you can pace yourself accordingly. Taking practice tests is the best way to work on your pacing. See how many questions you can leave blank and still get the score you want, and you'll have a better sense of what to aim at on the big day.

If you find yourself effortlessly hitting your target score when you take the practice tests, don't just pat yourself on the back. Set a higher target score and start gunning for that one. The purpose of buying this book and studying for the test is to improve your score as much as possible, so be sure to push your limits.

Know What You're Being Asked

You can't know the answer until you know the question. This might sound obvious, but many a point has been lost by the careless student who scans the answer choices hastily before properly understanding the question. Take the following example:

Mammalian cell membranes work to maintain a concentration gradient in which there is a high water concentration inside the cell and a high sodium concentration outside the cell. If the cell membrane contains transport channels, these channels would allow sodium to

(A)   flow out of the cell by simple diffusion
(B)   flow into the cell by simple diffusion
(C)   flow out of the cell by facilitated diffusion
(D)   flow into the cell through facilitated diffusion
(E)   flow into of the cell by phagocytosis

This is not a difficult question. The sodium will move by simple diffusion from a high concentration gradient to a low concentration gradient. But the question is long and contains a great deal of information, so that by the end, a hasty student might have mixed up whether there was a higher concentration of sodium inside or outside the cell. This sort of mix-up might happen to the hasty student on only a few questions, but a few questions are the difference between a 730 and a 680 on the SAT II Biology.

To avoid getting confused on any questions, take a moment to *understand* the question before answering it. Read the question, and then vocalize to yourself what the question is asking and what the pertinent information is. This process should not take more than a second or two. But those brief moments can make all the difference. For this question, once you've recognized what you're dealing with, you will have little trouble in correctly answering (C).

Think of the Answer Before Looking at the Answer Choices

This hint goes hand in hand with the last one. In fact, this hint provides a method to stop yourself from speeding through the test carelessly. Imagine the hasty student who read the last example question too quickly and thought that the sodium concentration was higher inside the cell than outside. The hasty student, of course, doesn't realize this error, and looks through the answers. And there sits choice (A), which is the right answer based on the information lodged in the hasty test-taker's head. So the hasty test-taker answers (A) and continues on her way, having lost points she should have gotten.

Biology Strategies

But if the hasty test-taker had instead tried to answer the question without looking at the answers, she wouldn't have been so hasty. Instead, she would have had to stop for a second, and look at the information in the question a second time; then she would have sorted everything out and gotten the question right. If you force yourself to answer the question before looking at the answer choices, you force yourself to come to grips with the question and therefore will cut down on the careless errors you might normally make.

Know How To Guess

ETS doesn't take off ¼ of a point for each wrong answer in order to punish you for guessing. They do it so as not to reward you for blind guessing. Suppose, without even glancing at any of the questions, you just randomly entered responses in the first 20 spaces on your answer sheet. Because there's a one-in-five chance of guessing correctly on any given question, odds are you would guess right for 4 questions and wrong for 16 questions. Your raw score for those 20 questions would then be:

$$4 \times 1 - 16 \times \frac{1}{4} = 0$$

Because of the ¼ point penalty for wrong answers, you would be no better off and no worse off than if you'd left those twenty spaces blank.

Now suppose in each of the first 20 questions you are able to eliminate just 1 possible answer choice so that you guess with a ¼ chance of being right. Odds are, you'd get 5 questions right and 15 questions wrong, giving you a raw score of:

$$5 \times 1 - 15 \times \frac{1}{4} = 1.25$$

All of a sudden, you're more than a point up. It's not much, but every little bit helps.

The lesson to be learned here is that blind guessing doesn't help, but educated guessing does. If you can eliminate even one of the five possible answer choices, *you must guess*. We'll discuss how to eliminate answer choices on certain special kinds of questions later in this chapter.

Guessing as Partial Credit

Some students feel that guessing is similar to cheating—that guessing correctly means getting credit where none is due. But instead of looking at guessing as an attempt to gain undeserved points, you should see it as a form of partial credit. For example, suppose you're stumped on the question mentioned earlier—which asks about sodium ions and transport channels in an animal's cell membrane—because you can't remember if the sodium should flow into the cell or out of the cell. But let's say you *do* know that phagocytosis occurs when a cell engulfs a particle that is much larger than an ion. And suppose you are pretty sure that the answer isn't simple diffusion, because sodium ions do not cross cell membranes without help. Don't you deserve something for that extra knowledge? Well, you do get something: when you look at this question, you can throw out (A), (B), and (E) as answer choices, leaving you with a one-in-two chance of getting the question right if you guess. Your extra knowledge gives you better odds of getting this question right, exactly as extra knowledge should.

Eliminate Wrong Answers

We've already said that if you can eliminate one answer in a question, the scoring odds are in your favor, and you should guess. This means that you shouldn't skip a question juts because you realize you don't know the right answer. Before skipping any question, check to see if you can at least eliminate an answer. For every question, you should go through a checklist of priorities:

- **First priority:** Answer the question correctly.

- **Second priority:** If you don't know the answer, try to eliminate answer choices and then guess.

- **Third priority:** If you can't eliminate any answer choices, move on to the next question.

On most questions, there will be at least one or two answer choices you can eliminate. There are also certain styles of question that lend themselves to particular processes of elimination.

Classification Questions

The weakness of classification questions is that the same five answer choices apply to several questions. Invariably, some of these answer choices will be tempting for some questions, but not for others.

<u>Questions 1–3</u> relate to the following molecules:

(A)   phospholipid
(B)   carbohydrate
(C)   protein
(D)   DNA
(E)   RNA

1.   Contains the nitrogenous base uracil

2.   Acts as storage for long strings of sugars

3.   One side is hydrophilic, while the other is hydrophobic

For instance, you can be pretty sure that uracil doesn't appear in protein, carbohydrates, or phospholipids, since nitrogenous bases are only found in RNA and DNA.

Another point that may help you guess in a pinch: you'll rarely find the same answer choice being correct for two different questions. True, the directions for classification questions explicitly state that an answer choice "may be used once, more than once, or not at all," but on the whole, the ETS people shy away from the "more than once" possibility. This is by no means a sure bet, but if you're trying to eliminate answers, you might want to eliminate those choices that you've already used on other questions in the same set.

If you're wondering, the answers to the above questions are 1 (E), 2 (B), and 3 (A).

"EXCEPT" Questions

"EXCEPT" questions are five-choice multiple-choice questions that contain a bunch of right answers and one wrong answer. The questions always contain an all-caps EXCEPT, LEAST, or some other, similar word. Even if you aren't sure of the answer (which is actually the wrong answer), you should be able to identify one or two of the answer choices as true statements and eliminate them.

Most birds are characterized by all of the following EXCEPT

(A)   four-chambered heart
(B)   strong, heavy bones
(C)   powerful lungs
(D)   eggs protected by hard shells
(E)   evolved from reptiles

Perhaps you're not sure which of the five answer choices is wrong. But you should be able to identify that birds *do* lay eggs protected by shells and that they evolved from dinosaurs. Already, you've eliminated two possible answers and can make a pretty good guess from there.

The answer is (B): the bones of birds are extremely light. Heavy bones would make flight much more difficult for birds.

"I, II, and III" Questions

"I, II, and III" questions are multiple-choice questions that provide you with three possible answers, and the five answer choices list different combinations of those three.

> A population of animals is split in two by the formation of a river through their territory. The two populations gain different characteristics due to the different natures of their new habitats. When the river disappears, the two populations can no longer interbreed. What has occurred?
>
> I.   Natural selection
> II. Convergent evolution
> III. Speciation
>
> (A)   I only
> (B)   II only
> (C)   I and III only
> (D)   II and III only
> (E)   I, II, and III

There's an upside and a downside to questions like this. Suppose you know that the scenario described by this question does involve speciation, but you aren't sure about natural selection or convergent evolution. The downside is that you can't get the right answer for sure. The upside is that you can eliminate (A) and (B) and significantly increase your chance of guessing the right answer. As long as you're not afraid to guess—and you should never be afraid to guess if you've eliminated an answer—these questions shouldn't be daunting. By the way, the answer is (C): changes in organisms' characteristics due to changes in habitat are a result of natural selection, and the inability of the members of a former population to interbreed after being separated for a long time is speciation.

Biology Strategies

Practice Tests

Practice Tests Are Your Best Friends

I N THIS CRAZY WORLD, THERE'S AT LEAST ONE thing that you can always take for granted: the SAT II Biology test will stay the same. From year to year and test to test, of the 60 core questions you have to answer on the SAT II Biology, about 10 will deal with genetics, 8 will cover ecology, 10 will deal with cellular biology, and so on. Obviously, different versions of the SAT II Biology aren't *exactly* the same: individual questions won't repeat from test to test. But the subjects you'll be tested on, and the way in which you'll be tested, *will* remain constant. This constancy can be of great benefit to you as you study for the test.

To show how you can use the similarity between different versions of the SAT II Biology test to your advantage, we provide a case study.

Taking Advantage of the Test's Regularity

One day, an eleventh grader named Molly Bloom sits down at the desk in her room and takes a practice test for the SAT II Biology. She's a bright young woman, and she gets only one question wrong. Molly checks her answers and then jumps from her chair and does a little happy dance that would be embarrassing if anyone else were around to see her.

After her euphoria passes, Molly begins to wonder which question she got wrong and returns to her chair. She discovers that the question dealt with mitosis. Looking over the question, Molly at first thinks the test made a mistake and that she was actually right, but then she realizes that she answered the question wrong because she had thought that anaphase preceded metaphase, when really it is the other way around. In thinking about the question, Molly realizes she didn't have the strongest grasp of the processes of mitosis in general. She takes a few minutes to study up on cell reproduction, and sorts out when the different phases take place and what happens in each. All this takes her about ten minutes, after which she vows never again to make a mistake on a question involving mitosis.

Analyzing Molly Bloom

Molly's actions seem minor. All she did was study a question she got wrong until she understood why she got it wrong and what she should have done to get it right. But think about the implications. Molly answered the question incorrectly because she didn't understand the topic it was testing, and the practice test pointed out her mistaken understanding in the most noticeable way possible: she got the question wrong.

After doing her admittedly goofy little dance, Molly wasn't content simply to see what the correct answer was and get on with her day; she wanted to see *how* and *why* she got the question wrong, and what she should have done, or needed to know, in order to get it right. So, with a look of determination, telling herself, "I will figure out why I got this question wrong, yes I will, yes," she spent a little while studying the question, discovered her mistaken understanding of mitosis, and then eliminated her misunderstanding of mitosis by studying the subject. If Molly were to take that same test again, she definitely would not get that question wrong.

"But she never will take that test again, so she's never going to see that particular question again," some poor sap who hasn't read this book might sputter. "She wasted her time. What a dork!"

Why That Poor Sap Really Is a Poor Sap

In some sense, that poor sap is correct: Molly never will take that exact practice test again. But the poor sap is wrong to call Molly derogatory names, because, as we know, the SAT II Biology is remarkably similar from year to year—both in the topics it covers and in the way it poses questions about those topics. Therefore, when Molly taught herself about mitosis, she actually learned how to answer the similar questions dealing with cell reproduction that will undoubtedly appear on every future practice test, and on the SAT II Biology that counts.

In studying the results of her practice test, in figuring out exactly why she got her one question wrong and what she should have known and done to get it right, Molly targeted a weakness and overcame it.

Molly and You

Molly has it easy. She took a practice test and only got one question wrong. Less than one percent of all people who take the SAT II Biology will be so lucky. Of course, the only reason Molly got that many right was so that we could use her as an easy example.

So, what if you take a practice test and get 15 questions wrong, and your errors span many of the major topics in biology? Well, you should do exactly what Molly did: take your test and study it. Identify every question you got wrong, figure out why you got it wrong, and then teach yourself what you should have done to get the question right. If you can't figure out your error, find someone who can.

Think about it. What does an incorrect answer mean? That wrong answer identifies a weakness in your test taking skills, whether that weakness is unfamiliarity with a particular topic or a tendency to be careless. If you got 15 questions wrong on a practice test, then each of those questions identifies a weakness in your ability to take the SAT II Biology or your knowledge about the topics the SAT II Biology tests. As you study each question and figure out why you got that question wrong, you are actually learning how to answer the very questions that will appear some Saturday in the future on the real SAT II Biology. You are discovering exactly where your weaknesses in biology lie and addressing them. You are learning not just to understand the principles you're being tested on, but also *the way* that ETS will test you. Practice tests do for you what simply studying biology cannot: beyond helping you understand biology, they prepare you specifically for the test you're going to take.

True, if you got 15 questions wrong, the first time you study your test will take a bit of time. Think of that time as an investment. If you study your practice test properly, you will be eliminating future mistakes. Since practice tests allow you to target your weaknesses, on each successive practice test you take, you will get fewer questions wrong, meaning less time spent studying those errors. Also, and more importantly, you'll be pinpointing what you need to study to get the score you want on the SAT II Biology, identifying and overcoming your weaknesses, and learning to answer an increasing variety of questions on the specific topics covered by the test. Taking practice tests and studying them will allow you to teach yourself how to recognize and handle whatever the SAT II Biology has to throw at you.

Taking a Practice Test

Through the example of Miss Molly Bloom, we've shown you why studying practice tests is an extremely powerful study tool. Now we'll explain how to use that tool.

Controlling Your Environment

Although a practice test is practice, and no one but you ever needs to see your scores, you should do everything in your power to make the practice test feel like the real SAT II Biology. The closer your practice resembles the real thing, the more helpful it will be. When taking a practice test, follow these rules:

- **Time yourself:** Don't give yourself any extra time. Be stricter with yourself than the meanest administrator would be. Don't give yourself time off for bathroom breaks. If you have to go to the bathroom, let the clock keep running; that's what would happen during the real SAT II.

- **Take the test in a single sitting:** Training yourself to endure an hour of test taking is part of your preparation.

- **Eliminate distractions:** Don't take the practice test in a room with lots of people walking through it. Go to a library, your bedroom, a well-lit closet— anywhere quiet.

Following these rules ensures that you won't cheat yourself as you study. If you aren't strict with yourself about the little details, it can be quite easy to put in hours of study time in which you're mostly staring into space or singing along with the radio. If you're going to take the time to study, you might as well make that time as productive and fruitful as possible.

Practice Test Strategy

You should take each practice test as if it were the real deal: go for the highest score you can get. This doesn't mean you should be more daring than you would be on the actual test, guessing blindly even when you can't eliminate an answer. It doesn't mean that you should speed through the test carelessly. The more closely your attitude and strategies during the practice test reflect those you'll employ during the actual test, the more accurately the practice test will reflect your strengths and weaknesses: you'll learn what areas you should study and how to pace yourself during the test.

Scoring Your Practice Test

After you take your practice test, you'll no doubt want to score it and see how you did. But don't just tally up your raw score. As a part of your scoring, you should keep a precise list of every question you got wrong and every question you skipped. This list will be your guide when you study your test.

Studying Your . . . No, Wait, Go Take a Break

You know how to have fun. Go do that for a while. Come back when you're refreshed.

Studying Your Practice Test

After grading your test, you should have a list of the questions you answered incorrectly or skipped. Studying your test involves going down this list and examining each question you answered incorrectly. As you study a question, make sure not just to learn the right answer but also to understand why you got the question wrong, and what you could have done to get the question right.

Why Did You Get the Question Wrong?

1. You thought you knew the answer, but, actually, you didn't.

2. You couldn't answer the question directly, but you knew the general principles involved. Using this knowledge, you managed to eliminate some answer choices and then guessed among the remaining answers; sadly, you guessed incorrectly.

3. You knew the answer, but somehow made a careless mistake.

You should know which of these reasons applies to every question you got wrong.

What You Could Have Done to Get the Question Right

The reasons you got a question wrong affect how you should think about it while studying your test.

If You Got a Question Wrong for Reason 1–Lack of Knowledge

A question answered incorrectly for Reason 1 identifies a weakness in your knowledge of the biology tested on the SAT II Biology. Discovering this wrong answer gives you an opportunity to target and eliminate that weakness, and perhaps related weaknesses as well.

For example, if you got a question wrong that dealt with the structure of RNA, first figure out why you were confused about RNA's structure, and then study up on the correct structure. But don't stop there. If you had some trouble with RNA structure, it's possible you're not so hot with RNA function. Take a quick look through RNA function to see if what you remember about it is complete and correct. If it is, great! If it isn't, take some time to study up on that as well. Remember, you will *not* see a question exactly like the question you got wrong, so there's no use in making sure you won't get that exact question wrong a second time. Instead, cut to the heart of the problem and understand the principles that would lead you to a correct answer on this question and any other related question.

If You Got a Question Wrong for Reason 2—Guessing Wrong

If you guessed wrong, review your guessing strategy. Did you guess intelligently? Could you have eliminated more answers? If yes, why didn't you? By thinking in this critical way about the decisions you made while taking the practice test, you can train yourself to make quicker, more decisive, and better decisions.

If you took a guess and chose the incorrect answer, don't let that sour you on guessing. Even as you go over the question and figure out if there was any way for you to have answered the question without having to guess, remind yourself that as long as you eliminated at least one answer and guessed—even if you got the question wrong— you followed the right strategy.

If You Got a Question Wrong for Reason 3—Carelessness

If you discover you got a question wrong because you were careless, it might be tempting to say to yourself, "Oh, I made a careless error," and assure yourself you won't do that again. That is not enough. You made that careless mistake for a reason, and you should try to figure out why. While getting a question wrong because you didn't know the answer constitutes a weakness in your knowledge about biology, making a careless mistake represents a weakness in your *method* of taking the test.

To overcome this weakness, you need to approach it in the same critical way you would approach a lack of knowledge. Study your mistake. Reenact your thought process on the problem and see where and how your carelessness came about. Were you rushing? Did you jump at the first answer that seemed right instead of reading all the answers? Do you have trouble telling the difference between the letters C and D? Know your error, and look it in the eye. If you learn precisely what your mistake was, you are much less likely to make that mistake again.

If You Left a Question Blank

It is also a good idea to study the questions you left blank on the test, since those questions constitute a reservoir of lost points. A blank answer is a result either of:

Total inability to answer a question.

Look to see if there was some way you might have been able to eliminate an answer choice or two and put yourself in a better position to guess. You should also make a particular point to study up on that topic in biology, since you clearly have a good deal of trouble with it.

Lack of time.

Look over the question and see whether you think you could have answered it. If you definitely could, then you know that you are throwing away points and probably working too slowly. If you couldn't, then carry out the steps above: study the relevant material and review your guessing strategy.

The Secret Weapon: Talking to Yourself

Yes, it's embarrassing. Yes, you'll look silly. But, first of all, no one will be around while you study. And second, talking to yourself is perhaps the best way to pound something into your brain. As you go through the steps of studying a question, you should talk them out. When you verbalize something to yourself, it makes it much harder to delude yourself into thinking that you're working if you're really not. Talking out the words makes you really think about them, and taking an active grip on your studying will make all the difference between a pretty good score and a great score.

SAT II Biology
Practice Test 1

BIOLOGY TEST 1 ANSWER SHEET

1. Ⓐ Ⓑ Ⓒ Ⓓ Ⓔ	26. Ⓐ Ⓑ Ⓒ Ⓓ Ⓔ	51. Ⓐ Ⓑ Ⓒ Ⓓ Ⓔ	76. Ⓐ Ⓑ Ⓒ Ⓓ Ⓔ
2. Ⓐ Ⓑ Ⓒ Ⓓ Ⓔ	27. Ⓐ Ⓑ Ⓒ Ⓓ Ⓔ	52. Ⓐ Ⓑ Ⓒ Ⓓ Ⓔ	77. Ⓐ Ⓑ Ⓒ Ⓓ Ⓔ
3. Ⓐ Ⓑ Ⓒ Ⓓ Ⓔ	28. Ⓐ Ⓑ Ⓒ Ⓓ Ⓔ	53. Ⓐ Ⓑ Ⓒ Ⓓ Ⓔ	78. Ⓐ Ⓑ Ⓒ Ⓓ Ⓔ
4. Ⓐ Ⓑ Ⓒ Ⓓ Ⓔ	29. Ⓐ Ⓑ Ⓒ Ⓓ Ⓔ	54. Ⓐ Ⓑ Ⓒ Ⓓ Ⓔ	79. Ⓐ Ⓑ Ⓒ Ⓓ Ⓔ
5. Ⓐ Ⓑ Ⓒ Ⓓ Ⓔ	30. Ⓐ Ⓑ Ⓒ Ⓓ Ⓔ	55. Ⓐ Ⓑ Ⓒ Ⓓ Ⓔ	80. Ⓐ Ⓑ Ⓒ Ⓓ Ⓔ
6. Ⓐ Ⓑ Ⓒ Ⓓ Ⓔ	31. Ⓐ Ⓑ Ⓒ Ⓓ Ⓔ	56. Ⓐ Ⓑ Ⓒ Ⓓ Ⓔ	81. Ⓐ Ⓑ Ⓒ Ⓓ Ⓔ
7. Ⓐ Ⓑ Ⓒ Ⓓ Ⓔ	32. Ⓐ Ⓑ Ⓒ Ⓓ Ⓔ	57. Ⓐ Ⓑ Ⓒ Ⓓ Ⓔ	82. Ⓐ Ⓑ Ⓒ Ⓓ Ⓔ
8. Ⓐ Ⓑ Ⓒ Ⓓ Ⓔ	33. Ⓐ Ⓑ Ⓒ Ⓓ Ⓔ	58. Ⓐ Ⓑ Ⓒ Ⓓ Ⓔ	83. Ⓐ Ⓑ Ⓒ Ⓓ Ⓔ
9. Ⓐ Ⓑ Ⓒ Ⓓ Ⓔ	34. Ⓐ Ⓑ Ⓒ Ⓓ Ⓔ	59. Ⓐ Ⓑ Ⓒ Ⓓ Ⓔ	84. Ⓐ Ⓑ Ⓒ Ⓓ Ⓔ
10. Ⓐ Ⓑ Ⓒ Ⓓ Ⓔ	35. Ⓐ Ⓑ Ⓒ Ⓓ Ⓔ	60. Ⓐ Ⓑ Ⓒ Ⓓ Ⓔ	85. Ⓐ Ⓑ Ⓒ Ⓓ Ⓔ
11. Ⓐ Ⓑ Ⓒ Ⓓ Ⓔ	36. Ⓐ Ⓑ Ⓒ Ⓓ Ⓔ	61. Ⓐ Ⓑ Ⓒ Ⓓ Ⓔ	86. Ⓐ Ⓑ Ⓒ Ⓓ Ⓔ
12. Ⓐ Ⓑ Ⓒ Ⓓ Ⓔ	37. Ⓐ Ⓑ Ⓒ Ⓓ Ⓔ	62. Ⓐ Ⓑ Ⓒ Ⓓ Ⓔ	87. Ⓐ Ⓑ Ⓒ Ⓓ Ⓔ
13. Ⓐ Ⓑ Ⓒ Ⓓ Ⓔ	38. Ⓐ Ⓑ Ⓒ Ⓓ Ⓔ	63. Ⓐ Ⓑ Ⓒ Ⓓ Ⓔ	88. Ⓐ Ⓑ Ⓒ Ⓓ Ⓔ
14. Ⓐ Ⓑ Ⓒ Ⓓ Ⓔ	39. Ⓐ Ⓑ Ⓒ Ⓓ Ⓔ	64. Ⓐ Ⓑ Ⓒ Ⓓ Ⓔ	89. Ⓐ Ⓑ Ⓒ Ⓓ Ⓔ
15. Ⓐ Ⓑ Ⓒ Ⓓ Ⓔ	40. Ⓐ Ⓑ Ⓒ Ⓓ Ⓔ	65. Ⓐ Ⓑ Ⓒ Ⓓ Ⓔ	90. Ⓐ Ⓑ Ⓒ Ⓓ Ⓔ
16. Ⓐ Ⓑ Ⓒ Ⓓ Ⓔ	41. Ⓐ Ⓑ Ⓒ Ⓓ Ⓔ	66. Ⓐ Ⓑ Ⓒ Ⓓ Ⓔ	91. Ⓐ Ⓑ Ⓒ Ⓓ Ⓔ
17. Ⓐ Ⓑ Ⓒ Ⓓ Ⓔ	42. Ⓐ Ⓑ Ⓒ Ⓓ Ⓔ	67. Ⓐ Ⓑ Ⓒ Ⓓ Ⓔ	92. Ⓐ Ⓑ Ⓒ Ⓓ Ⓔ
18. Ⓐ Ⓑ Ⓒ Ⓓ Ⓔ	43. Ⓐ Ⓑ Ⓒ Ⓓ Ⓔ	68. Ⓐ Ⓑ Ⓒ Ⓓ Ⓔ	93. Ⓐ Ⓑ Ⓒ Ⓓ Ⓔ
19. Ⓐ Ⓑ Ⓒ Ⓓ Ⓔ	44. Ⓐ Ⓑ Ⓒ Ⓓ Ⓔ	69. Ⓐ Ⓑ Ⓒ Ⓓ Ⓔ	94. Ⓐ Ⓑ Ⓒ Ⓓ Ⓔ
20. Ⓐ Ⓑ Ⓒ Ⓓ Ⓔ	45. Ⓐ Ⓑ Ⓒ Ⓓ Ⓔ	70. Ⓐ Ⓑ Ⓒ Ⓓ Ⓔ	95. Ⓐ Ⓑ Ⓒ Ⓓ Ⓔ
21. Ⓐ Ⓑ Ⓒ Ⓓ Ⓔ	46. Ⓐ Ⓑ Ⓒ Ⓓ Ⓔ	71. Ⓐ Ⓑ Ⓒ Ⓓ Ⓔ	96. Ⓐ Ⓑ Ⓒ Ⓓ Ⓔ
22. Ⓐ Ⓑ Ⓒ Ⓓ Ⓔ	47. Ⓐ Ⓑ Ⓒ Ⓓ Ⓔ	72. Ⓐ Ⓑ Ⓒ Ⓓ Ⓔ	97. Ⓐ Ⓑ Ⓒ Ⓓ Ⓔ
23. Ⓐ Ⓑ Ⓒ Ⓓ Ⓔ	48. Ⓐ Ⓑ Ⓒ Ⓓ Ⓔ	73. Ⓐ Ⓑ Ⓒ Ⓓ Ⓔ	98. Ⓐ Ⓑ Ⓒ Ⓓ Ⓔ
24. Ⓐ Ⓑ Ⓒ Ⓓ Ⓔ	49. Ⓐ Ⓑ Ⓒ Ⓓ Ⓔ	74. Ⓐ Ⓑ Ⓒ Ⓓ Ⓔ	99. Ⓐ Ⓑ Ⓒ Ⓓ Ⓔ
25. Ⓐ Ⓑ Ⓒ Ⓓ Ⓔ	50. Ⓐ Ⓑ Ⓒ Ⓓ Ⓔ	75. Ⓐ Ⓑ Ⓒ Ⓓ Ⓔ	100. Ⓐ Ⓑ Ⓒ Ⓓ Ⓔ

BIOLOGY E/M TEST

FOR BOTH BIOLOGY-E AND BIOLOGY-M, ANSWER QUESTIONS 1–60

Questions 1–3 refer to the following components of the circulatory system.

(A) Plasma
(B) Red blood cell
(C) White blood cell
(D) Hemoglobin
(E) Platelet

1. Iron-containing protein that can bind to oxygen molecules

2. Biconcave disc with no nucleus and no major organelles

3. Cell fragments that play a role in blood clotting

Questions 4–6 refer to the molecules of life.

(A) Amino acid
(B) Hydrocarbon chains
(C) Nitrogenous base
(D) Carbohydrates
(E) Protein

4. Contains carbon, hydrogen, and oxygen atoms in a ratio of about 1:2:1

5. One of the building blocks of a nucleotide

6. Found in lipids

Questions 7–9 refer to organisms of kingdom Animalia.

(A) Phylum Mollusca
(B) Phylum Cnidaria
(C) Phylum Arthropoda
(D) Phylum Annelida
(E) Phylum Echinodermata

7. Members have a foot, radula, and mantle

8. Encompasses more species than all other animal phyla combined

9. Includes sea urchins, sea cucumbers, and sea stars

Questions 10–12 refer to mitosis and meiosis.

(A) Chromosome
(B) Gamete
(C) Spindle
(D) Synapsis
(E) Crossing-over

10. A haploid sperm or ovum

11. A long strand of DNA and its associated proteins

12. The process by which pairs of homologous chromosomes join together to form a tetrad

GO ON TO THE NEXT PAGE ▶

Directions: Each of the questions or incomplete statements below is followed by five suggested answers or completions. Some questions pertain to a set that refers to a laboratory or experimental situation. Select the one choice that best answers the question and fill in the corresponding oval on the answer sheet.

13. The weather on Earth suddenly changes and the temperatures in the western U.S. get much hotter. Some rabbits in the region are more adaptive to the conservation of water than others. These rabbits survive and reproduce more effectively than the rabbits that do not have these adaptations. This is an example of

    (A) speciation
    (B) adaptive radiation
    (C) mutation
    (D) natural selection
    (E) Lamarckian evolution

14. Which organelle in the cell is involved in gene expression?

    (A) Vacuole
    (B) Lysosome
    (C) Cell wall
    (D) Ribosomes
    (E) Mitochondria

15. In a food web, a primary consumer is always a(n)

    (A) detritivore
    (B) carnivore
    (C) herbivore
    (D) saprophyte
    (E) autotroph

16. Which of the following is NOT true regarding xylem?

    (A) Carries water and minerals up from the root
    (B) Composed of dead cells
    (C) Provides structural support
    (D) Is responsible for distributing carbohydrates
    (E) Is sometimes called "wood"

17. A new animal has been discovered in Australia. This animal is warm-blooded, has hair, and gives birth to young just days after fertilization. The young finish developing in a pouch on the mother's body where they gain nourishment from milk stored in her mammary glands. To what group does this animal belong?

    (A) Placental mammals
    (B) Arthropods
    (C) Monotremes
    (D) Marsupials
    (E) Birds

18. In order for germination to occur, the seed of the *Calvaria major* tree had to pass through the digestive system of a Dodo bird. When the Dodo bird became extinct, so too did the tree. This is an example of

    (A) coevolution
    (B) competition
    (C) parasitism
    (D) niche separation
    (E) gene flow

19. What do proteins, carbohydrates, lipids, and nucleic acids all have in common?

    (A) All are building blocks of DNA.
    (B) All can become enzymes.
    (C) All contain carbon.
    (D) All can become hormones.
    (E) All contain nitrogen.

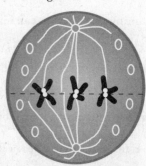

20. The cell in the diagram above is in the stage of mitosis called

    (A) anaphase
    (B) metaphase
    (C) prophase
    (D) telophase
    (E) interphase

21. A pregnant woman has just arrived at the hospital and is having contractions. She has elevated levels of what hormone?

    (A) Glucagon
    (B) Oxytocin
    (C) Testosterone
    (D) Thyroxin
    (E) Luteinizing hormone

GO ON TO THE NEXT PAGE

22. Which of the following is NOT a condition for Hardy-Weinberg equilibrium?

    (A) Large population size
    (B) Non-random mating
    (C) Absence of immigration or emigration
    (D) Random reproductive success
    (E) No mutation

23. Which of the following are true statements about cell size?

    I.   As cells grow larger, surface area increases more slowly than volume.
    II. As cells grow larger, surface area increases more rapidly than volume.
    III. Cells are small because their surface area and volume must be balanced.

    (A) I only
    (B) II only
    (C) III only
    (D) II and III only
    (E) I and III only

24. By what process does water cycle from the oceans to the atmosphere?

    (A) Runoff
    (B) Evaporation
    (C) Precipitation
    (D) Combustion
    (E) Photosynthesis

25. Members of the phylum Arthropoda possess all of the following characteristics except a(n)

    (A) open circulatory system
    (B) hard exoskeleton made of chitin
    (C) full digestive tract
    (D) 4-chambered heart
    (E) Malphigian tubules

26. A woman plants seeds in her garden. What type of plants could grow from those seeds?

    (A) Angiosperms
    (B) Fungi
    (C) Bryophytes
    (D) Ferns
    (E) Non-vascular plants

27. What is the correct pathway of food through the digestive system?

    (A) Esophagus, stomach, small intestine, large intestine, rectum
    (B) Stomach, esophagus, small intestine, rectum, large intestine
    (C) Esophagus, stomach, large intestine, small intestine, rectum
    (D) Rectum, esophagus, stomach, small intestines, large intestine
    (E) Stomach, small intestine, large intestine, esophagus, rectum

28. Which of the following is the best example of an ecological community?

    (A) A group of prairie dogs that live in the same area and interbreed
    (B) The abiotic environment in a prairie dog town
    (C) All of the plant and animal populations that live and interact in a prairie dog town
    (D) All of the prairie dogs in North America
    (E) A group of prairie dogs and the plant species that they eat

29. Just after a cell completes mitosis, it is cleaved into two cells, each with a full genetic complement. What is this process called?

    (A) Meiosis
    (B) Cytokinesis
    (C) Interphase
    (D) Prophase
    (E) Telophase

30. The dark reaction of photosynthesis occurs in the

    (A) grana
    (B) thylakoid spaces
    (C) intermembrane space
    (D) stroma
    (E) chlorophyll

GO ON TO THE NEXT PAGE

<u>Questions 31–32</u> refer to the experiment and diagrams below.

Students conducted an experiment by putting sugar into a fermentation tube (see diagram below) that contained a yeast solution. After five minutes, bubbles formed in the vertical segment of the tube. As time passed, more bubbles collected.

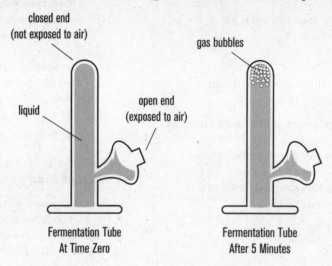

31. What process occurred in the vertical segment of the tube?

    (A) Aerobic respiration
    (B) Photosynthesis
    (C) Anaerobic respiration
    (D) Protein synthesis
    (E) The Krebs cycle

32. The bubbles produced in the tube were

    (A) carbon dioxide
    (B) oxygen
    (C) carbon monoxide
    (D) nitrous oxide
    (E) methane

GO ON TO THE NEXT PAGE

33. Yeast is a(n)

   (A) plant
   (B) fungus
   (C) lichen
   (D) animal
   (E) protist

34. After a runner has completed a marathon, she experiences some soreness in her legs. This is the result of

   I.   lactic acid fermentation
   III. alcoholic fermentation
   III. anaerobic respiration
   IV.   muscles running out of oxygen

   (A) I only
   (B) II only
   (C) I and III only
   (D) I, II, and IV only
   (E) I, III, and IV only

35. During glycolysis, ATP is used to split glucose into two

   (A) pyruvate molecules
   (B) fructose molecules
   (C) sucrose molecules
   (D) acetyl-CoA molecules
   (E) NADH molecules

Questions 36–39 refer to the illustration of the human heart below.

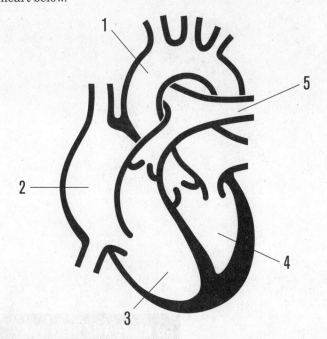

36. The area labeled 3 is which structure?

   (A) Right atrium
   (B) Left atrium
   (C) Right ventricle
   (D) Left ventricle
   (E) Aorta

37. Oxygen-poor blood can be found in the

   I.   aorta
   II.   right atrium
   III. pulmonary artery
   IV.   left atrium

   (A) I and II only
   (B) II and III only
   (C) I only
   (D) III and IV only
   (E) I, II, III, and IV

38. The function of the sinoatrial node is to

   (A) create red blood cells
   (B) stimulate cardiac muscles to contract in a regular and controlled rhythm
   (C) remove carbon dioxide from the blood
   (D) separate the atria from the ventricles
   (E) manufacture antigens

39. A heart with three chambers could belong to a

   (A) bird
   (B) reptile
   (C) mammal
   (D) jawless fish
   (E) human

GO ON TO THE NEXT PAGE

Questions 40–44 refer to the cell diagrams below.

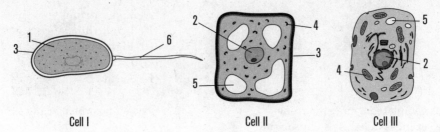

Cell I   Cell II   Cell III

40. Which of the above cells is eukaryotic?

   (A) I only
   (B) II only
   (C) I and II only
   (D) II and III only
   (E) III only

41. The area labeled 2 is called a

   (A) nucleus
   (B) vacuole
   (C) mitochondria
   (D) ribosome
   (E) cell wall

42. The cell wall of cell I is composed of

   (A) chitin
   (B) peptidoglycan
   (C) cellulose
   (D) a phospholipid bilayer
   (E) keratin

43. Cellular respiration takes place in the structure labeled

   (A) 1
   (B) 2
   (C) 3
   (D) 4
   (E) 5

44. The structure labeled 6 is used for

   (A) reproduction
   (B) movement
   (C) predator avoidance
   (D) thermoregulation
   (E) protein synthesis

GO ON TO THE NEXT PAGE

Questions 45–48 refer to the animals depicted below.

45. Which of the above organisms have young that develop in amniotic eggs?

    (A) 1, 2
    (B) 1, 2, 4
    (C) 1, 2, 5
    (D) 1, 2, 4, 5
    (E) 2, 4, 5

46. Which of the above organisms has a flexible skeleton made of cartilage?

    (A) 1
    (B) 2
    (C) 3
    (D) 4
    (E) 5

47. Organism 1 belongs to

    (A) the class Amphibia
    (B) the class Mammalia
    (C) the class Aves
    (D) the class Reptilia
    (E) the phylum Animalia

48. Which of the above organisms are ectothermic?

    (A) 1, 4, 5
    (B) 1, 2, 4, 5
    (C) 1, 5
    (D) 2, 3
    (E) 2, 3, 4

GO ON TO THE NEXT PAGE

Questions 49–52 refer to the diagram of neuron.

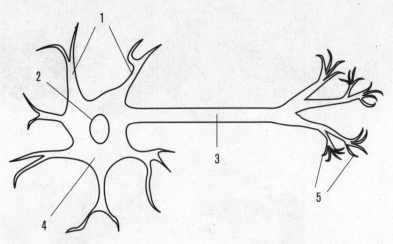

49. The structure labeled 1 is a(n)

(A) axon
(B) terminal branch
(C) cell body
(D) dendrite
(E) nucleus

50. The correct path of an electrical impulse through a neuron is

(A) axon, dendrite, cell body
(B) dendrite, axon, cell body
(C) cell body, dendrite, axon
(D) dendrite, cell body, axon
(E) axon, cell body, dendrite

51. The gap between one neuron and an adjacent neuron is called a

(A) synapse
(B) node of Ranvier
(C) voltage-gate
(D) threshold
(E) ganglia

52. The myelin sheath wraps around the structure labeled

(A) 1
(B) 2
(C) 3
(D) 4
(E) 5

GO ON TO THE NEXT PAGE

Questions 53–56 refer to the following case of a genetic disease.

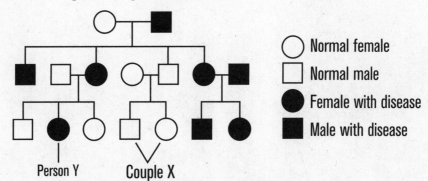

53. The above pedigree shows inheritance patterns that suggest that the genetic disease is

    (A) simple dominant
    (B) sex-linked dominant
    (C) simple recessive
    (D) sex-linked recessive
    (E) none of the above

54. What is the likelihood that person Y is homozygous for the disease?

    (A) 0%
    (B) 25%
    (C) 50%
    (D) 75%
    (E) 100%

55. If couple X has a child, what is the probability that the child will have the disease?

    (A) 0 %
    (B) 25 %
    (C) 50 %
    (D) 75 %
    (E) 100 %

56. Which of the following statements is NOT true?

    (A) Humans have 44 autosomes and 2 sex chromosomes.
    (B) Humans have 46 chromosomes.
    (C) If the fertilizing sperm carries an X chromosome, the child will be male.
    (D) Sex-linked traits are controlled by genes located on sex chromosomes.
    (E) Monosomy is the absence of one copy of a chromosome.

GO ON TO THE NEXT PAGE

Questions 57–60 refer to the diagram of the human endocrine system.

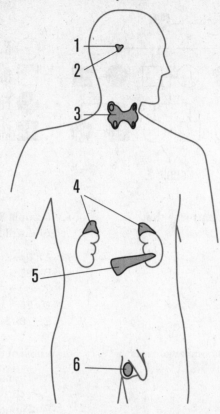

57. The structure labeled 6 is the

    (A) pituitary gland
    (B) adrenal gland
    (C) pancreas
    (D) thyroid
    (E) testis

58. The structure that releases the hormone insulin is

    (A) 1
    (B) 2
    (C) 3
    (D) 4
    (E) 5

59. A patient with low iodine intake and low levels of thyroxine is experiencing symptoms of low metabolic rate, obesity, and sluggishness. She likely has a problem with her

    (A) pituitary gland
    (B) thyroid gland
    (C) adrenal glands
    (D) testes
    (E) ovaries

60. Which of the following is NOT true regarding steroid hormones?

    (A) They are made of cholesterol.
    (B) They are hydrophilic.
    (C) They are lipids.
    (D) They react more slowly than peptide hormones.
    (E) Examples of steroid hormones are testosterone and estrogen.

GO ON TO THE NEXT PAGE ➡

BIOLOGY-E SECTION

If you are taking the Biology-E test, continue with questions 61–80.
If you are taking the Biology-M test, go to question 81 now.

<u>Directions:</u> Each of the questions or incomplete statements below is followed by five suggested answers or completions. Some questions pertain to a set that refers to a laboratory or experimental situation. For each question, select the one choice that is the best answer to the question and then fill in the corresponding oval on the answer sheet.

61. The part of the brain that regulates temperature and controls hunger and thirst is the

   (A) cerebrum
   (B) medulla oblongata
   (C) hypothalamus
   (D) cerebellum
   (E) brainstem

62. Which organelle(s) would you find in a plant cell but not in an animal cell?

   (A) Mitochondria
   (B) Ribosomes
   (C) Golgi body
   (D) Chloroplasts
   (E) Nucleus

63. Which of the following is NOT true of viruses?

   (A) Viruses are extremely small.
   (B) Viruses can only reproduce by using another cell's machinery.
   (C) The genetic material of a virus is never DNA.
   (D) Viruses do not fit well into the taxonomic system.
   (E) The life cycle of a virus includes attachment, penetration, replication, and release.

64. The maximum number of individuals that can be maintained in a given environment is called the

   (A) community
   (B) population
   (C) niche
   (D) climax community
   (E) carrying capacity

65. The diaphragm is part of the

   (A) digestive system
   (B) endocrine system
   (C) nervous system
   (D) respiratory system
   (E) skeletal system

66. If a farmer wants to increase the amount of nitrogen available to his plants, what should he do?

   I.   Add nitrogen-fixing legumes to his field.
   II. Add fertilizer to his field.
   III. Add denitrifying bacteria.

   (A) I only
   (B) II only
   (C) III only
   (D) I and II only
   (E) I, II, and III

GO ON TO THE NEXT PAGE

Questions 67–69 refer to a classic experiment with barnacles, as conducted by Joseph Cornell.

Both Barnacle Species are Present

Semibalanus is removed.
Chthamalus remains.

Chthamalus is removed.
Semibalanus remains.

▽ = Chthamalus
◀ = Semibalanus

67. The force keeping *Chthamalus* from occupying deeper water is

  (A) competition
  (B) predation
  (C) intolerance of deeper water
  (D) parasitism
  (E) coevolution

68. The force keeping *Semibalanus* from occupying shallower water is

  (A) competition
  (B) predation
  (C) intolerance of shallow water
  (D) parasitism
  (E) coevolution

69. Which of the following is NOT an accurate statement?

  (A) When both *Semibalanus* and *Chthamalus* are present, the niche *Chthamalus* occupies is smaller than the niche it would occupy if *Semibalanus* were absent.
  (B) Elimination of competing species is called "competitive exclusion."
  (C) A niche is simply where an organism lives.
  (D) When both *Semibalanus* and *Chthamalus* are present, the niche *Semibalanus* occupies is equal to the niche it would occupy if *Chthamalus* were absent.
  (E) Common use of scarce resources often leads to competition.

GO ON TO THE NEXT PAGE

Questions 70–73 refer to the diagrams of the food web and food chain below.

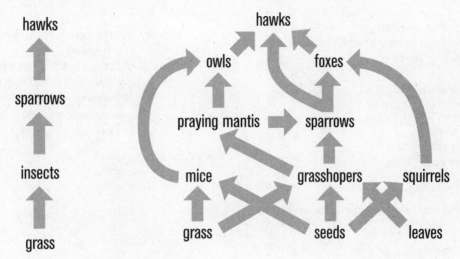

70. Which of the following is / are true regarding grasses?

   I.   They are autotrophs.
   II. They are primary producers.
   III. They cannot produce the energy and organic
        molecules necessary for life.
   IV. They are consumers.

   (A) I only
   (B) IV only
   (C) I and III only
   (D) I and II only
   (E) III and IV only

71. An example of a tertiary consumer is a

   (A) hawk
   (B) grasshopper
   (C) deer
   (D) sparrow
   (E) grass

72. Which of the following is NOT a true statement?

   (A) When a hawk eats a fox, not all energy is transferred
       from the fox to thehawk.
   (B) Food chains are a more accurate representation of
       trophic dynamics thanfood webs because they are
       more complex.
   (C) Grasshoppers consume seeds, so grasshoppers are
       considered primaryconsumers.
   (D) Most organisms in a community hunt for more than
       one kind of prey andare hunted by more than one
       predator.
   (E) The diagrams of the food chain and food web contain
       examples ofproducers andconsumers but not of
       decomposers.

73. Approximately how much energy would be available to
    organisms in the second trophic level if there were
    10,000 kcal available in the first trophic level?

   (A) 100,000 kcal
   (B) 10,000 kcal
   (C) 1,000 kcal
   (D) 100 kcal
   (E) 10 kcal

GO ON TO THE NEXT PAGE

Questions 74–76 refer to the following scenario.

An island is created by a volcanic eruption. Over the next 10,000 years, the island becomes populated by plants and animals from a nearby continent.

74. The process described is called

    (A) evolution
    (B) natural selection
    (C) primary succession
    (D) secondary succession
    (E) fixation

75. Compared with later successional stages, early successional stages have

    (A) more heterotrophic species
    (B) more biomass
    (C) higher productivity
    (D) more pioneer species
    (E) more soil nutrients

76. Which of the following is most similar to the volcanic island?

    (A) An old agricultural field that is no longer being cultivated
    (B) A forest that has been cleared of trees
    (C) An island that has been devastated by a hurricane
    (D) An area where a glacier has recently receded and exposed bare rock
    (E) A grassland that has recently caught on fire

GO ON TO THE NEXT PAGE

Questions 77–80 refer to the following map of the world.

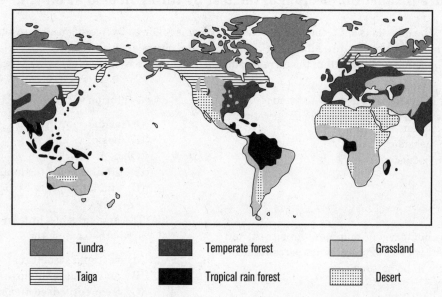

Tundra	Temperate forest	Grassland
Taiga	Tropical rain forest	Desert

77. Which of the regions has the greatest species diversity?

   (A) Tundra
   (B) Grassland
   (C) Taiga
   (D) Rainforest
   (E) Temperate deciduous forest

78. A biome that is characterized by spruce trees and moose is

   (A) tundra
   (B) grassland
   (C) taiga
   (D) desert
   (E) temperate deciduous forest

79. Which of the following biomes is INCORRECTLY matched with a representative organism?

   (A) Tundra – caribou
   (B) Grassland – bison
   (C) Temperate deciduous forest – squirrel
   (D) Rainforest – jaguar
   (E) Desert – bear

80. Rank the biomes in order from lowest to highest latitude.

   (A) Tundra, taiga, temperate deciduous forest, rainforest
   (B) Taiga, tundra, temperate deciduous forest, rainforest
   (C) Rainforest, temperate deciduous forest, tundra, taiga
   (D) Rainforest, temperate deciduous forest, taiga, tundra
   (E) Rainforest, taiga, tundra, temperate deciduous forest

GO ON TO THE NEXT PAGE

BIOLOGY-M SECTION

If you are taking the Biology-M test, continue with questions 81–100.
Be sure to start this section of the test by filling in oval 81 on your answer sheet.

Directions: Each of the questions or incomplete statements below is followed by five suggested answers or completions. Some questions pertain to a set that refers to a laboratory or experimental situation. For each question, select the one choice that is the best answer to the question and then fill in the corresponding oval on the answer sheet.

81. If the sequence of nucleotides in a DNA strand is CGTAAGC, the sequence of the complementary strand is

    (A) GCATTCG
    (B) CGTAAGC
    (C) CGAATGC
    (D) GCTTACG
    (E) GCAUUCG

82. If one parent is homozygous dominant for a trait, and the other parent is heterozygous, what percentage of their offspring will be heterozygous?

    (A) 0 %
    (B) 25 %
    (C) 50 %
    (D) 75 %
    (E) 100 %

83. Which of the following was NOT found in the early atmosphere of the Earth?

    (A) Hydrogen
    (B) Water
    (C) Ammonia
    (D) Methane
    (E) Oxygen

84. A solution with a pH of 8 is

    (A) acidic
    (B) basic
    (C) neutral
    (D) similar in pH to stomach fluid
    (E) similar in pH to hydrochloric acid

85. The appendix of a human and the wings of an ostrich are both examples of

    (A) vestigial structures
    (B) analogous structures
    (C) frequently used structures
    (D) homologous structures
    (E) budding

86. During the process of cellular respiration, which stage results in the greatestproduction of ATP?

    (A) Glycolysis
    (B) The Krebs cycle
    (C) The electron transport chain
    (D) The light reactions
    (E) The dark reactions

GO ON TO THE NEXT PAGE

Questions 87–90 refer to the genetic disease described below.

Hemophilia is a disease caused by a mutation on a sex chromosome. Hemophilia affects the blood's ability to clot.

87. Not all female individuals who carry the allele for hemophilia are affected by the disease, but all male individuals who carry the allele for hemophilia are affected by it. The disorder is

   (A) simple dominant
   (B) simple recessive
   (C) sex-linked dominant
   (D) sex-linked recessive
   (E) complex dominant

88. In order for a mutation to be inherited from one generation to another, it must

   (A) occur on a sex cell
   (B) occur on a somatic cell
   (C) occur on a protein
   (D) be disease-causing
   (E) be sex-linked

89. If a woman who is heterozygous for hemophilia marries a man who has hemophilia, what is the probability that their male child will have the disease?

   (A) 0 %
   (B) 25 %
   (C) 50 %
   (D) 75 %
   (E) 100 %

90. A photograph of the chromosomes of an individual cell is called a

   (A) pedigree
   (B) Punnett square
   (C) gene map
   (D) karyotype
   (E) test cross

GO ON TO THE NEXT PAGE

Questions 91–93 refer to the following experiment and its outcome.

In an experiment, students investigated the influence of temperature on the activity of an enzyme called amylase. Amylase breaks down starch (a polysaccharide composed of glucose monomers). Students filled four standard test tubes with amylase and starch solutions. Tube 1 was placed in an 80°C water bath, tube 2 in a 37°C water bath, tube 3 in a test-tube rack at room temperature, and tube 4 in a beaker of crushed ice. At 10-minute intervals, students tested samples from each test tube for the presence of starch.

The results are depicted in the following table.

Test Tube	Temperature (°C)	Time Until Starch Disappearance (min)
1	80	28
2	37	12
3	22	16
4	4	Over 30 minutes

91. Which of the following ranks the temperatures in order of fastest starch disappearance to slowest?

    (A) 37, 80, 22, 4
    (B) 4, 22, 80, 37
    (C) 37, 22, 80, 4
    (D) 80, 22, 37, 4
    (E) 4, 80, 22, 37

92. At what temperature was the enzyme optimally active?

    (A) 80°C
    (B) 37°C
    (C) 22°C
    (D) 4°C
    (E) A temperature higher than 80°C

93. Which of the following explains why starch was not broken down by the amylase when the solution was placed in an ice bath?

    I.   Amylase was denatured by high temperatures.
    II. At freezing temperatures, the velocity of the enzymatic reaction is exceedingly slow because substrate molecules are not colliding with active sites.
    III. An inhibitor molecule occupied all of the active sites on the amylase enzyme.

    (A) I only
    (B) II only
    (C) III only
    (D) I and III only
    (E) I, II, and III

GO ON TO THE NEXT PAGE

Questions 94–96 refer to the following figures of molecules.

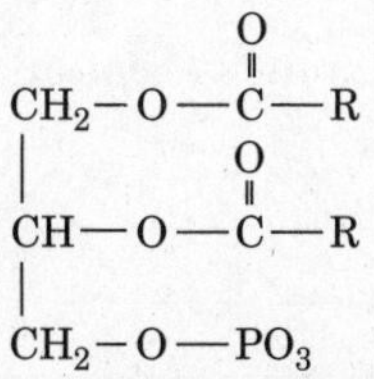

Figure 1 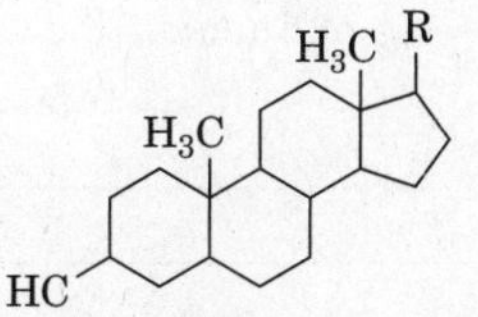   Figure 2 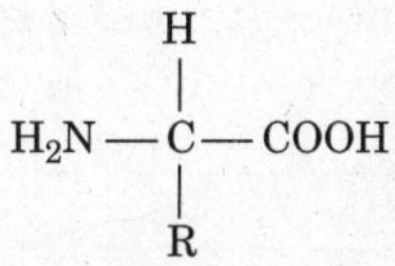   Figure 3 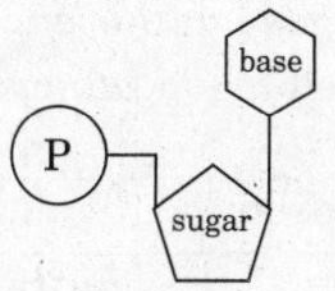   Figure 4 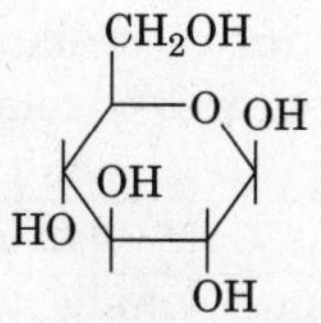   Figure 5

94. Which of the depicted molecules is found in DNA?

    (A) 1
    (B) 2
    (C) 3
    (D) 4
    (E) 5

95. Molecule 5 is a

    (A) protein
    (B) monosaccharide
    (C) starch
    (D) lipid
    (E) nucleic acid

96. Molecule 1 would most likely be found in

    (A) an amino acid
    (B) a cell membrane
    (C) DNA
    (D) a disaccharide
    (E) RNA

GO ON TO THE NEXT PAGE

<u>Questions 97–100</u>

A biologist visiting the Galápagos Islands encounters 10 similar species of finches. The different species all have different beak widths, which seem to be related to food choice.

Beak Width	Food Choice	Species
13 mm – 15 mm	Bud eaters	*Platyspiza crassirostris*
7 mm – 9 mm	Insect eaters	*Camarhynchus pallidus, Camarhynchus parvulus, Camarhynchus psittacula*
17 mm – 19 mm	Seed eaters	*Geospiza difficilis, Geospiza fuliginosa, Geospiza fortis, Geospiza magnirostris*
11 mm – 13 mm	Cactus eaters	*Geospiza conirostris, Geospiza scandens*

97. It is hypothesized that one common ancestor came from the mainland to the Galápagos Islands. The 10 species are thought to have evolved from that one common ancestor. This is an example of

   (A) Lamarckian evolution
   (B) convergent evolution
   (C) genetic drift
   (D) adaptive radiation
   (E) artificial selection

98. How is it that the 10 species can all coexist on the islands?

   (A) They all came from a common ancestor.
   (B) They all occupy different niches.
   (C) There is fierce competition among individuals of different species.
   (D) They all eat the same food.
   (E) They all occupy different biomes.

99. Based on the given data, if an unknown genetic disease were to wipe out most of the insects on the islands, which of the following would shape the beak width of the birds on the Galápagos?

   (A) Stabilizing selection
   (B) Directional selection
   (C) Disruptive selection
   (D) Speciation
   (E) Hardy-Weinberg equilibrium

100. Which of the following proves that *Platyspiza crassirostris* and *Geospiza scandens*, which both can have a beak width of 13 mm, are separate species?

   (A) They do not eat the same food.
   (B) They occupy different niches.
   (C) They cannot interbreed.
   (D) *Platyspiza crassirostris* are brightly colored, while *Geospiza scandens* are duller.
   (E) *Platyspiza crassirostris* live in trees, while *Geospiza scandens* make their home in cacti.

S T O P

IF YOU FINISH BEFORE TIME IS CALLED, YOU MAY CHECK YOUR WORK ON THIS TEST ONLY.
DO NOT TURN TO ANY OTHER TEST IN THIS BOOK.

SAT II Biology Test 1
Explanations

Answers to SAT II Biology Practice Test 1

Question Number	Correct Answer	Right	Wrong	Question Number	Correct Answer	Right	Wrong	Question Number	Correct Answer	Right	Wrong
1.	E			34.	E			67.	A		
2.	D			35.	A			68.	C		
3.	B			36.	C			69.	C		
4.	E			37.	B			70.	D		
5.	A			38.	B			71.	A		
6.	D			39.	B			72.	B		
7.	D			40.	D			73.	C		
8.	C			41.	A			74.	C		
9.	A			42.	B			75.	D		
10.	B			43.	D			76.	D		
11.	A			44.	B			77.	D		
12.	E			45.	A			78.	C		
13.	D			46.	E			79.	E		
14.	D			47.	D			80.	D		
15.	C			48.	A			81.	A		
16.	D			49.	D			82.	C		
17.	D			50.	D			83.	E		
18.	A			51.	A			84.	B		
19.	C			52.	C			85.	A		
20.	B			53.	A			86.	C		
21.	B			54.	A			87.	D		
22.	B			55.	A			88.	A		
23.	E			56.	C			89.	C		
24.	B			57.	E			90.	D		
25.	D			58.	E			91.	C		
26.	A			59.	B			92.	B		
27.	A			60.	B			93.	B		
28.	C			61.	C			94.	D		
29.	B			62.	D			95.	E		
30.	D			63.	C			96.	B		
31.	C			64.	E			97.	D		
32.	A			65.	D			98.	B		
33.	B			66.	D			99.	B		
								100.	C		

Your raw score for the SAT II Biology test is calculated from the number of questions you answer correctly and incorrectly. Once you have determined your composite score, use the conversion table on page **21** of this book to calculate your scaled score. To calculate your raw score, count the number of questions you answered correctly: _____

A

Count the number of questions you answered incorrectly, and multiply that number by $\frac{1}{4}$:

$$\underline{\hspace{2cm}} \times \frac{1}{4} = \underline{\hspace{2cm}}$$
B   C

Subtract the value in field C from value in field A: _____

D

Round the number in field D to the nearest whole number. This is your raw score: _____

E

Biology E/M Classification Questions

1. **(E)**   Organic and Biochemistry

An atom that contains a larger or smaller number of neutrons than usual is called an isotope. Nitrogen typically contains 7 protons and 7 neutrons; this form of nitrogen is called nitrogen-14. An isotope of nitrogen that contains 7 protons and 8 neutrons is called nitrogen-15.

2. **(D)**   Organic and Biochemistry

Electrons, protons, and neutrons are the main components of an atom. Both protons and neutrons can be found in the nucleus of the atom. The word "nucleus" refers to the central body of any object. Electrons appear around the nucleus within orbitals of varying energies. Protons have a positive charge, neutrons have a neutral charge, and electrons have a negative charge. The nucleus is thus positively charged and attracts the negatively charged electrons that are in the orbitals.

3. **(B)**   Organic and Biochemistry

An ion is an atom that either lacks or has extra electrons. The number of electrons in an atom is usually equal to the number of protons in the atom. If an atom has more electrons than protons, it will have a negative charge. If an atom has fewer electrons than protons, it will have a positive charge.

4. **(E)**   Ecology

An ecosystem consists of a community of organisms (biotic factors) and its abiotic environment. Abiotic factors are the non-living components of the ecosystem. Examples of abiotic factors are soil, water, and weather.

5. **(A)**   Ecology

"Biodiversity" is a term that refers to the number and types of different species in a given area or ecosystem. More species are found in tropical rainforests than in any other biome. The tropical rainforest therefore has the highest biodiversity.

6. **(D)**   Ecology

K-strategists are organisms that mature slowly, reproduce later in life, and bear few young. Humans are an example of a K-strategist. The opposite of K-strategists are R-strategists, which mature quickly, reproduce early in life, and produce numerous offspring. Insects are R-strategists.

7.   **(D)**   Genetics

Homozygous refers to a situation in which an organism's two alleles for a specific trait are identical (e.g., AA or aa). In contrast, heterozygous refers to a situation in which an organism's two alleles for a specific trait are different (e.g., Aa). Remember that "homo" means "same" and "hetero" means "different."

8.   **(C)**   Genetics

A gamete is a haploid sex cell. The male gamete is the sperm, and the female gamete is the egg. The gametes fuse during fertilization to make a diploid zygote that can develop into a diploid individual.

9.   **(A)**   Genetics

The phenotype is the physical expression of a certain trait. The genotype is the genetic makeup of the trait, as indicated by a set of alleles. For example, a person's phenotype for eye color is "blue," but their genotype for eye color is "bb."

10.   **(B)**   Organismal Biology

Invertebrates do not have internal skeletal structures that provide support, such as bones or cartilage. Some invertebrates, such as earthworms and jellyfish, have a hydrostatic skeleton that consists of fluid under pressure in a closed cavity. The fluid bathes and protects internal structures.

11.   **(A)**   Organismal Biology

Ligaments are tissues that hold adjacent bones together. It is easy to confuse ligaments with tendons. Tendons connect muscles with bones.

12.   **(E)**   Organismal Biology

Bones are rigid structures composed of living cells that are rooted in a matrix of calcium, phosphate salts, and collagen fibers. All vertebrates have bones.

Biology E/M Solitary Multiple Choice

13.   **(D)**   Evolution and Diversity

Natural selection is a mechanism of evolution. If a species produces more offspring than can survive, due to limited resources, predation, or disease, then there is competition among individuals for survival. Individuals within populations have different variations of traits, and some variations confer a survival advantage over others. Individuals with advantageous variations leave more offspring. In this case, the rabbits that are better adapted to the heat will survive and produce more offspring. Because the traits are heritable, the frequency of the successful variation will increase among the population.

14. **(D)**   The Cell

Ribosomes are cell structures that are involved in gene expression. On the ribosomes, the genetic material is translated into proteins, which work in the body to "express" the instructions embedded in the genetic code. Vacuoles serve as storage units within the cell. Lysosomes digest wastes. Cell walls provide structure and stability. Mitochondria are involved in energy production.

15. **(C)**   Ecology

Primary consumers eat primary producers (plants) and are always herbivores.

   The food chain represents "who is eaten by who" in a community. Primary producers are eaten by primary consumers. Primary consumers are eaten by secondary consumers. Secondary consumers are eaten by tertiary consumers , and so on, until the food chain ends.

16. **(D)**   Organismal Biology

Xylem carry water and minerals up from the root, are composed of dead cells, provide structural support, and are sometimes called "wood." Xylem are not involved in distributing carbohydrates. Carbohydrates such as glucose (produced in photosynthesis) are sources of food for the plant cells. Carbohydrates are carried by phloem.

17. **(D)**   Evolution and Diversity

Warm-blooded animals that have hair and mammary glands are called mammals. There are three types of mammals: placental mammals, marsupials, and monotremes. Placental mammals have young that develop completely within the placenta of the mother's uterus. Marsupials give birth to young just days after fertilization, and the minimally developed offspring finish development in a pouch on the mother's body. Monotremes reproduce by laying eggs. There are only three species of monotremes (the platypus and two species of echidnas), and they all live in Australia or New Guinea.

18. **(A)**   Ecology

This is an example of coevolution. Coevolution refers to the reciprocal evolutionary adjustments that take place between interacting members of an ecosystem.

19. **(C)**   Organic and Biochemistry

Proteins, carbohydrates, lipids, and nucleic acids are the building blocks of life and are called organic molecules. By definition, all organic molecules contain carbon.

20. **(B)** Genetics

During metaphase, chromosomes are aligned along the middle of the cell, half way between each of the mitotic spindle poles along a plane called the metaphase plate. One way to jog your memory about this is to remember that "meta" means "middle."

21. **(B)** Organismal Biology

Oxytocin is the hormone that stimulates contractions. A woman in labor would have elevated levels of oxytocin because she is experiencing contractions.

22. **(B)** Evolution and Diversity

The Hardy-Weinberg Theorem describes a gene pool in equilibrium (i.e., a non-evolving population). Hardy-Weinberg equilibrium requires a large population size, an absence of immigration or emigration, random reproductive success, no mutation, and random mating. If mating is non-random and individuals select mates that have particular heritable traits, then there will not be random mixing of gametes, and a change in gene frequency will occur over time. Remember that the definition of evolution is "the change in the allele frequencies in the gene pool over time."

23. **(E)** The Cell

Cells are small because surface area and volume must be balanced. As a cell increases in size, its surface area does not increase as rapidly as its volume. Substances are constantly moving in an out of cells across the cell surface. If the cell's surface area-to-volume ratio is too low, substances cannot move quickly enough across the cell's surface.

24. **(B)** Ecology

In the water cycle, water moves from oceans, rivers, and lakes to the atmosphere via evaporation.

25. **(D)** Evolution and Diversity

Arthropods do not have 4-chambered hearts. Arthropods have open circulatory systems, which means than there are no veins and, generally, no heart.

26. **(A)** Evolution and Diversity

Angiosperms have seeds, which are structures that consist of a plant embryo surrounded by a protective coating. Seeds are an adaptation for terrestrial life. Bryophytes reproduce through spores and require water for fertilization. Ferns, horsetails, and club mosses are all seedless, non-vascular plants. They also reproduce by spores and have flagellated sperm that require water. None of the non-vascular plants can produce seeds.

27. **(A)** Organismal Biology

The correct pathway of food through the digestive system is: esophagus, stomach, small intestine, large intestine, rectum.

28. **(C)** Ecology

The best representation of a community is all of the animal populations that live and interact in a prairie dog town. A community consists of all of the populations that interact in a given geographical area.

29. **(B)** Cell Processes

Cytokinesis is the final stage of cell division. A cell with duplicated contents splits into two independent cells.

30. **(D)** The Cell

The dark reaction phase of photosynthesis takes place in the stroma. During the dark reaction, the chloroplast produces the six-carbon compound that is the plants' "food" and produces the raw materials that are necessary for the next round of photosynthesis.

Biology E/M Group Multiple Choice

31. **(C)** Cell Processes

Cellular respiration is the process of extracting useful energy from carbohydrates. The yeast was extracting energy from the sugar. Because the tube was not exposed to oxygen in the vertical segment, respiration was anaerobic.

32. **(A)** Cell Processes

The bubbles that were produced in the tube were carbon dioxide molecules. All respiring organisms (humans, yeasts, plants, bacteria, etc.) expel carbon dioxide.

33. **(B)** Cell Processes or Evolution and Diversity

Yeast is a member of the kingdom Fungi.

34. **(E)** Cell Processes

Strenuous exercise can often cause a temporary oxygen shortage in muscles because the circulatory system cannot deliver oxygen as fast as the muscles use it. When muscles experience oxygen shortages, they have to respire anaerobically. The type of anaerobic respiration that is most common in vertebrate muscles is lactic acid fermentation. It is the buildup of lactic acid that often results in fatigue and soreness of muscles after strenuous exercise.

35. **(A)**   Cell Processes

During glycolysis, ATP is used to split glucose into pyruvate. Remember that the chemical formula for glycolysis is:

$$C_6H_{12}O_6 + 2ATP + 2NAD^+ \rightarrow 2Pyruvate + 4ATP + 2NADH$$

36. **(C)**   Organismal Biology

The structure labeled 3 is the right ventricle. Remember that a drawing of a heart is essentially a mirror image of the structure. Therefore, the structures on the left side of the page are the right atrium and right ventricle, and vice versa.

37. **(B)**   Organismal Biology

Let's trace the path of blood through the heart. Oxygen-poor blood returning from the body enters through the vena cava into the right atrium and then moves to the right ventricle. The right ventricle pumps the blood through the pulmonary artery to the lungs, where it is oxygenated. From the lungs, the pulmonary veins carry the newly oxygenated blood to the left atrium. Blood then moves to the left ventricle and is pumped out through the aorta to the rest of the body. Therefore, blood in the right atrium, right ventricle, and pulmonary artery is oxygen-poor. Blood in the pulmonary veins, left atrium, left ventricle, and aorta is oxygen-rich.

38. **(B)**   Organismal Biology

The sinoatrial node stimulates cardiac muscles to contract in a regular and controlled rhythm.

39. **(B)**   Organismal Biology

A heart with 3 chambers could belong to a reptile. Birds and mammals (including humans) have a 4-chambered heart. The circulatory system in fish consists of a single closed loop.

40. **(D)**   The Cell

Cell II is a plant cell, and cell III is an animal cell. Both plant and animal cells are eukaryotic. Like prokaryotes, eukaryotes are surrounded by a cell membrane and have cytoplasm and ribosomes. Unlike prokaryotes, eukaryotes contain organelles and a defined nucleus containing DNA. Examples of organelles are mitochondria, chloroplasts, Golgi bodies, and vacuoles.

41.   **(A)**   The Cell

The structure labeled 2 is the nucleus. The nucleus contains genetic material in the form of DNA. It is surrounded by a nuclear envelope and also houses a small, dark structure called the nucleolus.

42.   **(B)**   The Cell

Cell I is a prokaryotic cell. The cell walls of prokaryotes are composed of peptidoglycan. Both animal and plant cells are eukaryotic. However, animal cells do not have cell walls, while plant cells have cell walls made of cellulose.

43.   **(D)**   The Cell

Cellular respiration takes place in the structure labeled 4, which is a mitochondrion. Mitochondria are often called the "powerhouses" of a cell because they produce energy in the form of ATP.

44.   **(B)**   The Cell

The structure labeled 6 is a flagellum. The flagellum is a whiplike tail that helps propel cells through liquid.

45.   **(A)**   Evolution and Diversity

While fish, reptiles, and birds all lay eggs, not all three lay amniotic eggs. An amniotic egg is an egg with a hard shell that retains water. The amniotic egg is an adaptation that allows reptiles, birds, and egg-laying mammals to exist entirely on land.

46.   **(E)**   Evolution and Diversity

Sharks, eels, and rays are cartilaginous fish, which means that their skeletons are made of cartilage rather than bone.

47.   **(D)**   Evolution and Diversity

Organism 1 is an alligator. Alligators are reptiles. All reptiles belong to kingdom Animalia, phylum Chordata, and class Reptilia.

48.   **(A)**   Evolution and Diversity

An ectothermic animal is an animal whose body temperature is determined by its environment. Ectothermic animals are often called "cold-blooded." Vertebrates that evolved before birds are ectothermic. Fishes, sharks, and alligators are all ectothermic.

49.   **(D)**   Organismal Biology

The structure labeled 1 is a dendrite. A dendrite is a cytoplasmic extension of a neuron that receives electrical stimuli.

50. (D)   Organismal Biology

The correct path of an electrical impulse through a neuron is: dendrite, cell body, axon.

51. (A)   Organismal Biology

A synapse is the gap between the axon terminals of one neuron and the dendrite of another.

52. (C)   Organismal Biology

Myelin sheaths wrap around the axon. The sheath is composed of Schwann cells. The myelin sheath insulates the axon and helps speed movement of action potentials along the axon.

53. (A)   Genetics

The pedigree shows a trait with an inheritance pattern that is simple dominant. If a characteristic is due to a dominant gene, the affected individual must always have a parent showing that characteristic. If a trait is simple rather than sex-linked, males and females will be equally likely to inherit the trait.

54. (A)   Genetics

In order to get this question right, you have to first understand that the allele for the disease is simple dominant. Person Y has one parent with the disease and one without it, and neither of the siblings of person Y have the disease. Therefore, person Y's father (who does not have the disease) must be homozygous recessive (aa), while person Y's mother must be heterozygous (Aa). It is impossible for a person who has one homozygous recessive parent and one heterozygous parent to be homozygous dominant.

55. (A)   Genetics

The probability that the child will have or be a carrier of the disease is 0% because neither of the parents had the disease, so they could not pass it on to their offspring. Because the trait is simple dominant, anyone who shows the characteristic must have at least one dominant allele. In other words, a person who has the disease must have a homozygous dominant or heterozygous phenotype. Anyone who does not show the characteristic must not have any dominant alleles. In other words, a person who does not have the disease has a homozygous recessive genotype and can pass only recessive genes on to his or her offspring

56. (C)   Genetics

Each child receives one sex chromosome from each parent. Females have the genotype XX, and males have the genotype XY. The mother can produce gametes (eggs) with only X-chromosomes, but the father can produce gametes (sperm) with either an X-chromosome or a Y-chromosome. Since all of the eggs carry an X-chromosome, the sex of the child is determined by whether the sperm carries an X- or a Y-chromosome. If the sperm carries an X-chromosome, the baby will be female. If the sperm carries a Y-chromosome, the baby will be male.

57. **(E)**   Organismal Biology
Structure 6 is the testis. Testes are found in the scrotum of males, and they produce sperm as well as the hormone called testosterone.

58. **(E)**   Organismal Biology
The pancreas is the organ behind the stomach that secretes insulin. Insulin stimulates cells to absorb glucose from the bloodstream when glucose levels are high.

59. **(B)**   Organismal Biology
The thyroid gland requires iodine in order to produce a hormone called thyroxine. Thyroxine is a regulator of metabolism. A person with hypothyroidism has too little thyroxine. Their metabolism is consequently low, and the person suffers from fatigue and weight gain.

60. **(B)**   Organismal Biology
Steroid hormones are made of lipids and are hydrophobic, not hydrophilic. Because steroids are hydrophobic, they can easily pass into the bloodstream.

Biology E Solitary Multiple Choice

61. **(C)**   Organismal Biology
The hypothalamus is the part of the brain that regulates temperature and controls hunger and thirst.

62. **(D)**   The Cell
Plant cells have chloroplasts, but animal cells do not. Chloroplasts harness the sun's energy to produce carbohydrate food via photosynthesis.

63. **(C)**   Evolution and Diversity
The genetic material of viruses can be either DNA or RNA.

64. **(E)**   Ecology
"Carrying capacity" is the term for the maximum number of individuals that can be maintained in a given environment.

65. **(D)**   Organismal Biology

The diaphragm is a large muscle at the base of the chest cavity. It contracts and relaxes to facilitate inhalation and exhalation. The diaphragm is part of the respiratory system.

66. **(D)**   Ecology

Plants can only use nitrogen in the form of nitrates (NO_3^-). In order to increase the amount of nitrogen available to plants, the farmer could add nitrogen-fixing legumes, which are plants that convert atmospheric nitrogen to NO_3^-. He could also add fertilizer. Adding denitrifying bacteria would not work because they convert ammonia NH_3 from wastes and dead material into atmospheric nitrogen (N_2).

Biology E Group Multiple Choice

67. **(A)**   Ecology

Competition with *Semibalanus* is the force that kept *Chthamalus* from occupying deeper water. When *Semibalanus* (the competing species) was removed, *Chthamalus* was able to expand its niche.

68. **(C)**   Ecology

When *Chthamalus* was removed, *Semibalanus* was not able to expand its niche. *Semibalanus* is likely intolerant of shallow water.

69. **(C)**   Ecology

A niche is not simply where an animal lives but rather its habitat. A niche is the particular role that an organism plays in an environment—i.e., where it fits in the food chain, how and when it reproduces, time of day that it is active, and so on. An organism's fundamental niche is the entire range of conditions that an organism can tolerate. The realized niche is the part of the fundamental niche that an organism actually occupies. The realized niche is often smaller than the fundamental niche due to competition with other species for limited resources.

70. **(D)**   Ecology

Grasses are plants. Plants are autotrophs, which can harness solar energy from the sun to make their own chemical energy. Plants are the primary producers, and consumers feed on them.

71. **(A)**   Ecology

The hawk is at the top of this food chain and this food web. Tertiary consumers eat secondary consumers, which eat primary consumers, which eat primary producers. Tertiary consumers are carnivores.

72. (B) Ecology

A food web is a more accurate representation of trophic dynamics than a food chain because it is more complex and shows more interactions.

73. (C) Ecology

Each trophic level has only 10% of the energy available from the preceding trophic level. So, if there are 10,000 kcal available in the first trophic level, then there are 1,000 kcal available in the second trophic level. 10% of 10,000 is 1,000.

74. (C) Ecology

Primary succession occurs on a newly created habitat, such as a volcanic island or an area wiped clean by a receding glacier. Because a volcanic eruption causes bare rock to be exposed, there is no plant or animal life, and soil nutrient levels are extremely low. In contrast, secondary succession occurs in areas where there has been destruction of the habitat by an event such as fire, plowing, a hurricane, a flood, and so on. However, the destruction is not severe enough to remove all signs of life. There are residual plants and soil nutrients remaining in the area.

75. (D) Ecology

Pioneer species are the first organisms to colonize an empty habitat. They are usually small and fast growing. Later successional stages have more heterotrophic species because there is more plant life to support them. Likewise, later successional stages have more biomass because plant and animal life is more abundant. Later in succession, there are more plants to harness the sun's energy, so the environment is more productive. Soil nutrients accumulate over successional time, so later stages will have more soil nutrients.

76. (D) Ecology

The receding glacier is the only example in which bare rock is exposed and no residual plant life is present. Like the volcanic island, the receding glacier is an example of primary succession. The other examples are of secondary succession.

77. (D) Ecology

Tropical rainforests have the highest rainfall of all biomes, which results in the greatest plant and animal diversity.

78. **(C)**   Ecology

Taiga is a forested biome, where the trees are coniferous. Typical wildlife in the taiga are birds, small mammals, elk, moose, wolves, and grizzly bears.

79. **(E)**   Ecology

You would not find bears in a desert. Deserts are too dry and hot to support them.

80. **(D)**   Ecology

Latitude increases from 0° at the equator to 90° at the North Pole. The proper ranking of biomes from lowest to highest latitudes is: rainforest, temperate deciduous forest, taiga, tundra.

Biology M Solitary Multiple Choice

81. **(A)**   Cell Processes

DNA is a double-stranded helix. The first strand is complementary to its opposing strand. DNA has four nitrogenous bases—cytosine, guanine, adenine, and thymine. Cytosine always pairs with guanine, and adenine always pairs with thymine. Therefore, if one strand has the sequence consisting of CGTAAGC, then the complimentary strand will be GCATTCG.

82. **(C)**   Genetics

The best way to solve this question is to translate the information given into a Punnett square.

	B	b
B	BB	BB
B	Bb	Bb

50% of the offspring will have the heterozygous genotype Bb.

83. **(E)**   Evolution and Diversity

Oxygen was not a component of the atmosphere of the early earth.

84. **(B)**   Organic and Biochemistry

A solution with a pH of 8 is basic. The pH scale ranges from 0 to 14. A pH of 7 is neutral. The most acidic solutions have pHs approaching 0, while the most basic solutions have pHs approaching 14.

85. **(A)**   Evolution and Diversity

Vestigial structures are structures that evolved in the past but that no longer perform a useful function for the organism. The human appendix serves no actual function in the body, and though ostriches have wings, they cannot use them to fly.

86. **(C)**   Cell Processes

The electron transport chain results in the net production of 34 ATP. Glycolysis produces a net of only 2 ATP.

Biology M Group Multiple Choice

87. **(D)**   Genetics

The trait is sex-linked recessive. We know that hemophilia is sex-linked because it does not occur in equal percentages in males and females. We know that the trait is recessive because the fact that a woman (XX) carries one hemophiliac allele does not mean that she will have the disease.

88. **(A)**   Genetics

Mutations must occur on sex cells (gametes) if they are to be inherited. Only the genetic material in the sperm and egg will be passed on to one's children.

89. **(C)**   Genetics

Build a Punnett square to illustrate a cross of the mother (X normal / X hemophilia) and the father (X hemophilia / Y).

	X^h	Y
X^h	X^hX^h	X^hY
X	XX^h	XY

If they have a male child, he will have a 50% chance of being X^hY and a 50% chance of being XY. If the male is X^hY, he will have hemophilia because he does not have a normal X-chromosome. If they have a female child, she will have a 50% chance of being X^hX^h and a 50% chance of being XX^h. A female with the genotype X^hX^h will have hemophilia. A female with the genotype XX^h will be a carrier of the disease but will not have it.

90. **(D)**   Genetics

A karyotype is a photograph of the chromosomes of an individual cell.

91. **(C)**   Organic and Biochemistry

The starch disappeared first in the 37°C solution and then the 22°, 80°, and 4° solutions.

92. **(B)**   Organic and Biochemistry

Amylase is an enzyme that breaks down starch. The faster the starch disappears, the more active the enzyme is. The starch disappeared the fastest in the 37°C solution, so that is the temperature at which the starch is optimally active.

93. **(B)**   Organic and Biochemistry

Enzymes are denatured only at high temperatures. Therefore, the enzyme in this experiment would not become denatured when placed in an ice bath. There is no reason to think that an inhibitor molecule would outcompete the starch, as an inhibitor was not added to any of the test tubes. Molecules do have a lower velocity at lower temperatures. Therefore, the starch and the enzyme had less of a chance to "collide" in the solution. If the enzyme did not encounter the starch, it could not have broken it down.

94. **(D)**   Organic and Biochemistry

Figure 4 is a nitrogenous base. Nitrogenous bases are the building blocks of DNA. You can recognize nitrogenous bases by their characteristic base, sugar, and phosphate-group construction.

95. **(E)**   Organic and Biochemistry

Figure 5 is a glucose molecule. Glucose is a monosaccharide. Monosaccharides always have a chemical formula according to the ratio $C_1H_2O_1$.

96. **(B)**   Organic and Biochemistry

Molecule 1 is a phospholipid, which you should be able to identify from its glycerol component (CH_2, CH, and CH_2) and also from its phosphate (PO_3). Cell membranes are composed of a phospholipid bilayer.

97. **(D)**   Evolution and Diversity

The particular form of speciation that created Darwin's finches is called adaptive radiation. One species arrived in an area in which very few niches had been exploited. The single species diverged into many species, each occupying a different niche.

98. **(B)**   Evolution and Diversity

Many different species can occupy the islands because they occupy slightly different niches. A niche is the role that a species plays in an ecosystem—what it eats, what time of day it is active, how it finds food, its mating habits, and so on.

99. (B)   Evolution and Diversity

If the insects on the Galápagos were wiped out, finches that eat insects would lose their food source and be selected against. Since the finches that eat insects have the narrowest beaks, directional selection would occur against narrow beaks.

Based on the given table, you could say that *Geospiza fortis* is a seedeater.

100. (C)   Evolution and Diversity

The definition of a species is "a discrete group of organisms that can only breed within its own confines."

SAT II Biology
Practice Test 2

BIOLOGY TEST 2 ANSWER SHEET

1. Ⓐ Ⓑ Ⓒ Ⓓ Ⓔ	26. Ⓐ Ⓑ Ⓒ Ⓓ Ⓔ	51. Ⓐ Ⓑ Ⓒ Ⓓ Ⓔ	76. Ⓐ Ⓑ Ⓒ Ⓓ Ⓔ
2. Ⓐ Ⓑ Ⓒ Ⓓ Ⓔ	27. Ⓐ Ⓑ Ⓒ Ⓓ Ⓔ	52. Ⓐ Ⓑ Ⓒ Ⓓ Ⓔ	77. Ⓐ Ⓑ Ⓒ Ⓓ Ⓔ
3. Ⓐ Ⓑ Ⓒ Ⓓ Ⓔ	28. Ⓐ Ⓑ Ⓒ Ⓓ Ⓔ	53. Ⓐ Ⓑ Ⓒ Ⓓ Ⓔ	78. Ⓐ Ⓑ Ⓒ Ⓓ Ⓔ
4. Ⓐ Ⓑ Ⓒ Ⓓ Ⓔ	29. Ⓐ Ⓑ Ⓒ Ⓓ Ⓔ	54. Ⓐ Ⓑ Ⓒ Ⓓ Ⓔ	79. Ⓐ Ⓑ Ⓒ Ⓓ Ⓔ
5. Ⓐ Ⓑ Ⓒ Ⓓ Ⓔ	30. Ⓐ Ⓑ Ⓒ Ⓓ Ⓔ	55. Ⓐ Ⓑ Ⓒ Ⓓ Ⓔ	80. Ⓐ Ⓑ Ⓒ Ⓓ Ⓔ
6. Ⓐ Ⓑ Ⓒ Ⓓ Ⓔ	31. Ⓐ Ⓑ Ⓒ Ⓓ Ⓔ	56. Ⓐ Ⓑ Ⓒ Ⓓ Ⓔ	81. Ⓐ Ⓑ Ⓒ Ⓓ Ⓔ
7. Ⓐ Ⓑ Ⓒ Ⓓ Ⓔ	32. Ⓐ Ⓑ Ⓒ Ⓓ Ⓔ	57. Ⓐ Ⓑ Ⓒ Ⓓ Ⓔ	82. Ⓐ Ⓑ Ⓒ Ⓓ Ⓔ
8. Ⓐ Ⓑ Ⓒ Ⓓ Ⓔ	33. Ⓐ Ⓑ Ⓒ Ⓓ Ⓔ	58. Ⓐ Ⓑ Ⓒ Ⓓ Ⓔ	83. Ⓐ Ⓑ Ⓒ Ⓓ Ⓔ
9. Ⓐ Ⓑ Ⓒ Ⓓ Ⓔ	34. Ⓐ Ⓑ Ⓒ Ⓓ Ⓔ	59. Ⓐ Ⓑ Ⓒ Ⓓ Ⓔ	84. Ⓐ Ⓑ Ⓒ Ⓓ Ⓔ
10. Ⓐ Ⓑ Ⓒ Ⓓ Ⓔ	35. Ⓐ Ⓑ Ⓒ Ⓓ Ⓔ	60. Ⓐ Ⓑ Ⓒ Ⓓ Ⓔ	85. Ⓐ Ⓑ Ⓒ Ⓓ Ⓔ
11. Ⓐ Ⓑ Ⓒ Ⓓ Ⓔ	36. Ⓐ Ⓑ Ⓒ Ⓓ Ⓔ	61. Ⓐ Ⓑ Ⓒ Ⓓ Ⓔ	86. Ⓐ Ⓑ Ⓒ Ⓓ Ⓔ
12. Ⓐ Ⓑ Ⓒ Ⓓ Ⓔ	37. Ⓐ Ⓑ Ⓒ Ⓓ Ⓔ	62. Ⓐ Ⓑ Ⓒ Ⓓ Ⓔ	87. Ⓐ Ⓑ Ⓒ Ⓓ Ⓔ
13. Ⓐ Ⓑ Ⓒ Ⓓ Ⓔ	38. Ⓐ Ⓑ Ⓒ Ⓓ Ⓔ	63. Ⓐ Ⓑ Ⓒ Ⓓ Ⓔ	88. Ⓐ Ⓑ Ⓒ Ⓓ Ⓔ
14. Ⓐ Ⓑ Ⓒ Ⓓ Ⓔ	39. Ⓐ Ⓑ Ⓒ Ⓓ Ⓔ	64. Ⓐ Ⓑ Ⓒ Ⓓ Ⓔ	89. Ⓐ Ⓑ Ⓒ Ⓓ Ⓔ
15. Ⓐ Ⓑ Ⓒ Ⓓ Ⓔ	40. Ⓐ Ⓑ Ⓒ Ⓓ Ⓔ	65. Ⓐ Ⓑ Ⓒ Ⓓ Ⓔ	90. Ⓐ Ⓑ Ⓒ Ⓓ Ⓔ
16. Ⓐ Ⓑ Ⓒ Ⓓ Ⓔ	41. Ⓐ Ⓑ Ⓒ Ⓓ Ⓔ	66. Ⓐ Ⓑ Ⓒ Ⓓ Ⓔ	91. Ⓐ Ⓑ Ⓒ Ⓓ Ⓔ
17. Ⓐ Ⓑ Ⓒ Ⓓ Ⓔ	42. Ⓐ Ⓑ Ⓒ Ⓓ Ⓔ	67. Ⓐ Ⓑ Ⓒ Ⓓ Ⓔ	92. Ⓐ Ⓑ Ⓒ Ⓓ Ⓔ
18. Ⓐ Ⓑ Ⓒ Ⓓ Ⓔ	43. Ⓐ Ⓑ Ⓒ Ⓓ Ⓔ	68. Ⓐ Ⓑ Ⓒ Ⓓ Ⓔ	93. Ⓐ Ⓑ Ⓒ Ⓓ Ⓔ
19. Ⓐ Ⓑ Ⓒ Ⓓ Ⓔ	44. Ⓐ Ⓑ Ⓒ Ⓓ Ⓔ	69. Ⓐ Ⓑ Ⓒ Ⓓ Ⓔ	94. Ⓐ Ⓑ Ⓒ Ⓓ Ⓔ
20. Ⓐ Ⓑ Ⓒ Ⓓ Ⓔ	45. Ⓐ Ⓑ Ⓒ Ⓓ Ⓔ	70. Ⓐ Ⓑ Ⓒ Ⓓ Ⓔ	95. Ⓐ Ⓑ Ⓒ Ⓓ Ⓔ
21. Ⓐ Ⓑ Ⓒ Ⓓ Ⓔ	46. Ⓐ Ⓑ Ⓒ Ⓓ Ⓔ	71. Ⓐ Ⓑ Ⓒ Ⓓ Ⓔ	96. Ⓐ Ⓑ Ⓒ Ⓓ Ⓔ
22. Ⓐ Ⓑ Ⓒ Ⓓ Ⓔ	47. Ⓐ Ⓑ Ⓒ Ⓓ Ⓔ	72. Ⓐ Ⓑ Ⓒ Ⓓ Ⓔ	97. Ⓐ Ⓑ Ⓒ Ⓓ Ⓔ
23. Ⓐ Ⓑ Ⓒ Ⓓ Ⓔ	48. Ⓐ Ⓑ Ⓒ Ⓓ Ⓔ	73. Ⓐ Ⓑ Ⓒ Ⓓ Ⓔ	98. Ⓐ Ⓑ Ⓒ Ⓓ Ⓔ
24. Ⓐ Ⓑ Ⓒ Ⓓ Ⓔ	49. Ⓐ Ⓑ Ⓒ Ⓓ Ⓔ	74. Ⓐ Ⓑ Ⓒ Ⓓ Ⓔ	99. Ⓐ Ⓑ Ⓒ Ⓓ Ⓔ
25. Ⓐ Ⓑ Ⓒ Ⓓ Ⓔ	50. Ⓐ Ⓑ Ⓒ Ⓓ Ⓔ	75. Ⓐ Ⓑ Ⓒ Ⓓ Ⓔ	100. Ⓐ Ⓑ Ⓒ Ⓓ Ⓔ

BIOLOGY E/M TEST

FOR BOTH BIOLOGY-E AND BIOLOGY-M, ANSWER QUESTIONS 1–60

Directions: Each set of lettered choices below refers to the numbered questions or statements immediately following it. Select the one lettered choice that best answers each question or best fits each statement, and then fill in the corresponding oval on the answer sheet. A choice may be used once, more than once, or not at all in each set.

Questions 1–3 refer to the following parts of the human digestive system.

(A) Salivary glands
(B) Gall bladder
(C) Stomach
(D) Large intestine
(E) Liver

1. Contains symbiotic bacteria such as *E. coli*

2. Has a pH of less than 2 due to secretions of hydrochloric acid

3. Where bile is stored and concentrated

Questions 4–6 refer to members of the kingdom Plantae.

(A) Bryophytes
(B) Gymnosperms
(C) Seedless vascular plants
(D) Angiosperms
(E) Legumes

4. Divided into two subgroups—monocots and dicots

5. Include club mosses, horsetails, and ferns

6. Lack true roots, stems, and leaves

Questions 7–9 refer to the world's biomes.

(A) Taiga
(B) Tropical rainforest
(C) Tundra
(D) Savanna
(E) Desert

7. Exhibits radical temperature changes between night and day

8. Covered by ice sheets for the majority of the year

9. Has the highest rainfall of all biomes and the greatest plant and animal diversity

Questions 10–12 refer to the following components of DNA synthesis.

(A) Transcription
(B) Replication
(C) Messenger RNA
(D) Translation
(E) Transfer RNA

10. The process of assembling an RNA molecule that is complementary to a strand of DNA

11. The process of creating an exact copy of a double helix of DNA

12. Carries a specific amino acid to a growing polypeptide chain

GO ON TO THE NEXT PAGE

BIOLOGY E/M TEST—Continued

Directions: Each of the questions or incomplete statements below is followed by five suggested answers or completions. Some questions pertain to a set that refers to a laboratory or experimental situation. For each question, select the best answer to the question and fill in the corresponding oval on the answer sheet.

13. Peristalsis during digestion and constriction of bronchioles during breathing are both actions of muscles that are

    (A) striated and involuntary
    (B) smooth and involuntary
    (C) striated and voluntary
    (D) smooth and voluntary
    (E) striated and smooth

14. A lion stalks an antelope, kills it, and then eats it. Which set of terms best describes the lion?

    (A) Prey, consumer, heterotroph
    (B) Predator, producer, heterotroph
    (C) Predator, consumer, heterotroph
    (D) Carnivore, consumer, autotroph
    (E) Prey, producer, autotroph

15. Which of the following is NOT true of enzymes?

    (A) Enzymes lower the activation energy for a reaction.
    (B) A single enzyme cannot be used repeatedly in many reactions.
    (C) Enzymes are catalytic proteins.
    (D) Enzymes are substrate-specific.
    (E) Enzyme performance is affected by temperature and pH.

16. What component of the circulatory system is responsible for fighting off infectious diseases?

    (A) Red blood cells
    (B) White blood cells
    (C) Hemoglobin
    (D) Platelets
    (E) Lymph

17. A community made up of a species of grass, deer, and wolves exists in equilibrium. The deer eat the grass, and the wolves eat the deer. What would likely happen to the deer population if a disease suddenly eliminated the wolf population from the community?

    (A) The deer population would increase exponentially.
    (B) The deer population would increase exponentially, then crash and level off.
    (C) The deer population would remain the same.
    (D) The deer population would crash, then increase and level off.
    (E) The deer population would crash.

18. An example of a mutualistic relationship is

    (A) A tapeworm fills a man's digestive system and makes him malnourished.
    (B) A spider kills and eats its partner after mating.
    (C) A bird helps pollinate a plant while getting nutrients from the plant.
    (D) A bird eats the insects flushed up by grazing cattle but does not harm or help the cattle.
    (E) A swarm of mosquitoes bites children at a picnic.

19. In a plant cell, respiration occurs in

    (A) chloroplasts
    (B) thylakoids
    (C) ribosomes
    (D) the nucleus
    (E) mitochondria

20. ATP is required for

    (A) passive transport
    (B) facilitated diffusion
    (C) osmosis
    (D) active transport
    (E) diffusion

21. Sweat glands and sebaceous glands would be found in

    (A) the epidermis
    (B) the hypodermis
    (C) the dermis
    (D) hair follicles
    (E) keratin follicles

GO ON TO THE NEXT PAGE

22. Which of the following is not required in order for evolution to occur?

    (A) More organisms must be born than can survive to reproduce.
    (B) There must be phenotypic variation among organisms in a population.
    (C) The phenotypic variations must be heritable (passed from parent to offspring).
    (D) A better trait must be acquired over an individual's lifetime.
    (E) Some phenotypic variations must be more beneficial to survival than others.

23. Rods and cones can be found in the

    (A) eyes
    (B) skin
    (C) ears
    (D) nose
    (E) taste buds

24. Rank the following bonds in order from strongest to weakest.

    (A) Ionic bond, hydrogen bond, polar covalent bond
    (B) Polar covalent bond, ionic bond, hydrogen bond
    (C) Hydrogen bond, ionic bond, polar covalent bond
    (D) Ionic bond, polar covalent bond, hydrogen bond
    (E) Hydrogen bond, polar covalent bond, ionic bond

25. A freshman moves into a college dorm. For the first month, he has a hard time studying at his desk because of his three noisy roommates. After a while, he is able to ignore the noise and study well. This is an example of

    (A) habituation
    (B) imprinting
    (C) conditioning
    (D) associative learning
    (E) instinctual behavior

26. Turner's Syndrome (XO) is a chromosomal disorder that can be diagnosed by

    (A) pedigree analysis
    (B) biochemical analysis
    (C) Punnett square analysis
    (D) karyotyping
    (E) blood type analysis

27. A scientist observes that an organism has the following characteristics: a hard shell, bilateral symmetry, a complete digestive tract and circulatory system, and a single muscular structure for movement. This organism belongs to the phylum

    (A) Mollusca
    (B) Arthropoda
    (C) Cnidaria
    (D) Porifera
    (E) Platyhelminthes

28. When a protein loses its three-dimensional structure, it is said to be

    (A) activated
    (B) denatured
    (C) nucleated
    (D) dehydrated
    (E) hydrolyzed

29. A human sex cell has

    (A) the same number of chromosomes as a somatic cell
    (B) 48 chromosomes
    (C) 46 chromosomes
    (D) 23 chromosomes
    (E) a diploid number of chromosomes

30. Members of the same class are more closely related than members of the same

    (A) species
    (B) genus
    (C) family
    (D) phylum
    (E) order

GO ON TO THE NEXT PAGE

Questions 31–34 refer to the following diagram of a nephron.

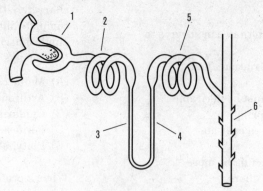

31. Most reabsorption occurs in structure

    (A) 2
    (B) 3
    (C) 4
    (D) 5
    (E) 6

32. Which of the following does not enter structure 1?

    (A) Water
    (B) Salts
    (C) Red blood cells
    (D) Amino acids
    (E) Urea

33. The correct pathway for the elimination of urine is

    (A) kidney, ureter, bladder, urethra
    (B) kidney, bladder, ureter, urethra
    (C) bladder, ureter, kidney, urethra
    (D) bladder, urethra, kidney, ureter
    (E) ureter, kidney, bladder, urethra

34. Nitrogenous wastes are the result of the metabolic breakdown of

    (A) disaccharides and polysaccharides
    (B) amino acids and nucleic acids
    (C) lipids and phospholipids
    (D) vitamins and minerals
    (E) carbohydrates and monosaccharides

GO ON TO THE NEXT PAGE

<u>Questions 35–36</u> refer to an experiment with reptiles.

A certain rare lizard is found only in New Zealand. This lizard has temperature-dependent sex determination, which means that the sex of its offspring is determined by the temperature at which its eggs are incubated. Scientists conducted an experiment to study the pattern of sex determination in the reptile. They incubated the eggs at different temperatures during each half of incubation and noted the sex of the hatchlings.

35. Which of the following statements is supported by the data?

 (A) If an egg is kept at a temperature less than 25°C during the first half of incubation, the lizard will always be male.
 (B) If an egg is kept at a temperature greater than 25°C during the first half of incubation, the lizard will always be female.
 (C) If an egg is kept at a temperature less than 25°C during the second half of incubation, the lizard will always be male.
 (D) The sex of the lizard is determined by the temperature during the first half of incubation.
 (E) The sex of the lizard is determined by the temperature during the second half of incubation.

36. Based on this data, what effect could global warming have on this population of lizards?

 (A) The population will grow exponentially.
 (B) There will be more males than females.
 (C) There will be more females than males.
 (D) The sex ratio of the population will stay the same.
 (E) There will not be enough males to fertilize the eggs that females lay.

GO ON TO THE NEXT PAGE

Questions 37–39 relate to the aquatic food chain below.

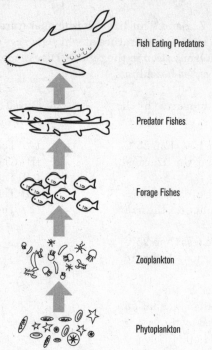

Fish Eating Predators

Predator Fishes

Forage Fishes

Zooplankton

Phytoplankton

37. The forage fishes are

    (A) primary producers
    (B) consumers
    (C) autotrophs
    (D) saprophytes
    (E) secondary producers

38. Which trophic level would have the most energy?

    (A) Fish-eating predators
    (B) Predator fishes
    (C) Forage fishes
    (D) Zooplankton
    (E) Phytoplankton

39. A pesticide production plant accidentally dumps DDT into the bay. The average amount of DDT found in a forage fish is 2 parts per million, while the average amount found in a fish-eating predator is 10 parts per million. This is an example of

    (A) amplification
    (B) biomagnification
    (C) energy loss
    (D) chemosynthesis
    (E) biodampening

GO ON TO THE NEXT PAGE

Questions 40–42 refer to a breeding experiment using plants with unknown genotypes. The plant phenotypes include a plant with red flowers and a plant with white flowers.

	Offspring	
Cross	**Red**	**White**
I. Red is self-pollinated	100	0
II. White is self-pollinated	0	100
III. Red is cross-pollinated with white	100	0
IV. Red is cross-pollinated with white	50	50

40. In which of the crosses is at least one parent homozygous for red flowers?

    (A) I only
    (B) III only
    (C) IV only
    (D) I and III only
    (E) I and IV only

41. If the offspring in Cross III had all been pink, then the gene for flower color would be an example of

    (A) complete dominance
    (B) incomplete dominance
    (C) codominance
    (D) complete recessiveness
    (E) polygenetics

42. If the red progeny of Cross III are self-pollinated, what is the probability that an individual offspring will be red?

    (A) 0%
    (B) 25%
    (C) 50%
    (D) 75%
    (E) 100%

GO ON TO THE NEXT PAGE

Questions 43–44 refer to the following sequence of nucleotides in an mRNA strand.

AAAGCGCUAGCUCUG

43. What would be the nucleotide sequence on the strand of tRNA that will associate with this mRNA?

    (A) TTTCGCGATCGACAC
    (B) UUUCGCGAUCGAGAC
    (C) CAGAGCUAGCGCUUU
    (D) CACAGCTAGCGCTTT
    (E) AAAGCGCUAGCUCUG

44. The mRNA strand will travel

    (A) from the nucleus to the Golgi apparatus
    (B) from the nucleus to the ribosomes
    (C) from the ribosomes to the cytoplasm
    (D) to find an amino acid
    (E) to the nucleus from the cytoplasm

Questions 45–48 refer to the following laboratory exercise.

Students in a laboratory were given 5 unknown solutions and asked to correctly identify them. The solutions were: water, glucose syrup, a pure protein shake, salt water, and vegetable oil. Students ran 4 tests.

Silver Nitrate Test – A solution containing chloride will turn brown when silver nitrate is added.

Sudan Test – A solution containing fats will turn red when Sudan IV is added.

Biuret Test – A solution containing proteins will turn purple when NaOH and $CuSO_4$ are added.

Benedict's Test – A solution containing monosaccharides will turn greenish yellow when Benedict's solution is added.

45. Solution B contains

    (A) lipids
    (B) nucleic acids
    (C) chloride ions
    (D) carbohydrates
    (E) amino acids

46. The correct identity of Solution A is

    (A) water
    (B) glucose syrup
    (C) protein shake
    (D) salt water
    (E) vegetable oil

47. A student added a test reagent to his solution, and the solution turned red. What reagent did he add?

    (A) Protein shake
    (B) Vegetable oil
    (C) Salt water
    (D) Water
    (E) Glucose syrup

48. A polymer of amino acids is called a

    (A) monosaccharide
    (B) polysaccharide
    (C) triglyceride
    (D) polypeptide
    (E) nucleic acid

GO ON TO THE NEXT PAGE

Questions 49–52 refer to the following illustrations of osmosis that is occurring in an animal and a plant cell in three different solutions.

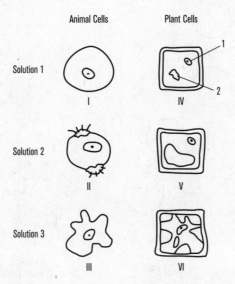

49. With respect to cells III and VI, the surrounding solution is

    (A) hypertonic
    (B) isotonic
    (C) hypotonic
    (D) subtonic
    (E) supertonic

50. The function of structure 2 is to

    (A) house the genetic material
    (B) synthesize proteins
    (C) digest wastes
    (D) protect the cell
    (E) store fluid and other materials

51. Cell II swelled and then burst due to

    (A) diffusion of salt from the solution into the cell
    (B) diffusion of salt from the cell into the solution
    (C) diffusion of water from the solution into the cell
    (D) diffusion of water from the cell into the solution
    (E) mismatched electrical charges in the cell

52. The plant cell and the animal cell are different because

    (A) the plant is a prokaryote, and the animal is a eukaryote
    (B) an animal cell has a nucleus, but a plant cell does not
    (C) a plant cell has a cell membrane, but an animal cell does not
    (D) a plant cell has a cell wall, but an animal cell does not
    (E) an animal cell has mitochondria, but a plant cell does not

GO ON TO THE NEXT PAGE

Questions 53–56 refer to gametogenesis in a human.

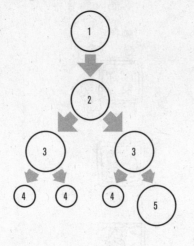
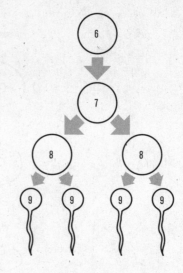

53. How many chromosomes are in structures 1 and 6?

  (A) 48
  (B) 46
  (C) 24
  (D) 23
  (E) 0

54. The polar bodies are numbered

  (A) 3
  (B) 4
  (C) 5
  (D) 8
  (E) 9

55. What process occurs to create structure 8 from structure 7?

  (A) Mitosis
  (B) Meiosis I
  (C) Meiosis II
  (D) Fertilization
  (E) Oogenesis

56. The processes depicted occur in the

  (A) fallopian tubes and prostate gland
  (B) vagina and penis
  (C) uterus and urethra
  (D) ovaries and testes
  (E) cervix and vas deferens

GO ON TO THE NEXT PAGE

Questions 57–60 refer to the cross-section of a leaf.

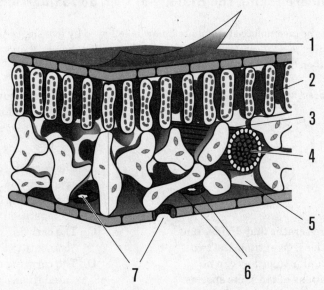

57. Gases diffuse in and out of the leaf through structure

    (A) 3
    (B) 4
    (C) 5
    (D) 6
    (E) 7

58. Which of the following would not be found in structure 2?

    (A) Thylakoid
    (B) Chlorophyll
    (C) Stroma
    (D) Guard cells
    (E) Granum

59. All of the following are true regarding structure 4 EXCEPT

    (A) It is comprised of sieve elements
    (B) It distributes the products of photosynthesis
    (C) It is comprised of living cells
    (D) It can carry materials both up and down the plant body
    (E) It will become wood

60. If structure 1 were very thick, and structure 7 were closed during the warmest part of the day, then this plant likely lives in the

    (A) desert
    (B) taiga
    (C) rainforest
    (D) temperate deciduous forest
    (E) ocean

GO ON TO THE NEXT PAGE

BIOLOGY-E SECTION

If you are taking the Biology-E test, continue with questions 61–80.
If you are taking the Biology-M test, go to question 81 now.

<u>Directions:</u> Each of the questions or incomplete statements below is followed by five suggested answers or completions. Some questions pertain to a set that refers to a laboratory or experimental situation. For each question, select the one choice that is the best answer to the question and then fill in the corresponding oval on the answer sheet.

61. Counter-current exchange occurs in the respiratory system of

    (A) jellyfish
    (B) insects
    (C) frogs
    (D) humans
    (E) birds

62. An earthquake creates a large crater that divides one population into two populations. Over time, the two populations become so dissimilar that they can no longer be considered populations of the same species. What process occurred?

    (A) Adaptive radiation
    (B) Allopatric speciation
    (C) Convergent evolution
    (D) Hardy-Weinberg equilibrium
    (E) Larmackian evolution

63. In times of favorable environmental conditions, a particular population of organisms grows at nearly exponential speed. In times of unfavorable environmental conditions, however, the population crashes. Which of the following is likely NOT true of the organisms in the population?

    (A) They reproduce early in life.
    (B) They reproduce asexually.
    (C) They have a short life span.
    (D) They have young that require extensive parental supervision.
    (E) They display little variation between individuals.

64. Suppose that a botanical disease were to destroy aspen trees in Rocky Mountain National Park. What would happen with respect to the elk population that feeds on aspen trees?

    (A) The carrying capacity would decrease due to competition for space.
    (B) The carrying capacity would decrease due to competition for food.
    (C) The carrying capacity would increase due to competition for space.
    (D) The carrying capacity would increase due to predation.
    (E) The carrying capacity would increase due to disease.

65. Evolution occurs at the level of the

    (A) individual
    (B) population
    (C) community
    (D) ecosystem
    (E) biome

66. In the diagram of a root, the purpose of structure 1 is to

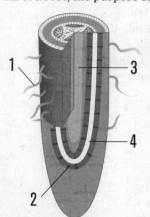

    (A) increase the absorptive area of the roots
    (B) produce new cells
    (C) keep CO_2 out of the plant
    (D) close the stomata
    (E) store chloroplasts

GO ON TO THE NEXT PAGE

<u>Questions 67–69</u> refer to the following experiment.

A group of students in Texas decided to conduct an experiment with a group of students in Alaska. At the beginning of the school year, the classes in Texas and Alaska collected and dried grasses from nearby natural areas. The students put 5 grams of grass in each of 20 mesh bags. They kept 10 bags and mailed 10 bags to the students in the other state. When the bags from the other state arrived, the students took all 20 bags (10 from Texas and 10 from Alaska) to a field and nailed them to the ground in random locations. At the end of the school year, the students collected the bags and weighed them.

Here are their results:

Samples at Texas Site	Average Initial Weight	Average End Weight
Bags from Texas	5 grams	2.3 grams
Bags from Alaska	5 grams	2.8 grams

Samples at Alaska Site	Average Initial Weight	Average End Weight
Bags from Alaska	5 grams	3.9 grams
Bags from Texas	5 grams	4.1 grams

67. Which bags had the greatest change in weight?

(A) The bags from Texas that were kept in Texas
(B) The bags from Alaska that were sent to Texas
(C) The bags from Alaska that were kept in Alaska
(D) The bags from Texas that were sent to Alaska
(E) The bags from Texas and Alaska had an equal change in weight.

68. Why did the bags lose weight?

(A) Grass fell out of the bags.
(B) Water evaporated from the bags.
(C) The grass grew in the bags.
(D) Microorganisms broke down the compounds in the grass and fed on them.
(E) The grass harnessed carbon dioxide from the atmosphere.

69. The experiment taught the students about the process of

(A) photosynthesis
(B) production
(C) decomposition
(D) succession
(E) secondary consumption

GO ON TO THE NEXT PAGE

Questions 70–71 refer to the following illustration of the carbon cycle.

70. The process by which carbon dioxide is transferred from the rabbit to the atmosphere is called

    (A) photosynthesis
    (B) erosion
    (C) carbonation
    (D) respiration
    (E) assimilation

71. When the rabbit eats the flower, the flower's carbon matter

    (A) remains entirely in the rabbit until it dies and decomposes
    (B) partially remains in the rabbit until death, and partially is given off as waste
    (C) is eliminated by the rabbit through waste
    (D) is given off into the atmosphere via respiration
    (E) is processed by bacteria that release the carbon as carbon dioxide

GO ON TO THE NEXT PAGE

Questions 72–75 refer to the following diagram of a flower.

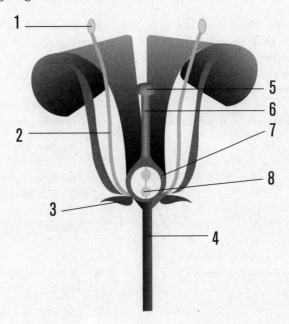

72. In order to fertilize the plant, pollen must land on structure

   (A) 1
   (B) 2
   (C) 3
   (D) 4
   (E) 5

73. Which structure will develop into fruit after fertilization?

   (A) Pollen
   (B) Sepal
   (C) Pistil
   (D) Ovules
   (E) Ovary

74. The plant in the diagram could be a

   (A) fern
   (B) bryophyte
   (C) conifer
   (D) dicot
   (E) gymnosperm

75. A plant that has small and drab flowers is mostly likely to be pollinated by

   (A) bees
   (B) birds
   (C) ants
   (D) wind
   (E) arthropods

GO ON TO THE NEXT PAGE

Questions 76–78 refer to the following experiment.

Two species of birds compete for seeds. These birds are susceptible to a parasite that affects their overall health. A researcher decided to count the number of seeds that the birds ate when they were free of parasites and the number of seeds that they ate when they were infected.

76. What is the number of seeds that species 2 consumed when infected by parasites?

    (A) 70
    (B) 35
    (C) 60
    (D) 20
    (E) 80

77. After the birds were infected by parasites, the total number of seeds eaten by bothspecies combined

    (A) increased
    (B) decreased
    (C) stayed the same
    (D) was greater than 100
    (E) was greater than 150

78. Based on the graph, what can you conclude about the effects of the parasite on competition?

    (A) Parasites have no influence on competition.
    (B) When parasites are present, species 1 is the better competitor.
    (C) When parasites are absent, species 1 is the better competitor.
    (D) Parasites affect the digestive system of the birds.
    (E) Parasites increase species 1's ability to gather, consume, and digest seeds.

Questions 79–80 refer to the following scenario.

A woman hikes to the top of Mt. Denali in Alaska. Her hike starts in an area populated by coniferous trees and ends in an area where the vegetation is very short and the soil is permanently frozen 1 meter below the surface.

79. Which of the following statements describes the woman's hike?

    (A) She hiked from temperate deciduous forest to tundra.
    (B) She hiked from tundra to taiga.
    (C) She hiked from taiga to grassland.
    (D) She hiked from taiga to tundra.
    (E) She hiked from tundra to temperate deciduous forest.

80. An increase in altitude often shows the same change in biomes as

    (A) traveling west along the equator
    (B) traveling east along the equator
    (C) traveling north from the equator
    (D) traveling south from the North Pole to the South Pole
    (E) traveling north toward the equator

GO ON TO THE NEXT PAGE

BIOLOGY-M SECTION

If you are taking the Biology-M test, continue with questions 81–100.
Be sure to start this section of the test by filling in oval 81 on your answer sheet.

<u>Directions:</u> Each of the questions or incomplete statements below is followed by five suggested answers or completions. Some questions pertain to a set that refers to a laboratory or experimental situation. For each question, select the one choice that is the best answer to the question and then fill in the corresponding oval on the answer sheet.

81. The sides of the DNA "ladder" are made of

    (A) nitrogenous bases
    (B) deoxyribose and a phosphate group
    (C) thymine, adenine, guanine, and cytosine
    (D) uracil, adenine, guanine, and cytosine
    (E) ribose and a phosphate group

82. What is the correct arrangement of the "heads" and "tails" of the phospholipids in the phospholipid bilayer?

    (A) Head, tail, tail, head
    (B) Tail, head, tail, head
    (C) Tail, tail, head, head
    (D) Head, tail, head, tail
    (E) Tail, head, head, tail

83. A good example of a set of homologous structures is

    (A) a person's fingers and toes
    (B) the paw of a tiger and the paw of another tiger
    (C) the wing of an insect and the fin of a whale
    (D) the arm of a man and the wing of a bat
    (E) the appendix and the tonsils

84. Which of the following requires oxygen?

    (A) Glycolysis
    (B) Photosynthesis
    (C) Lactic acid fermentation
    (D) Alcoholic fermentation
    (E) The Krebs cycle

85. If you find fossilized seashells 3 feet below the surface of a sedimentary rock and fossilized trees 7 feet below the surface, you can infer that the region was

    (A) a forest before it was covered by ocean
    (B) a grassland before it was a forest
    (C) covered by an ocean before it was a forest
    (D) populated by tropical insects
    (E) a desert after it was a forest

86. Red-green color blindness is an X-linked trait. If a woman is red-green colorblind, and both of her parents have normal vision, what are the genotypes of her mother and father? (X' denotes that a chromosome is positive for red-green colorblindness.)

    (A) Mother is X'X, father is X'Y
    (B) Mother is XX, father is X'Y
    (C) Mother is XX, father is XY
    (D) Mother is X'X, father is XY
    (E) Mother is X'X', father is X'Y

GO ON TO THE NEXT PAGE

Questions 87–90 refer to the illustrations of the stages of mitosis in a human.

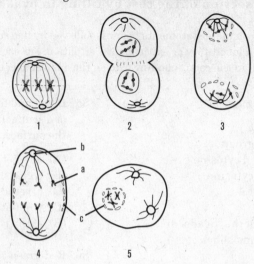

87. Put the illustrations in the order in which they would occur during mitosis.

   (A) 2, 3, 4, 1, 5
   (B) 3, 5, 4, 2, 1
   (C) 1, 2, 3, 4, 5
   (D) 5, 4, 2, 3, 1
   (E) 5, 1, 4, 3, 2

88. The two halves of the X-shaped structure labeled "a" are called

   (A) chromatids
   (B) chromosomes
   (C) centrioles
   (D) centromeres
   (E) microtubules

89. The process occurring in diagram 4 is called

   (A) anaphase
   (B) telophase
   (C) cell division
   (D) cytokinesis
   (E) splitting

90. The two cells that are produced will be

   (A) genetically identical, haploid, somatic cells
   (B) genetically identical, diploid, sex cells
   (C) genetically different, haploid, sex cells
   (D) genetically identical, diploid, somatic cells
   (E) genetically different, diploid, somatic cells

GO ON TO THE NEXT PAGE

Questions 91–92 refer to cellular respiration.

Turtles often will stay underwater for long periods of time during the winter. The graph below depicts the accumulation of lactic acid in the bodies of turtles that were under water for different time periods (5, 15, and 25 days) during winter hibernation.

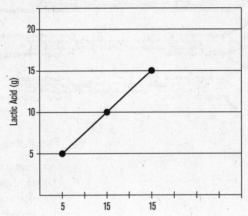

91. Based on the graph, what would you predict would be the amount of lactic acid in a turtle that has been under water for 35 days?

   (A) 5 g
   (B) 10 g
   (C) 15 g
   (D) 20 g
   (E) 25 g

92. What is the most likely cause of the accumulation of lactic acid in the bodies ofthe turtles?

   (A) Muscles in the turtles were breaking down after periods of inactivity.
   (B) There was not enough oxygen in the brain to support glycolysis.
   (C) There was not enough oxygen in the blood to support glycolysis.
   (D) There was not enough oxygen in the blood for the Krebs cycle and electron transport chain.
   (E) The CO_2 in the bloodstream inhibited the Krebs cycle.

GO ON TO THE NEXT PAGE

Questions 93–96 refer to the diagram of muscle tissue below.

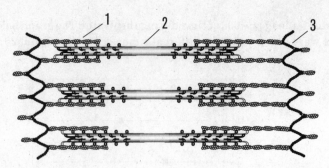

93. Structure 1 is called

    (A) actin
    (B) myosin
    (C) sarcomere
    (D) myofibril
    (E) thin filament

94. Which of the following is NOT correct?

    (A) Muscle contractions are stimulated by neurons.
    (B) ATP is needed for muscle contractions.
    (C) During muscle contractions, the sarcomere shortens.
    (D) During muscle contractions, the actin and myosin shorten.
    (E) When a muscle is fully contracted, the actin and myosin completely overlap one another.

95. This arrangement of muscle fibers is found in

    (A) smooth muscle only
    (B) cardiac muscle only
    (C) skeletal muscle only
    (D) smooth and cardiac muscle
    (E) skeletal and cardiac muscle

96. Muscles and bones are similar in that

    (A) both are made of living cells rooted in a matrix of calcium
    (B) both produce blood cells
    (C) both grow when you exercise regularly
    (D) both are flexible
    (E) both help support and protect parts of the body

GO ON TO THE NEXT PAGE

<u>Questions 97–100</u> refer to human blood types.

There is a mix-up of three babies at a hospital, and the nurse does not know which baby belongs to which parents. She thinks that she may be able to solve the problem by looking at the blood types of the parents and the babies. There are four phenotypes for blood: A, B, AB, and O.

Baby One's blood type is B. Baby Two's blood type is O. Baby Three's blood type is A.

The parents' blood types are:

Mr. Robinson - Type A	Mr. Lincoln - Type A	Mr. Smith - Type B
Mrs. Robinson - Type A	Mrs. Lincoln - Type AB	Mrs. Smith - Type B

97. Which is NOT a possible match?

(A) Baby Two - Mr. & Mrs. Smith
(B) Baby Three - Mr. & Mrs. Robinson
(C) Baby One - Mr. & Mrs. Smith
(D) Baby Three - Mr. & Mrs. Lincoln
(E) Baby Two - Mr. & Mrs. Lincoln

98. If the genotypes of Mr. and Mrs. Smith are both BB, then their baby could be

(A) Baby One only
(B) Baby Two only
(C) Baby Three only
(D) Baby One or Baby Two
(E) Baby One or Baby Three

99. The A and B alleles for blood type are

(A) recessive
(B) incompletely dominant
(C) codominant
(D) homologous
(E) analogous

100. Which two genotypes can be "crossed" to yield all four possible blood types?

(A) AB and AB
(B) Ai andBi
(C) O and AB
(D) O and O
(E) AA and Bi

S T O P

IF YOU FINISH BEFORE TIME IS CALLED, YOU MAY CHECK YOUR WORK ON THIS TEST ONLY.
DO NOT TURN TO ANY OTHER TEST IN THIS BOOK.

SAT II Biology Test 2
Explanations

Answers to SAT II Biology Practice Test 2

Question Number	Correct Answer	Right	Wrong	Question Number	Correct Answer	Right	Wrong	Question Number	Correct Answer	Right	Wrong
1.	D			34.	B			67.	A		
2.	C			35.	E			68.	D		
3.	B			36.	B			69.	C		
4.	D			37.	B			70.	D		
5.	C			38.	E			71.	B		
6.	A			39.	B			72.	E		
7.	E			40.	D			73.	E		
8.	C			41.	B			74.	D		
9.	B			42.	D			75.	D		
10.	A			43.	B			76.	C		
11.	B			44.	B			77.	B		
12.	E			45.	C			78.	C		
13.	B			46.	B			79.	D		
14.	C			47.	B			80.	C		
15.	B			48.	D			81.	B		
16.	B			49.	A			82.	A		
17.	B			50.	E			83.	D		
18.	C			51.	C			84.	E		
19.	E			52.	D			85.	A		
20.	D			53.	B			86.	D		
21.	C			54.	B			87.	E		
22.	D			55.	B			88.	A		
23.	A			56.	D			89.	A		
24.	D			57.	E			90.	D		
25.	A			58.	D			91.	D		
26.	D			59.	E			92.	D		
27.	A			60.	A			93.	A		
28.	B			61.	E			94.	C		
29.	D			62.	B			95.	C		
30.	D			63.	D			96.	E		
31.	A			64.	B			97.	E		
32.	C			65.	B			98.	A		
33.	A			66.	A			99.	C		
								100.	B		

Your raw score for the SAT II Biology test is calculated from the number of questions you answer correctly and incorrectly. Once you have determined your composite score, use the conversion table on page **21** of this book to calculate your scaled score. To calculate your raw score, count the number of questions you answered correctly: _____
                                                                        A

Count the number of questions you answered incorrectly, and multiply that number by $\frac{1}{4}$:

$$\underline{\quad\quad} \times \frac{1}{4} = \underline{\quad\quad}$$
$\quad\quad$ B $\qquad\qquad\qquad$ C

Subtract the value in field C from value in field A: _____
                                                     D

Round the number in field D to the nearest whole number. This is your raw score: _____
                                                                                  E

Biology E/M Classification Questions

1.   **(D)**   Organismal Biology
The large intestine contains mutually symbiotic bacteria such as *E. coli*. The bacteria feed on indigestible material and produce vitamin K, which is absorbed into the body. The primary function of the large intestine is to compact waste before it leaves the body through the anus. No digestion takes place in the large intestine, and very little fluid is absorbed there.

2.   **(C)**   Organismal Biology
The stomach secretes hydrochloric acid and thus has a very low pH. The concentrated acid breaks proteins and connective tissues into smaller subunits. The low pH also serves to kill potentially harmful bacteria that may have been ingested along with food.

3.   **(B)**   Organismal Biology
Bile is produced by the liver but is stored and concentrated in the gall bladder. Bile is a substance that emulsifies fats and promotes the absorption of fat-soluble vitamins (A, D, E, and K) and fatty acids.

4.   **(D)**   Evolution and Diversity
Angiosperms are flowering plants. Angiosperms are divided into two subgroups— monocots and dicots. Monocots have one cotyledon (seed leaf), flower parts in groups of three, and parallel venation in the leaves. Dicots have two cotyledons, flower parts in groups of four or five, and netlike venation in the leaves.

5.   **(C)**   Evolution and Diversity
Club mosses, horsetails, and ferns are all seedless vascular plants. They have a vascular system with both xylem and phloem. Seedless vascular plants have spores rather than seeds and require water for fertilization.

6.   **(A)**   Evolution and Diversity
Bryophytes are the seedless, nonvascular plants such as mosses, liverworts, and hornworts. Bryophytes have no vascular tissue (xylem and phloem) and therefore cannot have roots, stems, or leaves, which are complex structures that contain vascular tissue. Bryophytes must absorb and distribute water and nutrients by osmosis and diffusion.

7. **(E)**   Ecology
The desert biome exhibits radical temperature changes between night and day. There is typically little vegetation or cloud cover to keep the ground from getting hot during the day or to keep heat from escaping during the night.

8. **(C)**   Ecology
The tundra is often covered by ice for the majority of the year. The soil is often permanently frozen a few feet below the surface—a condition called "permafrost."

9. **(B)**   Ecology
Tropical rainforests have the highest rainfall (100–180 inches per year) of all of the biomes. It is the most species-rich biome and probably contains over half of the world's terrestrial species.

10. **(A)**   Cell Processes
Transcription is the process by which a messenger RNA strand is created from the information in a strand of DNA. The mRNA strand will be a complement of the DNA. Transcription occurs in the nucleus and is one of the steps of protein synthesis.

11. **(B)**   Cell Processes
Replication is the process by which an exact copy of DNA is made. Replication occurs during the interphase stage of mitosis.

12. **(E)**   Cell Processes
Transfer RNA are single strands of RNA that temporarily carry amino acids to the ribosomes, where polypeptide chains are assembled. The tRNA has an anti-codon on one side and an amino acid on the other. The tRNA carries an amino acid that corresponds to a particular mRNA codon.

Biology E/M Solitary Multiple Choice

13. **(B)**   Organismal Biology
Smooth muscle is also called involuntary muscle. You cannot consciously control the contractions of smooth muscle. Smooth muscle is involved in processes such as digestion, respiration, and circulation.

14. **(C)**   Ecology
The lion is a predator because it stalks and kills another organism—the prey. The lion is a consumer rather than a producer. Consumers must eat other organisms to get

energy and organic molecules necessary for life. Consumers are also called heterotrophs. Producers, or autotrophs, can harness the energy of the sun to make their own organic food.

15. (B)   Organic and Biochemistry

A single enzyme can be used repeatedly in many reactions because enzymes are not "used up" or altered when they aid in a chemical reaction.

16. (B)   Organismal Biology

Blood contains three types of specialized cells. White blood cells aid in fighting off disease. Red blood cells transport oxygen. Platelets release a hormone that causes clotting and thereby prevents blood loss when the body is wounded.

17. (B)   Ecology

When the wolves disappear from the community, the deer suddenly have no predators. In other words, fewer deer will be eaten by wolves, and thus, the carrying capacity for deer in the population will increase. The deer population will begin to grow exponentially, but at some point, a generation will be produced that needs to eat more grass than actually exists in the community. At this point, the deer population has grown larger than the carrying capacity, and it will crash until it reaches the actual carrying capacity of the community.

18. (C)   Ecology

A mutualistic relationship is one in which both partners in the relationship benefit. Both the bird and the plant benefit from their association with one another. The bird gains nourishment from the pollen and helps the plant reproduce by pollinating the flower.

19. (E)   Cell Processes

Respiration occurs in the mitochondria of plant cells, just as it does in animal cells. Students often forget that plants have mitochondria as well as chloroplasts. Plants can produce carbohydrates via photosynthesis in the chloroplasts. However, plants cells also have to catabolize carbohydrates, so they must have mitochondria.

20. (D)   The Cell

ATP is required for active transport. Active transport is needed when a cell has to transport a substance *against* its normal concentration gradient. This requires energy in the form of ATP. In passive transport (diffusion, facilitated diffusion, and osmosis), a substance moves *along* its concentration gradient—from an area of high concentration to an area of low concentration. Passive transport does not require the input of energy.

21. **(C)**   Organismal Biology
Sweat and sebaceous glands are found in the dermis of the skin. The skin has three layers: the epidermis, the dermis, and the hypodermis. The epidermis is the topmost layer that is exposed to the outside environment. The dermis is the middle layer and contains blood vessels, sweat glands, and sebaceous glands. The hypodermis is the deepest layer and is composed mostly of fat cells and loose connective tissue.

22. **(D)**   Evolution and Diversity
In order for evolution to occur, there have to be more organisms born than can survive and reproduce. There has to be phenotypic variation among organisms, and some variations have to be more beneficial for survival than others. The variations have to be heritable (genetic). (D) is the correct answer because it is impossible for an individual to acquire or lose genetic traits over his or her lifetime.

23. **(A)**   Organismal Biology
Rods and cones are photoreceptors in the retina of the eye. Rods respond to dim light. Cones are responsible for detecting colors.

24. **(D)**   Organic and Biochemistry
Ionic bonds are stronger than polar bonds. Hydrogen bonds are simply weak dipole-dipole attractions and are not as strong as ionic or covalent bonds.

25. **(A)**   Organismal Biology
Habituation is a learned behavior in which an individual loses sensitivity to an unimportant or non-harmful stimulus. Habituation allows an individual to conserve time and energy. While the noise in the student's dorm room was not physically harmful to him, it did keep him from concentrating on his studies. When the student learned to ignore the noise, his studying was more effective.

26. **(D)**   Genetics
Karyotyping would detect Turner's Syndrome, a genetic disorder that involves a missing X-chromosome. A karyotype in an enlarged photograph of an individual cell's chromosomes. Chromosomes are lined up in homologous pairs according to size. Missing, extra, or abnormal chromosomes can be identified by looking at a karyotype. None of the other types of analysis would detect a disorder in the chromosomes.

27. **(A)**   Evolution and Diversity

Members of phylum Mollusca have a hard shell, bilateral symmetry, a complete digestive tract, and circulatory system, and they move by means of a single muscular structure (called a foot). None of the other phyla display all of these characteristics.

28. **(B)**   Organic and Biochemistry

When a protein loses its three-dimensional shape, it is said to be denatured. A protein
may unravel as a result of a deviation from normal in the pH, temperature, salt concentration, or other factors in its surrounding environment.

29. **(D)**   Cell Processes

Human sex cells have 23 chromosomes. Sex cells, also called gametes, are haploid and
have half the number of chromosomes as those found in the diploid autosomal, or
somatic, cells.

30. **(D)**   Evolution and Diversity

The classification system is a hierarchical system. The following are ranked from most
inclusive to least inclusive: kingdom, phylum, class, order, family, genus, species. All of
the individuals in the same class are also in the same kingdom and phylum but not necessarily in the same order, family, genus, or species.

Biology E/M Group Multiple Choice

31. **(A)**   Organismal Biology

Most reabsorption of water and other important molecules, such as sodium, glucose,
and amino acids, occurs in structure 2, the proximal convoluted tubule. By the time the
filtrate reaches the loop of Henle, it has lost about 75% of its original volume. The filtrate is called urine after reabsorption occurs.

32. **(C)**   Organismal Biology

As the filtrate passes into Bowman's capsule (structure 1), molecules such as red blood
cells and large proteins are filtered out by the high pressure and narrow capillaries of
the glomerulus. The filtrate that enters Bowman's capsule contains water, salts, amino
acids, glucose, and urea.

33. **(A)**   Organismal Biology

The correct pathway for the elimination of urine is: kidney, ureter, bladder, urethra.

34. **(B)**   Organismal Biology

Nitrogenous wastes are the result of the metabolism of amino acids and nucleic acids. Remember that each amino acid has an amino group which contains nitrogen and hydrogen. Each nucleic acid has a nitrogenous base (adenine, guanine, cytosine, thymine, and uracil) that contains nitrogen. None of the other molecules mentioned in the answer choices contain nitrogen, so they cannot break down into nitrogenous wastes.

35. **(E)**   Ecology

The temperature during the second half of incubation could predict the sex of the hatchling. Even if you knew the incubation temperature during the first half of incubation, you still could not say definitively what the sex of the hatchling would be. If you knew the incubation temperature during the second half of incubation, you could say that if the temperature were > 25°C, the hatchling would be male, and if the temperature were < 25°C, the hatchling would be female.

36. **(B)**   Ecology

Global warming would increase temperatures. Higher temperatures would enable the production of more male hatchlings.

37. **(B)**   Ecology

Forage fishes are consumers. They must obtain energy and nutrients from other organisms.

38. **(E)**   Ecology

The majority of energy in a food chain or food web is concentrated in the lowest trophic level. In this case, phytoplankton are in the lowest trophic level. Each trophic level has only 10% of the energy that was contained within the preceding trophic level.

39. **(B)**   Ecology

As some chemicals travel through the trophic levels in a food chain, they become more and more concentrated. This process is called biomagnification.

40. **(D)**   Genetics

Based on the given data, you can see that every time a red flowered plant is crossed with another plant (red or white), some of the offspring are always red. This means that when a red plant is crossed with a white one, they do not always yield white offspring. The red allele is dominant, and the white allele is recessive. Once you know that the red allele is dominant, you can make a Punnett square for each of the crosses and guess the alleles of the gametes until you come up with the correct ratios of red and white offspring. Cross I and cross III both contain homozygous red parents.

Cross I		
	R	R
R	RR	RR
R	RR	RR

100 % red progeny

Cross II		
	r	r
r	Rr	rr
r	Rr	rr

100% white progeny

Cross III		
	R	R
r	Rr	Rr
r	Rr	Rr

100 % red progeny

Cross IV		
	R	r
r	Rr	rr
r	Rr	rr

50 % red progeny and
50% white progeny

41. **(B)** Genetics

The offspring in Cross III all have the genotype Rr. Since red is the dominant allele, the offspring are all red. If the offspring were all pink, then you could infer that the alleles for flower color show incomplete dominance, a condition in which two different alleles are both expressed in a heterozygote. The resulting phenotype is intermediate between the two homozygous phenotypes.

42. **(D)** Genetics

If you self-pollinate the progeny from Cross III, the offspring would have a 75% chance of being red, as shown in the Punnett square below.

	R	r
R	RR	Rr
r	Rr	rr

75% red progeny and
25% white progeny

43. **(B)** Genetics

The strands of tRNA and mRNA are complementary (exact opposites). If there is an adenine molecule in a particular position on one strand, the complementary strand contains uracil in that position. If there is guanine in one strand, the complementary strand contains cytosine. The sequence of tRNA for the given mRNA would be UUUCGCGAUCGAGAC.

44. **(B)**   Genetics

As part of protein synthesis, mRNA is made from DNA that is housed in the nucleus. After mRNA is made, it moves out of the nucleus to the ribosomes, where protein synthesis will occur.

45. **(C)**   Organic and Biochemistry

Solution B gave a positive result for the silver nitrate test. The explanation of the silver nitrate test tells you that silver nitrate is an indicator of the presence of chloride ions.

46. **(B)**   Organic and Biochemistry

Solution A gave a positive result for Benedict's Test. There must be monosaccharides in the solution. Of the solutions given, dilute glucose syrup stands out because glucose is a monosaccharide.

47. **(B)**   Organic and Biochemistry

If you look at the descriptions of each test, the only test that shows a positive result by turning red is the Sudan test. The Sudan test, as stated in the question, identifies the presence of fats. Of the five answer choices, only vegetable oil contains fats.

48. **(D)**   Organic and Biochemistry

A polymer of amino acids is known as a polypeptide.

49. **(A)**   Cell Structure

Cells III and VI are shriveled because they have lost water in a hypertonic solution. A hypertonic solution contains a greater concentration of dissolved solutes than the environment within the cell. Since water will diffuse from an area of low solute concentration to an area of high solute concentration until the concentrations are balanced, the water inside the cells will flow outward, and the cells will shrivel.

50. **(E)**   Cell Structure

Structure 2 is a vacuole. The vacuole stores just about anything in a plant cell, from water to nutrients and waste. Vacuoles fill up when cells are put in a hypotonic environment.

51. **(C)**   Cell Structure

The cell had a greater concentration of solutes than the surrounding solution. Because water moves from an area of high solute concentration to an area of low solute concentration, water diffused into the cell from the surrounding solution. The concentrations did not equilibrate before the cell had taken in so much water that the plasma membrane was compromised and the cell burst.

52. **(D)**   Cell Structure

Plant cells have a cell wall, and animal cells do not. Both plant and animal cells are eukaryotic and both have a cell membrane, a nucleus, and mitochondria.

53. **(B)**   Genetics

Structures 1 and 6 are the primary oocyte and the spermatogonium, which are diploid cells each containing 46 chromosomes. When the process of oogenesis is complete, 1 haploid egg and 3 polar bodies will have been produced. When the process of spermatogenesis is complete, 4 haploid sperm will have been produced. Collectively, these processes are known as gametogenesis because they produce the gametes.

54. **(B)**   Genetics

The polar bodies are represented by the number 4. Polar bodies are haploid cells that are much smaller than the egg. The polar bodies eventually disintegrate.

55. **(B)**   Genetics

Meiosis I is the process that creates structure 8, which is haploid, from structure 7, which is diploid. Meiosis II, which does not involve a 50% decrease in the number of chromosomes, creates haploid structure 9 from haploid structure 8. Mitosis does not occur in either oogenesis or spermatogenesis. Fertilization is the event when two haploid gametes meet and fuse into a diploid embryo.

56. **(D)**   Genetics

The processes depicted are oogenesis, which occurs in the ovaries, and spermatogenesis, which occurs in the testes. These are the processes by which the egg and sperm are formed.

57. **(E)**   Organismal Biology

Diffusion of gases occurs through structures on the underside of the leaf, called stomata, which are labeled 7 in the diagram. The opening and closing of the stomata is controlled by the guard cells.

58. **(D)**   Organismal Biology

Structure 2 is a chloroplast. Chloroplasts contain stacks of flattened compartments. Each compartment is a thylakoid, and a stack of thylakoids is called a granum. Chlorophyll is located within the thylakoids, and the fluid that lies outside the thylakoids is called the stroma. Guard cells are not part of the chloroplast.

59. **(E)**   Organismal Biology

Structure 4 is phloem. Phloem is made of living cells and is comprised of sieve elements and companion cells. The purpose of the phloem is to transport nutrients up and down the plant. Wood is made not from phloem but from xylem.

60. **(A)**   Organismal Biology

Structure 1 is the cuticle. Plants that live in desert climates, where water is limiting, have thick cuticles to preserve water. Another adaptation for conserving water is closing the stomata during the hottest part of the day when evaporative demand is highest.

Biology E Solitary Multiple Choice

61. **(E)**   Organismal Biology

Counter-current exchange occurs in the respiratory system of birds. The respiratory system of birds uses air sacs to maintain a constant, counter-current, unidirectional flow of air across the lung surfaces.

62. **(B)**   Evolution and Diversity

Allopatric speciation refers to a situation in which a geographic barrier splits a population and the two separated populations evolve into two separate species.

63. **(D)**   Ecology

Populations that perform exceedingly well in favorable conditions but exceedingly poorly in unfavorable conditions probably do not have very much variation among individuals. If variation existed, more individuals would be able to adapt to new environmental conditions, and the population would be better equipped to survive. Populations with little variation and fast population growth in favorable conditions are usually asexual, reproduce early in life, and have short life spans. But this type of population generally does not have young that need intensive parental care. The effort needed to provide such care would limit the speed of the population's growth.

64. **(B)**   Ecology

The disease reduces the amount of forage (aspen trees) that is available to the elk. The carrying capacity is reduced due to a shortage of food. Carrying capacity is the maximum number of individuals that can be supported by the available resources.

65. **(B)**   Evolution and Diversity

Evolution occurs at the level of the population. Individuals cannot evolve, nor can a community, ecosystem, or biome. Do not confuse succession with evolution. Evolution is the change in allele frequencies in a population over time. Succession is the gradual change in the plant and animal communities in an area after a disturbance or the creation of a new substrate (e.g., volcanic island formation). Succession does not involve a change in the genetic make-up of organisms. Succession involves the migration of species into an area.

66. **(A)**   Organismal Biology

Structure 1 is a root hair, the purpose of which is to increase the absorptive capacity of the root.

Biology E Group Multiple Choice

67. **(A)**   Ecology

To get the change in weight for each set of bags, subtract the final weight from the initial weight. The bags from Texas that were kept in Texas lost the most weight (2.7 grams).

68. **(D)**   Ecology

The bags lost weight because microorganisms broke down the plant matter and fed on it—a process called decomposition. The bags did not lose weight because grass fell out of them. The bags did not lose weight from evaporation because the plants were dried before they were put into the bags. The plants were not alive, so they could not photosynthesize (i.e. harness CO_2 and light in order to grow).

69. **(C)**   Ecology

The process that the students learned about is called decomposition.

70. **(D)**   Ecology

Cellular respiration (glycolysis, Krebs cycle, and the electron transport chain) is the process by which plants and animals break down carbohydrates for energy and release carbon dioxide as a byproduct.

71. **(B)**   Ecology

When a rabbit eats a flower, it absorbs what carbon matter it can and gives off the rest as waste. The carbon that is absorbed and incorporated into the rabbit's body is returned to the environment when the rabbit dies and decomposes. It's true that rabbits give off carbon dioxide through respiration, but this carbon dioxide is not directly related to the carbon that the rabbit ingests from the flower.

72. **(E)**   Organismal Biology

Pollen must land on the stigma in order to fertilize the female. Pollen is the male gamete. The male reproductive parts of the plant are the anther and the filament, which collectively are known as the stamen. The female reproductive parts of the plant are the stigma, style, and ovary. The female parts collectively are known as the pistil.

73. **(E)**   Organismal Biology

The ovary will develop into fruit after fertilization. The ovary encloses the ovules, which will develop into seeds.

74. **(D)**   Organismal Biology

This plant could be a dicot. Angiosperms are the only plant group that has flowers. The angiosperms are divided into monocots and dicots. All of the other choices are not in the angiosperm division.

75. **(D)**   Organismal Biology

Plants grow colorful flowers or give off attractive scents to attract animal pollinators such as birds and bees. If a plant has small, drab flowers, it indicates that the plant does not need to attract animal pollinators. Of the answer choices, only wind and pollinated plants do not rely on animals.

76. **(C)**   Ecology

The results of this experiment are represented in a bar graph. To read the graph, look at the top of the bar for species 2 when it is infected by parasites. Follow the top of the bar to the y-axis, and you will see that the species consumed 60 seeds.

77. **(B)**   Ecology

The total number of seeds consumed by both species was 105 when the birds were not infected by parasites and 80 when the birds were infected by parasites. The total number of seeds eaten decreased (from 105 to 80) when the birds were infected.

78. **(C)**   Ecology

When there are no parasites present, species 1 eats more seeds than species 2. When there are parasites present, species 2 eats more seeds than species 1. So, species 1 is the better competitor when no parasites are present, and species 2 is the better competitor when parasites are present.

79. **(D)**   Ecology

The woman hiked from taiga to tundra. Taiga usually is populated by conifers and is cold and wet. Tundra has short vegetation, and the soil is permanently frozen a few feet below the surface.

80. **(C)**   Ecology

The sequential change in biomes as one travels higher in altitude is similar to the change seen as one travels north or south from the equator (increase in latitude).

Biology M Solitary Multiple Choice

81. **(B)**   Organic and Biochemistry

The sides of the DNA ladder are composed of deoxyribose and phosphate. The "rungs" of the ladder are composed of the nitrogenous bases (adenine, guanine, thymine, and cytosine).

82. **(A)**   The Cell

The correct arrangement of tails and heads in a phospholipid bilayer is "head" "tail" "tail" "head." The hydrophilic phosphorous heads face the watery regions on the inside and outside of the cell. The hydrophobic tails, which are chains of carbon and hydrogen, face each other in the water-free junction.

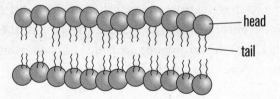

83. **(D)**   Evolution and Diversity

A good example of a set of homologous structures is the arm of a man and the wing of a bat. Homologous structures are structures in different species that are similar because of common ancestry.

84. (E) Cell Processes

The Krebs cycle cannot proceed unless the electron transport chain (ETC) is also working. The ETC requires oxygen to be the final acceptor of electrons. Glycolysis and fermentation processes are part of anaerobic respiration and do not require oxygen.

85. (A) Evolution and Diversity

The particular layers of rock in which fossils are found can give clues about the relative ages of the fossils. If fossils are found in the same geographic area, the fossils in the upper layers are generally from an earlier era. Sedimentary rock is created when sediment is deposited and covered by more and more layers of sediment. Very gradually, heat and pressure cause the sediment to harden, and any organic material trapped in that sediment also hardens and becomes a fossil.

86. (D) Genetics

Red-green colorblindness is a recessive trait carried on the X-chromosome. Since both of the parents have normal vision, they must each have one normal X-chromosome. The father only has one X-chromosome, so his genotype must be XY. In order for the daughter to have red-green colorblindness, her mother has to be a carrier of the disorder. Thus, her mother must be heterozygous for the trait, so her genotype is X'X.

Biology M Group Multiple Choice

87. (E) Cell Processes

The correct order of the steps in mitosis is: prophase (5), metaphase (1), anaphase (4), telophase (3), cytokineses (2).

88. (A) Cell Processes

The two halves of the X-shaped structure are called chromatids. After a chromosome replicates, the two new chromosomes are joined together in the middle region (the centromere). Together, the two chromatids are called a chromosome and the cell is still considered to be diploid, even though the DNA is replicated.

89. (A) Cell Processes

During anaphase, the chromatids separate into individual chromosomes and are pulled to opposite poles of the cell.

90. **(D)**   Cell Processes

Mitosis is a process that creates two daughter cells that are genetically identical to both each other and the parent cell. Mitosis creates diploid cells (46 chromosomes) that are somatic cells, not sex cells.

91. **(D)**   Cell Processes

You can draw an extension of the line on the graph, using the same slope as in the previous sets of points. At 35 days, you could predict that there would be 20g of lactic acid accumulated in the body.

92. **(D)**   Organismal Biology

A lack of oxygen underwater means that the Krebs cycle and the electron transport chain cannot proceed because oxygen is required for the final electron acceptor in the ETC. Glycolysis, in contrast, does not require oxygen and can occur in both aerobic and anaerobic environments. Anaerobic respiration can involve alcoholic or lactic acid fermentation, depending on the species. These turtles were generating lactic acid through anaerobic respiration.

93. **(A)**   Organismal Biology

Structure 1 is called actin. Actin is the thin filament that is connected to the ends of the Z-lines. Myosin in the thick filament that does not connect to the ends of the Z-lines.

94. **(C)**   Organismal Biology

During muscle contractions, the actin and myosin fibers do not shorten; they simply overlap more. The overlap brings the Z-lines closer together, and the sarcomere shortens.

95. **(C)**   Organismal Biology

Muscle units with this arrangement of actin and myosin are called sarcomeres. Sarcomeres are found in skeletal muscle.

96. **(E)**   Organismal Biology

Muscles and bones are similar in that they both serve as support for and protection of the body's various parts.

97. **(E)**   Genetics

Human blood types are determined by the presence or absence of two alleles, A and B, which code for antigen A and antigen B, respectively. If no antigen is present, then the blood type is called O. When both A and B alleles are present, they are both fully expressed, and the person has the blood type AB. The possible blood types are:

Genotypes		Phenotypes
AA and Ai	→	Type A
AB	→	Type AB
BB and Bi	→	Type B
ii	→	Type O

To answer this question, you can guess at the genotypes of the parents to see whether they could possibly have a child with a given blood type. For example, Mrs. Lincoln's phenotype is AB, so her genotype has to be AB. Mr. Lincoln's phenotype is A, so his genotype could be either AA or Ai.

Possible Cross 1	A	A
A	AA	AA
B	AB	AB

Possible Cross 2	A	i
A	AA	Ai
B	AB	Bi

Looking at the crosses, you can see that the Lincolns could not have a baby with type O blood.

98. **(A)**   Genetics

If Mr. and Mrs. Smith both have the genotype BB, then any child they had would have a 100% chance of having type B blood.

99. **(C)**   Genetics

Because both the A and B alleles are fully expressed when they occur together, the alleles are codominant.

100. **(B)**   Genetics

The only cross that can give all possible blood types (A, B, AB, and O) is Ai × Bi.

SAT II Biology
Practice Test 3

131

BIOLOGY TEST 3 ANSWER SHEET

1. Ⓐ Ⓑ Ⓒ Ⓓ Ⓔ	26. Ⓐ Ⓑ Ⓒ Ⓓ Ⓔ	51. Ⓐ Ⓑ Ⓒ Ⓓ Ⓔ	76. Ⓐ Ⓑ Ⓒ Ⓓ Ⓔ
2. Ⓐ Ⓑ Ⓒ Ⓓ Ⓔ	27. Ⓐ Ⓑ Ⓒ Ⓓ Ⓔ	52. Ⓐ Ⓑ Ⓒ Ⓓ Ⓔ	77. Ⓐ Ⓑ Ⓒ Ⓓ Ⓔ
3. Ⓐ Ⓑ Ⓒ Ⓓ Ⓔ	28. Ⓐ Ⓑ Ⓒ Ⓓ Ⓔ	53. Ⓐ Ⓑ Ⓒ Ⓓ Ⓔ	78. Ⓐ Ⓑ Ⓒ Ⓓ Ⓔ
4. Ⓐ Ⓑ Ⓒ Ⓓ Ⓔ	29. Ⓐ Ⓑ Ⓒ Ⓓ Ⓔ	54. Ⓐ Ⓑ Ⓒ Ⓓ Ⓔ	79. Ⓐ Ⓑ Ⓒ Ⓓ Ⓔ
5. Ⓐ Ⓑ Ⓒ Ⓓ Ⓔ	30. Ⓐ Ⓑ Ⓒ Ⓓ Ⓔ	55. Ⓐ Ⓑ Ⓒ Ⓓ Ⓔ	80. Ⓐ Ⓑ Ⓒ Ⓓ Ⓔ
6. Ⓐ Ⓑ Ⓒ Ⓓ Ⓔ	31. Ⓐ Ⓑ Ⓒ Ⓓ Ⓔ	56. Ⓐ Ⓑ Ⓒ Ⓓ Ⓔ	81. Ⓐ Ⓑ Ⓒ Ⓓ Ⓔ
7. Ⓐ Ⓑ Ⓒ Ⓓ Ⓔ	32. Ⓐ Ⓑ Ⓒ Ⓓ Ⓔ	57. Ⓐ Ⓑ Ⓒ Ⓓ Ⓔ	82. Ⓐ Ⓑ Ⓒ Ⓓ Ⓔ
8. Ⓐ Ⓑ Ⓒ Ⓓ Ⓔ	33. Ⓐ Ⓑ Ⓒ Ⓓ Ⓔ	58. Ⓐ Ⓑ Ⓒ Ⓓ Ⓔ	83. Ⓐ Ⓑ Ⓒ Ⓓ Ⓔ
9. Ⓐ Ⓑ Ⓒ Ⓓ Ⓔ	34. Ⓐ Ⓑ Ⓒ Ⓓ Ⓔ	59. Ⓐ Ⓑ Ⓒ Ⓓ Ⓔ	84. Ⓐ Ⓑ Ⓒ Ⓓ Ⓔ
10. Ⓐ Ⓑ Ⓒ Ⓓ Ⓔ	35. Ⓐ Ⓑ Ⓒ Ⓓ Ⓔ	60. Ⓐ Ⓑ Ⓒ Ⓓ Ⓔ	85. Ⓐ Ⓑ Ⓒ Ⓓ Ⓔ
11. Ⓐ Ⓑ Ⓒ Ⓓ Ⓔ	36. Ⓐ Ⓑ Ⓒ Ⓓ Ⓔ	61. Ⓐ Ⓑ Ⓒ Ⓓ Ⓔ	86. Ⓐ Ⓑ Ⓒ Ⓓ Ⓔ
12. Ⓐ Ⓑ Ⓒ Ⓓ Ⓔ	37. Ⓐ Ⓑ Ⓒ Ⓓ Ⓔ	62. Ⓐ Ⓑ Ⓒ Ⓓ Ⓔ	87. Ⓐ Ⓑ Ⓒ Ⓓ Ⓔ
13. Ⓐ Ⓑ Ⓒ Ⓓ Ⓔ	38. Ⓐ Ⓑ Ⓒ Ⓓ Ⓔ	63. Ⓐ Ⓑ Ⓒ Ⓓ Ⓔ	88. Ⓐ Ⓑ Ⓒ Ⓓ Ⓔ
14. Ⓐ Ⓑ Ⓒ Ⓓ Ⓔ	39. Ⓐ Ⓑ Ⓒ Ⓓ Ⓔ	64. Ⓐ Ⓑ Ⓒ Ⓓ Ⓔ	89. Ⓐ Ⓑ Ⓒ Ⓓ Ⓔ
15. Ⓐ Ⓑ Ⓒ Ⓓ Ⓔ	40. Ⓐ Ⓑ Ⓒ Ⓓ Ⓔ	65. Ⓐ Ⓑ Ⓒ Ⓓ Ⓔ	90. Ⓐ Ⓑ Ⓒ Ⓓ Ⓔ
16. Ⓐ Ⓑ Ⓒ Ⓓ Ⓔ	41. Ⓐ Ⓑ Ⓒ Ⓓ Ⓔ	66. Ⓐ Ⓑ Ⓒ Ⓓ Ⓔ	91. Ⓐ Ⓑ Ⓒ Ⓓ Ⓔ
17. Ⓐ Ⓑ Ⓒ Ⓓ Ⓔ	42. Ⓐ Ⓑ Ⓒ Ⓓ Ⓔ	67. Ⓐ Ⓑ Ⓒ Ⓓ Ⓔ	92. Ⓐ Ⓑ Ⓒ Ⓓ Ⓔ
18. Ⓐ Ⓑ Ⓒ Ⓓ Ⓔ	43. Ⓐ Ⓑ Ⓒ Ⓓ Ⓔ	68. Ⓐ Ⓑ Ⓒ Ⓓ Ⓔ	93. Ⓐ Ⓑ Ⓒ Ⓓ Ⓔ
19. Ⓐ Ⓑ Ⓒ Ⓓ Ⓔ	44. Ⓐ Ⓑ Ⓒ Ⓓ Ⓔ	69. Ⓐ Ⓑ Ⓒ Ⓓ Ⓔ	94. Ⓐ Ⓑ Ⓒ Ⓓ Ⓔ
20. Ⓐ Ⓑ Ⓒ Ⓓ Ⓔ	45. Ⓐ Ⓑ Ⓒ Ⓓ Ⓔ	70. Ⓐ Ⓑ Ⓒ Ⓓ Ⓔ	95. Ⓐ Ⓑ Ⓒ Ⓓ Ⓔ
21. Ⓐ Ⓑ Ⓒ Ⓓ Ⓔ	46. Ⓐ Ⓑ Ⓒ Ⓓ Ⓔ	71. Ⓐ Ⓑ Ⓒ Ⓓ Ⓔ	96. Ⓐ Ⓑ Ⓒ Ⓓ Ⓔ
22. Ⓐ Ⓑ Ⓒ Ⓓ Ⓔ	47. Ⓐ Ⓑ Ⓒ Ⓓ Ⓔ	72. Ⓐ Ⓑ Ⓒ Ⓓ Ⓔ	97. Ⓐ Ⓑ Ⓒ Ⓓ Ⓔ
23. Ⓐ Ⓑ Ⓒ Ⓓ Ⓔ	48. Ⓐ Ⓑ Ⓒ Ⓓ Ⓔ	73. Ⓐ Ⓑ Ⓒ Ⓓ Ⓔ	98. Ⓐ Ⓑ Ⓒ Ⓓ Ⓔ
24. Ⓐ Ⓑ Ⓒ Ⓓ Ⓔ	49. Ⓐ Ⓑ Ⓒ Ⓓ Ⓔ	74. Ⓐ Ⓑ Ⓒ Ⓓ Ⓔ	99. Ⓐ Ⓑ Ⓒ Ⓓ Ⓔ
25. Ⓐ Ⓑ Ⓒ Ⓓ Ⓔ	50. Ⓐ Ⓑ Ⓒ Ⓓ Ⓔ	75. Ⓐ Ⓑ Ⓒ Ⓓ Ⓔ	100. Ⓐ Ⓑ Ⓒ Ⓓ Ⓔ

BIOLOGY E/M TEST

FOR BOTH BIOLOGY-E AND BIOLOGY-M, ANSWER QUESTIONS 1–60

Directions: Each set of lettered choices below refers to the numbered questions or statements immediately following it. Select the one lettered choice that best answers each question or best fits each statement, and then fill in the corresponding oval on the answer sheet. A choice may be used once, more than once, or not at all in each set.

Questions 1–3 refer to the components of cells.

    (A) Ribosome
    (B) Cell wall
    (C) Mitochondria
    (D) Cell membrane
    (E) Golgi complex

1.   Produces energy for the cell

2.   Where proteins are packaged for secretion

3.   Composed of cellulose in plant cells

Questions 4–6 refer to the organic compounds crucial to the storage and transfer of information.

    (A) Nucleic acids
    (B) Steroids
    (C) Phospholipids
    (D) Polypeptides
    (E) Polysaccharides

4.   Take the form of starch in plants and glycogen in animals

5.   Form the fundamental structure of the cell membrane

6.   The primary structure in hydrophobic hormones

Questions 7–9 refer to components of a human heart.

    (A) Right ventricle
    (B) Aorta
    (C) Right atrium
    (D) Pulmonary artery
    (E) Atrioventricular node

7.   The chamber where blood returns to the heart

8.   Carries deoxygenated blood to the lungs

9.   Causes the walls of the ventricles to contract

Questions 10–12 refer to different types of consumers.

    (A) Autotroph
    (B) Heterotroph
    (C) Primary consumer
    (D) Saprophyte
    (E) Secondary consumer

10. A carnivore that eats an herbivore

11. An organism that can use solar energy and carbon dioxide to make organic molecules

12. An organism that decomposes waste and dead material

GO ON TO THE NEXT PAGE

Directions: Each of the questions or incomplete statements below is followed by five suggested answers or completions. Some questions pertain to a set that refers to a laboratory or experimental situation. For each question, select the best answer to the question and fill in the corresponding oval on the answer sheet.

13. If a carbon atom has 6 protons, 7 neutrons, and 6 electrons, then that carbon atom is a(n)

    (A) cation
    (B) anion
    (C) isotope
    (D) metal
    (E) electrically charged element

14. Which of the following statements is NOT true?

    (A) Prokaryotic cells are evolutionarily more advanced than eukaryotic cells.
    (B) Prokaryotic cells have no nucleus.
    (C) Plant cells are eukaryotic.
    (D) Prokaryotic cell walls are composed of peptidoglycan.
    (E) Eukaryotic cells have mitochondria.

15. A rat in a cage flinches when a burst of noise is played over a loudspeaker. The burst is played twice an hour. Otherwise, the rat is treated normally. After one day, the rat no longer flinches when the sound is played. This is an example of

    (A) aberrant behavior
    (B) learned behavior
    (C) habituation
    (D) conditioning
    (E) instinctual behavior

16. The prairie of North America and the steppe of Russia—both grasslands— are examples of the same

    (A) biome
    (B) ecosystem
    (C) biosphere
    (D) community
    (E) habitat

17. The theory that there are short periods of rapid evolution followed by long periods with little or no evolution is called

    (A) gradualism
    (B) Lamarckism
    (C) punctuated equilibrium
    (D) natural selection
    (E) creationism

18. A lizard in the genus *Cnemidophorus* can reproduce when the female's eggs divide mitotically without being fertilized by sperm. This type of reproduction is called

    (A) sexual reproduction
    (B) parthenogenesis
    (C) regeneration
    (D) budding
    (E) hermaphrodism

19. A microscope with a 10x ocular lens and a 20x objective lens will produce a total magnification of

    (A) 10x
    (B) 20x
    (C) 30x
    (D) 200x
    (E) 2,000x

20. When a plant loses water through its leaves, the process is called

    (A) photosynthesis
    (B) precipitation
    (C) respiration
    (D) percolation
    (E) transpiration

21. Epinephrine and norepinephrine are the "fight-or-flight" hormones that are released by the

    (A) pituitary gland
    (B) thyroid gland
    (C) adrenal glands
    (D) hypothalamus
    (E) pancreas

GO ON TO THE NEXT PAGE

22. During the Great Depression, many farmers stopped plowing their fields and abandoned them. The abandoned fields subsequently underwent ecological changes through a process known as

    (A) evolution
    (B) population dynamics
    (C) primary succession
    (D) secondary succession
    (E) ecosystem maintenance

23. A plant in a windowsill bends toward the light. This is an example of

    (A) photoperiodism
    (B) thigmotropism
    (C) gravitropism
    (D) photorespiration
    (E) phototropism

24. The Krebs cycle takes place in the

    (A) cytoplasm of the cell
    (B) chloroplasts
    (C) matrix of the mitochondria
    (D) inner membrane of the mitochondria
    (E) thylakoid of the mitochondria

25. A scientist places three substances into three different beakers of water. The first substance dissolves, the second substance does not dissolve, and the third substance dissolves. Which of the following is the most likely identification of the components of each of the substances:

    (A) Substance 1: ionic compounds
        Substance 2: isotopes
        Substance 3: nonpolar molecules
    (B) Substance 1: polar molecules
        Substance 2: ionic compounds
        Substance 3: molecules with hydrogen bonds
    (C) Substance 1: ionic compounds
        Substance 2: polar molecules
        Substance 3: molecules with hydrogen bonds
    (D) Substance 1: isotopes
        Substance 2: molecules with hydrogen bonds
        Substance 3: ionic compounds
    (E) Substance 1: polar molecules
        Substance 2: nonpolar molecules
        Substance 3: ionic compounds

26. In a eukaryotic cell, where can DNA be found?

    (A) Ribosomes and nucleus
    (B) Nucleus only
    (C) Nucleus and mitochondria
    (D) Golgi complex only
    (E) Cytoplasm

27. Which of the following characteristics would most likely be associated with an ocean organism that feeds exclusively on dead organic matter?

    (A) Is exclusively unicellular
    (B) Has a silicate shell
    (C) Is also autotrophic
    (D) Lives in the photo zone
    (E) Has poor eyesight

28. When two substances are placed in a cup filled with distilled water, nothing happens. When a third substance is added to the cup, the first two substances combine, while the third remains unchanged. The third substance is a(n)

    (A) amino acid
    (B) enzyme
    (C) lipid
    (D) carbohydrate
    (E) heavy metal

29. The uncontrolled growth of cells is called

    (A) gametogenesis
    (B) budding
    (C) cytokinesis
    (D) cancer
    (E) mitosis

30. The similar appearance of the wing of an insect and the wing of a bird are examples of what process?

    (A) Speciation
    (B) Adaptive radiation
    (C) Stabilizing selection
    (D) Convergent evolution
    (E) Divergent evolution

GO ON TO THE NEXT PAGE

Questions 31–35 refer to the experiment described below.

Aquatic plants called *Elodea* were placed in four different jars of distilled water. Each jar was exposed to a different wavelength of light. Jar 1 was exposed to blue light (λ = 440 nm), Jar 2 was exposed to orange light (λ = 600 nm), Jar 3 was exposed to sunlight (all wavelengths), and Jar 4 was kept in the dark. The amount of dissolved oxygen in the jars was measured once per minute for 15 minutes, using a dissolved oxygen probe.

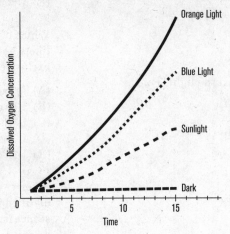

31. At the end of the experiment, which jar had the highest dissolved oxygen concentration?

    (A) Jar 1
    (B) Jar 2
    (C) Jar 3
    (D) Jar 4
    (E) Jars 1 and 2 had equally high concentrations of dissolved oxygen.

32. In Jar 1, oxygen concentrations

    (A) were initially high and then decreased
    (B) stayed the same
    (C) increased rapidly and then leveled off
    (D) decreased rapidly and then leveled off
    (E) increased steadily

33. The substances in a leaf that absorb light are called

    (A) stomata
    (B) guard cells
    (C) thylakoids
    (D) pigments
    (E) ATP

34. In this experiment, dissolved oxygen comes from the breakdown of

    (A) H_2O during photosynthesis
    (B) CO_2 during respiration
    (C) both CO_2 and H_2O during photosynthesis
    (D) carbohydrates during respiration
    (E) H_2O during respiration

35. Based on the results of this experiment, you could conclude that

    (A) orange light is absorbed more than blue light
    (B) blue light is reflected more than orange light
    (C) sunlight is not a good light for growing plants
    (D) plants do not absorb all wavelengths of light equally
    (E) plants that are kept in the dark will create more oxygen than plants that are kept in the light

GO ON TO THE NEXT PAGE

Questions 36–38 relate to the following diagram of fossils found in sedimentary rock.

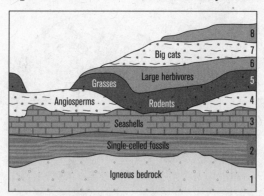

36. During the time that layer 3 was deposited, the environment was most likely a

    (A) desert
    (B) sea or ocean
    (C) tropical rainforest
    (D) tundra
    (E) deciduous forest

37. Which of the following mammals lived earliest in this area?

    (A) Big cats
    (B) Large herbivores
    (C) Rodents
    (D) Impossible to tell
    (E) All of the mammals lived at the same time.

38. What can you say about the fossil depicted below?

    (A) It is from what was a very social animal.
    (B) It is from an ancestor of the modern-day bear.
    (C) It had a coat made of black fur.
    (D) It was a carnivore.
    (E) It was an herbivore.

39. Which of the following events might create a gap in the fossil record?

    I.   Mass extinction
    II. Erosion
    III. Volcanic activity

    (A) I
    (B) II
    (C) I and III only
    (D) II and III only
    (E) I, II, and III

GO ON TO THE NEXT PAGE

Questions 40–43 refer to the following drawing of a cell.

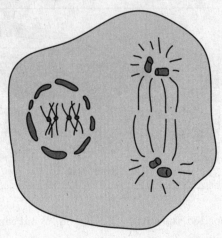

40. The phase depicted is

 (A) prophase I of mitosis
 (B) interphase of mitosis
 (C) interphase of meiosis
 (D) prophase I of meiosis
 (E) prophase II of meiosis

41. The homologous chromosomes are engaged in a process called

 (A) cytokinesis
 (B) substitution
 (C) replication
 (D) crossing-over
 (E) translation

42. The exchange of genetic material between homologous chromosomes during the production of sperm and eggs is important because it

 (A) produces offspring that are genetically identical to the parent
 (B) increases the number of genetic combinations in the gametes
 (C) decreases the genetic variation caused by independent assortment
 (D) results in faster reproduction
 (E) creates alleles that were not present in either parent

43. Mitosis and meiosis are similar because both

 (A) result in the production of gametes in humans
 (B) involve independent assortment
 (C) result in the production of two identical daughter cells
 (D) involve replication of DNA
 (E) have two cell divisions

GO ON TO THE NEXT PAGE

Questions 44–48 refer to the vertebrate digestive system.

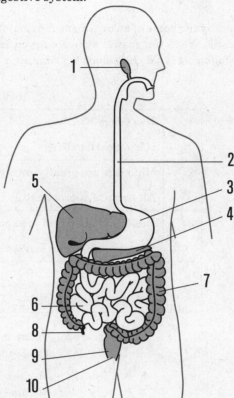

44. Structure 2 pushes food down into the stomach through successive waves of smooth muscle contractions called

    (A) diaphragm contractions
    (B) peristaltic contractions
    (C) Braxton-Hix contractions
    (D) diastolic contractions
    (E) hepatic contractions

45. The majority of the digestion and absorption occurs in structure

    (A) 3
    (B) 4
    (C) 5
    (D) 6
    (E) 7

46. Bile plays an important role in the digestion process because it

    (A) chemically digests starches that would otherwise be eliminated as waste
    (B) controls *E. coli* activity in the large intestine
    (C) emulsifies fat globules to increase surface area for eventual chemical digestion
    (D) protects the gall bladder from infection
    (E) enhances the absorptive power of the villi

47. Excessive acid in the stomach can result in a hole in the wall of the organ. What is this hole called?

    (A) Tumor
    (B) Cancer
    (C) Boil
    (D) Ulcer
    (C) Hemorrhoid

48. Structure 1 secretes

    (A) proteases to break down proteins
    (B) salivary amylase to break down carbohydrates
    (C) emulsifiers to break up fats
    (D) lipases to break down lipids
    (E) proteases to break down carbohydrates

GO ON TO THE NEXT PAGE

<u>Questions 49–51</u> refer to the dichotomous key below.

Taxonomists use dichotomous keys to identify the name of an organism. A dichotomous key has a series of two-part questions based on the characteristics of the organisms. When you answer a question, you are led to the next question and ultimately to the name of the unknown organism. The following is a dichotomous key for animals in a natural history collection.

1. ladybug   2. centipede   3. spider

4. grasshopper   5. moth

Dichotomous Key

1.	Has 6 legs . . . . go to 2
	Has more than 6 legs . . . . go to 4
2.	Hind legs are greatly enlarged . . . . Orthoptera
	All legs are approximately the same size. . . . . go to 3
3.	Has hard wings that are spotted . . . . Coleoptera
	Has soft wings that are striped . . . . Lepidoptera
4.	Has 8 leg . . . . Arachnida
	Has more than 8 legs . . . . Chilopoda

49. Organism #1 is a(n)

    (A) Orthoptera
    (B) Chilopoda
    (C) Lepidoptera
    (D) Coleoptera
    (E) Arachnida

50. All of the organisms shown are members of phylum

    (A) Insecta
    (B) Arthropoda
    (C) Animalia
    (D) Echinodermata
    (E) Arachnida

51. Another example of a member of this phylum would be a(n)

    (A) snail
    (B) clam
    (C) earthworm
    (D) lobster
    (E) jellyfish

52. Organisms in the same phylum would definitely also be in the same

    (A) class
    (B) family
    (C) order
    (D) genus
    (E) kingdom

53. Individuals from two separate species that share an evolutionary ancestor may

    I.   have identical genetic codes
    II. be able to produce viable offspring
    III. follow similar stages of embryological development

    (A) I only
    (B) II only
    (C) III only
    (D) I and II only
    (E) I and III only

GO ON TO THE NEXT PAGE

BIOLOGY E/M TEST—*Continued*

Questions 54–57 refer to the following drawing of an individual's chromosomes, arranged by size.

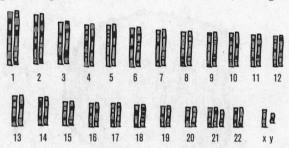

54. The above drawing is of a

    (A) pedigree
    (B) DNA helix
    (C) Punnett square
    (D) karyotype
    (E) gene sequence

55. How many individual chromosomes are shown?

    (A) 22
    (B) 46
    (C) 45
    (D) 23
    (E) 47

56. The individual whose chromosomes are shown here has a disorder called

    (A) disjunction
    (B) trisomy of chromosome 21
    (C) nondisjunction of the Y-chromosome
    (D) polyploidy
    (E) monosomy of the X-chromosome

57. This individual received

    (A) an X-chromosome from the mother and a Y from the father
    (B) a Y-chromosome from the mother and an X-chromosome from the father
    (C) an X- and a Y-chromosome from the mother and no sex chromosome from the father
    (D) an X-chromosome from the mother and no sex chromosome from the father
    (E) an X- and a Y-chromosome from both the mother and father

GO ON TO THE NEXT PAGE

/ 4 1

Questions 58–60 refer to the following diagram of a cross-section of a tree.

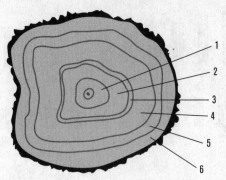

58. What is the approximate age of this tree?

   (A) 6 years
   (B) 15 years
   (C) 30 years
   (D) 150 years
   (E) 60 years

59. Which ring indicates a year in which rainfall was low?

   (A) 1
   (B) 2
   (C) 3
   (D) 4
   (E) 5

60. The tree rings are made of

   (A) live tissue
   (B) meristematic tissue
   (C) phloem
   (D) xylem
   (E) palisade layers

GO ON TO THE NEXT PAGE

BIOLOGY-E SECTION

If you are taking the Biology-E test, continue with questions 61–80.
If you are taking the Biology-M test, go to question 81 now.

<u>Directions:</u> Each of the questions or incomplete statements below is followed by five suggested answers or completions. Some questions pertain to a set that refers to a laboratory or experimental situation. For each question, select the one choice that is the best answer to the question and then fill in the corresponding oval on the answer sheet.

61. Evolution is defined as

    (A) a population in Hardy-Weinberg equilibrium
    (B) a change in the inhabitants of a community over time
    (C) a change in gene frequency over time
    (D) inheritance of acquired traits
    (E) survival of the fittest

62. Soil, water, rainfall, and temperature are examples of

    (A) communities
    (B) habitats
    (C) biotic factors
    (D) abiotic factors
    (E) climate

63. Clusters of neurons are known as

    (A) ganglia
    (B) Nodes of Ranvier
    (C) receptors
    (D) Schwann cells
    (E) axons

64. Which of the following is NOT a characteristic of members of the kingdom Fungi?

    (A) Often live as decomposers
    (B) Are heterotrophic
    (C) Secrete enzymes to digest their food externally
    (D) Spend most of their life cycle in the haploid state
    (E) Have cell walls made of cellulose

65. In a food chain, roughly what percentage of energy is transferred from one trophic level to the next?

    (A) 100 %
    (B) 80 %
    (C) 50 %
    (D) 10 %
    (E) 1 %

66. The first animals that were fully adapted to live their entire life cycle on land are the

    (A) amphibians
    (B) reptiles
    (C) birds
    (D) mammals
    (E) crustaceans

GO ON TO THE NEXT PAGE

Questions 67–69 refer to organismal biology

A group of students trained their pets to push a lever that released a treat. The pets were two rats, a guinea pig, a hamster, and a ferret. At the beginning of the experiment, the students showed the pets the lever and helped them push the lever down to retrieve the treat. The students then conducted trials in which they put each pet in a box with a lever and observed whether or not the pet pushed the lever to get the treat. Between each of the trials, the students again showed their pets the way in which to get a treat by pressing the lever. The students stopped doing demonstrations between trials once all of the pets were successful at pushing the lever. The following table shows the results of the experiment.

Trial Number	Rat 1	Rat 2	Guinea Pig	Hamster	Ferret
1	unsuccessful	unsuccessful	unsuccessful	unsuccessful	unsuccessful
2	unsuccessful	unsuccessful	unsuccessful	unsuccessful	successful
3	successful	unsuccessful	unsuccessful	unsuccessful	successful
4	successful	successful	unsuccessful	successful	successful
5	successful	successful	successful	successful	successful
6	successful	successful	successful	successful	successful

67. The type of behavior exhibited by the pets in this experiment is called

   (A) imprinting
   (B) instinctual behavior
   (C) habituation
   (D) conditioning or associative learning
   (E) a fixed-action pattern

68. Which of the following statements is supported by the data from the experiment?

   (A) The two rats both got the treat in Trial 3.
   (B) The guinea pig and the hamster both learned at the same rate.
   (C) The ferret was the first of the pets to have a successful trial.
   (D) The hamster did not like the treat that she was given.
   (E) Animals of the same species will perform equally well.

69. If in Trials 7, 8 and 9, the animals do not receive a treat when they press the lever, what is the best prediction of what would happen?

   (A) Some or all of the animals would not press the lever in Trial 10.
   (B) All of the animals would continue to press the lever indefinitely.
   (C) The animals would try to destroy the lever.
   (D) The ferret would eat the hamster.
   (E) The ferret would be the last animal to stop pressing the lever.

GO ON TO THE NEXT PAGE

<u>Questions 70–73</u> refer to the following germination experiment.

A seed cannot sprout until oxygen and water penetrate the seed coat. An experiment was conducted to determine what effect water, heat, cold, and scarification had on the germination of seeds. Scarification is the process of mechanically wearing down the seed coat. Two seed types were used in this experiment. One seed type had a very hard seed coat, and the other had a moderately soft seed coat. For 5 days prior to planting, seeds were either soaked in water, passed through the digestive system of a Guinea pig (scarification), exposed to 100°F, exposed to 30°F, or left at ambient temperatures. The seeds were then planted. Every 5 days, the number of seed sprouts from each treatment was counted.

Seeds with hard coats

Treatment	Cumulative % of Germinated Seeds				
	Day 5	Day 10	Day 15	Day 20	Day 25
Water	25%	45%	55%	65%	70%
Heat	15%	25%	45%	50%	55%
Cold	10%	20%	30%	35%	40%
Scarification	60%	75%	75%	75%	75%
Ambient temperature	15%	30%	50%	60%	60%

Seeds with soft coats

Treatment	Cumulative % of Germinated Seeds				
	Day 5	Day 10	Day 15	Day 20	Day 25
Water	5%	7%	7%	9%	10%
Heat	10%	15%	45%	65%	70%
Cold	10%	15%	35%	40%	40%
Scarification	2%	3%	3%	4%	4%
Ambient temperature	15%	30%	50%	60%	65%

70. During which treatment did the hard-coated seeds germinate the earliest?

(A) Water
(B) Heat
(C) Cold
(D) Scarification
(E) Ambient temperature

71. During which treatment did the greatest percentage of soft-coated seeds germinate?

(A) Water
(B) Heat
(C) Cold
(D) Scarification
(E) Ambient temperature

72. Which treatment served as the control for this experiment?

(A) Water
(B) Heat
(C) Cold
(D) Scarification
(E) Ambient temperature

73. Which of the following statements is an acceptable interpretation of this data?

(A) A seed cannot germinate unless it has been soaked in water.
(B) Exposing seeds to heat and cold increases germination by equal amounts.
(C) Angiosperms and gymnosperms have different requirements for germination.
(D) Monocots and dicots have different requirements for germination.
(E) Seeds with hard coats germinated better when they were scarified, but seeds with soft coats were too damaged by scarification and didn't germinate.

GO ON TO THE NEXT PAGE

BIOLOGY E SECTION—*Continued*

Questions 74–76 refer to the following graph of body temperature as a function of ambient, or environmental, temperature.

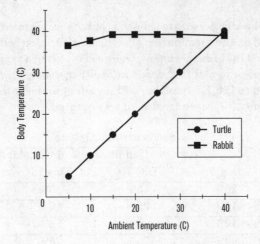

74. Turtles are

   (A) ectotherms and absorb most of their body heat from their surroundings
   (B) endotherms and absorb most of their body heat from their surroundings
   (C) ectotherms and derive most of their body heat from their own metabolism
   (D) endotherms and derive most of their body heat from their own metabolism
   (E) cold-blooded and derive most of their body heat from their own metabolism

75. If the rabbit were put in a room that was 27°C, you could predict that its body temperature would be about

   (A) 27°C
   (B) 27°F
   (C) 37°C
   (D) 37°F
   (E) 98.6°C

76. Which of the following is incorrectly matched?

   (A) Reptiles - ectotherms
   (B) Birds - ectotherms
   (C) Amphibians - ectotherms
   (D) Mammals - endotherms
   (E) Fish - ectotherms

GO ON TO THE NEXT PAGE

BIOLOGY E SECTION—*Continued*

Questions 77–80 refer to climate diagrams, as discussed below.

Climate diagrams are graphs that show the relationship between temperature and precipitation over the course of the year in a given geographic local. By looking at a climatograph for a given region, you can get an idea of what the environment is like, i.e., how dry or wet it is, how long the growing season lasts, how constant conditions are, and so on. When you read a climatograph, the months of the year are on the x-axis, temperature is on the left-hand y-axis, and precipitation is on the right-hand y-axis.

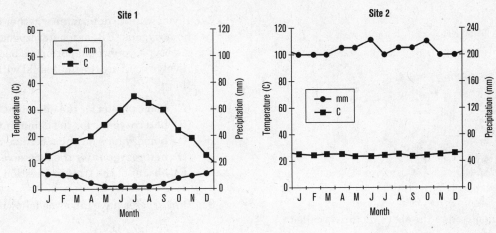

77. The average temperature at Site 1 in April is

   (A) 10°C
   (B) 15°C
   (C) 22°C
   (D) 30°C
   (E) 35°C

78. Which of the following is NOT a correct statement?

   (A) At Site 1, the temperature line lies above the precipitation line.
   (B) Temperature varies more during the course of the year at Site 1 than it does at Site 2.
   (C) At Site 2, the temperature line lies above the precipitation line, indicating that conditions are dry.
   (D) At Site 1, average monthly precipitation is always below 20 mm.
   (E) At Site 2, the average monthly temperature is always above 20°C, and the average monthly rainfall is always above 100 mm.

79. Based on the climatographs, in what biomes could the two sites be found?

   (A) Site 1 – tropical rainforest; Site 2 – arctic tundra
   (B) Site 1 – desert; Site 2 – taiga
   (C) Site 1 – temperate deciduous forest; Site 2 – desert
   (D) Site 1 – temperate grassland; Site 2 – arctic tundra
   (E) Site 1 – desert; Site 2 – tropical rainforest

80. Tropical rainforests are generally found

   (A) at high latitudes
   (B) at high altitudes
   (C) on all seven continents
   (D) near the poles
   (E) within 30° latitude of the equator

GO ON TO THE NEXT PAGE

BIOLOGY-M SECTION

If you are taking the Biology-M test, continue with questions 81–100.
Be sure to start this section of the test by filling in oval 81 on your answer sheet.

Directions: Each of the questions or incomplete statements below is followed by five suggested answers or completions. Some questions pertain to a set that refers to a laboratory or experimental situation. For each question, select the one choice that is the best answer to the question and then fill in the corresponding oval on the answer sheet.

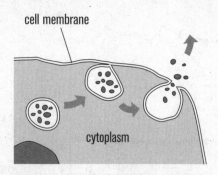

cell membrane

cytoplasm

81. The process depicted in the above picture is called

    (A) phagocytosis
    (B) cytoplasmic streaming
    (C) exocytosis
    (D) pinocytosis
    (E) osmosis

82. The number of nucleotides that are needed to code for a specific amino acid is

    (A) 1
    (B) 2
    (C) 3
    (D) 4
    (E) 6

83. Which of the following organisms is the most primitive in evolutionary terms?

    (A) Starfish
    (B) Jellyfish
    (C) Sponge
    (D) Tapeworm
    (E) Spider

84. If you want to determine whether an individual has a homozygous (BB) or a heterozygous (Bb) dominant genotype, you would perform a back cross, which involves mating the individual with another individual that is

    (A) homozygous for the dominant trait
    (B) heterozygous for the dominant trait
    (C) homozygous for the recessive trait
    (D) heterozygous for the recessive trait
    (E) absent of the trait in question

85. Prokaryotes have all of the following EXCEPT

    (A) circular DNA
    (B) cell wall
    (C) cytoplasm
    (D) ribosomes
    (E) nucleus

86. A scientist uses the rate of change in a protein called cytochrome c to calculate the point at which humans and chimpanzees last shared a common ancestor. The protein is an example of a(n)

    (A) fossil
    (B) acquired trait
    (C) vestigial structure
    (D) homologous structure
    (E) molecular clock

GO ON TO THE NEXT PAGE

Questions 87–90 refer to cell processes.

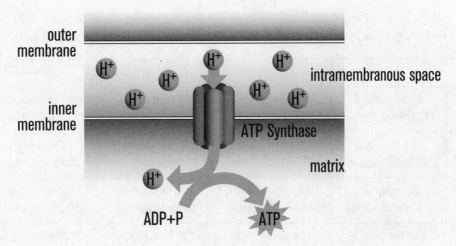

87. The process depicted is called

   (A) transcription
   (B) photosynthesis
   (C) Krebs cycle
   (D) the electron transport chain
   (E) glycolysis

88. When H⁺ ions move through ATP synthase, they are

   (A) using energy from ATP to move against their
       concentration gradient
   (B) using energy from ATP to move along their
       concentration gradient
   (C) producing ATP as they move against their
       concentration gradient
   (D) producing ATP as they move along their
       concentration gradient
   (E) producing AMP as they move along their
       concentration gradient

89. The final electron acceptor in this process is

   (A) water
   (B) oxygen
   (C) carbon
   (D) nitrogen
   (E) hydrogen

90. Which of the following processes is INCORRECTLY
    matched with the location at which it occurs?

   (A) Glycolysis – membrane of the mitochondria
   (B) Krebs cycle – matrix of the mitochondria
   (C) Electron transport chain – membrane of
       mitochondria
   (D) Anaerobic respiration – cytoplasm
   (E) Photosynthesis - chloroplasts

49

BIOLOGY M SECTION—*Continued*

Questions 91–94 refer to the following experiment.

A group of students in Mr. Olsen's biology class conducted an experiment to test the effects of activity on heart rate and breathing rate. They measured their pulse rate after doing a variety of activities for 5 minutes each.

Activity	John	Maria	Beth	Steven	Mr. Olsen
Sitting still	68 beats/min 17 breaths/min	70 beats/min 18 breaths/min	68 beats/min 16 breaths/min	67 beats/min 17 breaths/min	80 beats/min 20 breaths/min
Walking	77 beats/min 22 breaths/min	85 beats/min 21 breaths/min	77 beats/min 20 breaths/min	77 beats/min 20 breaths/min	88 beats/min 22 breaths/min
Jumping rope	100 beats/min 36 breaths/min	115 beats/min 38 breaths/min	120 beats/min 38 breaths/min	130 beats/min 40 breaths/min	135 beats/min 45 breaths/min
Running	120 beats/min 45 breaths/min	100 beats/min 37 breaths/min	120 beats/min 38 breaths/min	125 beats/min 36 breaths/min	140 beats/min 47 breaths/min
Lying down	66 beats/min 16 breaths/min	68 beats/min 16 breaths/min	63 beats/min 15 breaths/min	65 beats/min 15 breaths/min	79 beats/min 19 breaths/min

91. Whose heart rate increased the most between sitting still and walking?

   (A) John
   (B) Maria
   (C) Beth
   (D) Steven
   (E) Mr. Olsen

92. For which activity did each person reach his or her maximum breathing rate?

   (A) Walking only
   (B) Lying down only
   (C) Jumping rope only
   (D) Running only
   (E) Jumping rope or running

93. Which of the following statements is NOT supported by the data?

   (A) Each person's heart rate was greater when sitting than it was when lying down.
   (B) When pulse rate increases, the breathing rate decreases.
   (C) While sitting still, the females (Maria and Beth) had a higher average heart rate than the males (John, Steven, and Mr. Olsen).
   (D) Each person's breathing rate was greater after jumping rope than it was after walking.
   (E) Mr. Olsen had his highest pulse rate after running.

94. The role of the lungs is to

   (A) take in oxygen and remove carbon dioxide from the blood
   (B) carry carbon dioxide from various parts of the body
   (C) take in oxygen and remove carbon monoxide from the blood
   (D) carry oxygen to various parts of the body
   (E) add hemoglobin molecules to the blood

GO ON TO THE NEXT PAGE

Questions 95–97 refer to separating amino acids using chromatography paper.

Amino acids from a protein can be separated from one another and identified by paper chromatography. A group of students in a laboratory class were asked to identify the amino acids in a particular protein. A drop of the protein was put at the base of Lane 1 on a sheet of chromatography paper, and different known amino acids were put in the other lanes. The chromatography paper was then placed upright in a solvent solution. As the solvent moved up the paper, it carried the amino acids with it until the amino acids bound to the paper and would move no further. Nonpolar amino acids move farther up the chromatography paper than polar amino acids.

Lane 1: Protein X

Lane 2: Arginine

Lane 3: Methionine

Lane 4: Threonine

Lane 5: Valine

Lane 6: Histidine

Lane 7: Glutamine

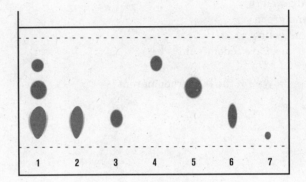

95. The Protein X in Lane 1 contains the following amino acids:

(A) Arginine, methionine, and valine
(B) Arginine, threonine, and valine
(C) Arginine, valine, and histidine
(D) Glutamine, histidine, valine, and methionine
(E) Arginine, methionine, glutamine

96. Of the amino acids used, which is the most nonpolar?

(A) Arginine
(B) Methionine
(C) Threonine
(D) Valine
(E) Histidine

97. Which of the following is NOT a component of an amino acid?

(A) Hydrogen
(B) Amino group
(C) Carboxyl group
(D) Nitrogenous base
(E) A variable "R" group

GO ON TO THE NEXT PAGE

Questions 98–100 refer to Mendelian genetics.

PARENTS		OFFSPRING	
Tall, Green	X Short, Yellow	33 Tall, Green	0 Short, Yellow

98. In this example, what are the dominant alleles for size and color?

   (A) Tall and yellow
   (B) Tall and green
   (C) Short and green
   (D) Short and yellow
   (E) Tall and short are codominant

99. What is the genotype of the tall, green parent?

   (A) Tt, Gg
   (B) TT, GG
   (C) TT, gg
   (D) Tt, GG
   (E) tt, gg

100. If you were to cross two tall, green plants that were both heterozygous for height and color, the phenotypic ratio of the offspring would be

   (A) 9 tall green, 3 tall yellow, 3 short green, 1 short yellow
   (B) 1 tall green, 3 tall yellow, 3 short green, 9 short yellow
   (C) 3 tall green, 3 tall yellow, 3 short green, 1 short yellow
   (D) 1 tall green, 3 tall yellow, 3 short green, 3 short yellow
   (E) 9 tall green, 1 tall yellow, 1 short green, 3 short yellow

S T O P

IF YOU FINISH BEFORE TIME IS CALLED, YOU MAY CHECK YOUR WORK ON THIS TEST ONLY.
DO NOT TURN TO ANY OTHER TEST IN THIS BOOK.

SAT II Biology Test 3
Explanations

Answers to SAT II Biology Practice Test 3

Question Number	Correct Answer	Right	Wrong	Question Number	Correct Answer	Right	Wrong	Question Number	Correct Answer	Right	Wrong
1.	C			34.	A			67.	D		
2.	E			35.	D			68.	C		
3.	B			36.	B			69.	A		
4.	E			37.	D			70.	D		
5.	C			38.	E			71.	B		
6.	B			39.	D			72.	E		
7.	C			40.	D			73.	E		
8.	D			41.	D			74.	A		
9.	E			42.	B			75.	C		
10.	E			43.	D			76.	B		
11.	A			44.	B			77.	C		
12.	D			45.	D			78.	C		
13.	C			46.	C			79.	E		
14.	A			47.	D			80.	E		
15.	C			48.	B			81.	C		
16.	A			49.	D			82.	C		
17.	C			50.	B			83.	C		
18.	B			51.	D			84.	C		
19.	D			52.	E			85.	E		
20.	E			53.	C			86.	E		
21.	C			54.	D			87.	D		
22.	D			55.	E			88.	D		
23.	E			56.	B			89.	B		
24.	C			57.	A			90.	A		
25.	E			58.	A			91.	B		
26.	C			59.	C			92.	E		
27.	E			60.	D			93.	B		
28.	B			61.	C			94.	A		
29.	D			62.	D			95.	B		
30.	D			63.	A			96.	C		
31.	C			64.	E			97.	D		
32.	E			65.	D			98.	B		
33.	D			66.	B			99.	B		
								100.	A		

Your raw score for the SAT II Biology test is calculated from the number of questions you answer correctly and incorrectly. Once you have determined your composite score, use the conversion table on page **21** of this book to calculate your scaled score. To calculate your raw score, count the number of questions you answered correctly: _____

A

Count the number of questions you answered incorrectly, and multiply that number by $\frac{1}{4}$:

$$\underline{\hspace{2cm}}_{B} \times \frac{1}{4} = \underline{\hspace{2cm}}_{C}$$

Subtract the value in field C from value in field A: _____

D

Round the number in field D to the nearest whole number. This is your raw score: _____

E

Biology E/M Classification Questions

1. (C)   The Cell

Mitochondria are sometimes called the "powerhouse" of the cell because they convert carbohydrates into energy through a process called cellular respiration. The Krebs cycle and electron transport chain occur in the mitochondria.

2. (E)   The Cell

The Golgi complex is the site where proteins are packaged for export out of the cell.

3. (B)   The Cell

Plant cells have cell walls composed of cellulose. Prokaryotes have cell walls composed of peptidoglycan. Animal cells do not have cell walls.

4. (E)   Organic and Biochemistry

Plants and animals store excess sugars as polysaccharides (3 or more monosaccharides that are linked together). The storage polysaccharide in plants is starch; in animals it is glycogen.

5. (C)   Organic and Biochemistry

Phospholipids are what give the cell membrane its "fluid" characteristics. Each phospholipid consists of a glycerol molecule with two fatty acid chains and a phosphate group attached to it. The cell membrane is a phospholipid bilayer.

6. (B)   Organic and Biochemistry

There are two major classes of hormones: steroid hormones and peptide hormones. Steroid hormones have a steroid as their fundamental unit, and because they are hydrophobic, they can easily cross cell membranes. Peptide hormones are composed of amino acids and cannot cross cell membranes. Testosterone is often used as an example of a steroid hormone. Insulin is often used as an example of a peptide hormone.

7. (C)   Organismal Biology

The superior and inferior vena cava return deoxygenated blood from the body to the right atrium of the heart.

8. **(D)**   Organismal Biology

The pulmonary artery carries deoxygenated blood from the right ventricle to the lungs, where it will pick up oxygen and release carbon dioxide. The pulmonary artery is the only artery that carries deoxygenated blood.

9. **(E)**   Organismal Biology

The atrioventricular node fires an electrical impulse that stimulates the contraction of the ventricles. This contraction forces blood out of the heart and into the aorta and pulmonary arteries.

10. **(E)**   Ecology

A secondary consumer is always a carnivore that eats an herbivore. Primary consumers are herbivores because they eat primary producers, i.e., plants. Secondary consumers eat primary consumers. Any animal that eats another animal is a carnivore.

11. **(A)**   Ecology

An autotroph is an organism that can use solar energy and carbon dioxide to make organic molecules by a process called photosynthesis. Autotrophs are also called primary producers.

12. **(D)**   Ecology

A saprophyte or decomposer is an organism that derives its energy from feeding on dead and waste materials.

Biology E/M Solitary Multiple Choice

13. **(C)**   Organic and Biochemistry

An atom that has gained or lost one or more neutrons is called an isotope. Carbon-12 is the most abundant form of carbon. It has 6 protons, 6 neutrons, and 6 electrons. The example given is carbon-13, which has 6 protons, 7 neutrons, and 6 electrons.

14. **(A)**   The Cell

Prokaryotic cells are smaller and structurally less complex than eukaryotic cells and are therefore considered to be more primitive than eukaryotic cells.

15. **(C)**   Organismal Biology

Habituation occurs when a non-harmful stimulus that would normally cause an animal to respond is repeated over and over again until the animal learns to ignore it. The scenario describing the rat and the loud noise played twice an hour fits this description.

16. **(A)**   Ecology

A biome is a group of communities that have the same general climate and life forms. Grasslands receive 10–60 inches per year. They are too dry to support many trees but wet enough to support grass and shrub species. Common animals found in grasslands include large herbivores, small burrowing animals, birds, and insects.

17. **(C)**   Evolution and Diversity

The theory of punctuated equilibrium states that evolution occurs in spurts followed by long periods of little or no change. This theory is more recent than the theory of gradualism, which suggests that gradual change over time leads to the formation of new species.

18. **(B)**   Organismal Biology

Parthenogenesis is a type of non-sexual reproduction in which unfertilized eggs divide mitotically and the resulting offspring have genes that are identical to their mothers'. Parthenogenic populations are typically all female. Since there is no independent assortment or crossing-over involved in asexual reproduction, there is less genetic variation in parthenogenic populations. Parthenogenesis allows a population to grow quickly, but the limited variation in the offspring makes these populations very vulnerable to extreme environmental changes. Populations that use sexual reproduction grow more slowly but have more variation and are therefore more resistant to changes in the environment.

19. **(D)**   The Cell

In order to get the total magnification of a microscope, you must multiply the magnification of the ocular lens by the magnification of the objective lens. In this example, the ocular lens has a magnification of 10x, and the objective lens has a magnification of 20x, which yields a total magnification of 200x.

20. **(E)**   Organismal Biology

Transpiration is the loss of water from a leaf's stomata.

21. **(C)**   Organismal Biology

The adrenal glands secrete hormones that help the body respond to stress. Epinephrine and norepinephrine are the "fight or flight" hormones. They cause an increase in heart and breathing rates, an increase in blood sugar, and a dilation of the pupils.

22. **(D)**   Evolution and Diversity

Succession is the progressive change in an ecological community. It occurs when current species are displaced by new immigrant species. Succession is said to lead ultimately to a stable climax community in which the essential makeup of the populations within the community will stay constant. Primary succession occurs in areas where there are no traces of plant life, such as a newly formed volcanic island. Secondary succession occurs in areas where there has been previous plant growth. An abandoned field is a classic example of a site for secondary succession.

23. (E)   Organismal Biology

Tropisms are hormone-mediated responses to stimuli. There are three main tropisms. Phototropism is the tendency of a plant to grow toward light. Gravitropism is the tendency of a plant to grow either with or against gravity. Thigmotropism is a reaction to touch that causes the touched part of the plant to either thicken or recoil.

24. (C)   Cell Processes

The Krebs cycle occurs after glycolysis, is part of aerobic cellular respiration, and takes place in the matrix of the mitochondria. The Krebs cycle produces energy-laden NADH and $FADH_2$. NADH and $FADH_2$ go to the mitochondrial membrane, where the electron transport chain transfers their energy to ATP.

25. (E)   Organic and Biochemistry

To answer this question, you need to know how different types of compounds or molecules dissolve in water. Because the hydrogen atoms in a water molecule have a slight positive charge and the oxygen has a slight negative charge, ions and polar heads of molecules are attracted to the part of the water molecule that has a charge opposite of theirs. These attractive forces mean that polar and ionic compounds dissolve well in water while nonpolar molecules do not. Knowing that an atom is an isotope doesn't tell you whether it is polar or nonpolar, so if all you know about an atom is that it is an isotope, you cannot make much of a guess as to whether it will or won't dissolve. Once you know which sorts of molecules or atoms dissolve readily in water, the question becomes simply a matter of mix-and-match. As it turns out, only the final choice, (E), puts the substances in an order from which you are likely to get the first and third substances to dissolve, while the second substance does not dissolve.

26. (C)   The Cell

Eukaryotic cells house their DNA in the nucleus. However, eukaryotic cells also have mitochondria, and mitochondria have their own DNA and can make some of their own proteins. Mitochondria are thought to have originated from symbiotic primitive prokaryotes.

27. **(E)** Ecology

Ocean scavengers that feed on dead organic matter generally live in the aphotic zone, the deepest regions of the ocean, where light can't penetrate. These organisms are often multicellular, are not autotrophic, and may or may not have silicate shells. One characteristic that most denizens of the aphotic zone share is poor eyesight. There is no evolutionary reason for an organism that lives in a region without light to have good eyesight.

28. **(B)** Organic and Biochemistry

Enzymes are proteins that lower the activation energy needed for specific chemical reactions to occur. The enzymes bond to the two substrates and help bind them together. The enzymes are not themselves altered during this process. The third substance, which causes the first two substances to combine while remaining unchanged itself, is therefore an enzyme.

29. **(D)** Cell Processes

Cancer is a disease caused by an uncontrolled growth of cells. Cancer can result from environmentally caused genetic mutations. For example, smoking has been shown to cause lung cancer.

30. **(D)** Evolution and Diversity

The wings of insects and birds share similar characteristics because they perform similar functions for their respective organisms—the power of flight. Because these body parts perform such similar functions, over time, they have evolved certain physical similarities. This process, in which organisms that belong to different evolutionary paths develop similar body parts because those body parts perform similar functions, is called convergent evolution.

Biology E/M Group Multiple Choice

31. **(C)** Cell Processes

At the end of the experiment, the jar that had been exposed to sunlight, Jar 3, had the highest concentration of dissolved oxygen. This suggests that the rate of photosynthesis was fastest in Jar 3.

32. **(E)** Cell Processes

Jar 1 was exposed to blue light. The dissolved oxygen concentration in Jar 1 increased steadily throughout the duration of the experiment.

33. (D) Cell Processes

The substances in a plant that absorb light energy are called pigments. Chlorophyll is the primary plant pigment. It absorbs blue and red light and reflects green and yellow light. There are other pigments that absorb different wavelengths of light.

34. (A) Cell Processes

The dissolved oxygen (O_2) in the water increases because the plants are photosynthesizing. The general equation for photosynthesis is:

$$6CO_2 + 6H_2O + \text{light energy} \rightarrow C_6H_{12}O_6 + 6O_2$$

The oxygen molecules come from H_2O, which is broken down during photosynthesis.

35. (D) Cell Processes

This experiment shows us that the plant does not absorb all types of wavelengths equally. In this experiment, the pigments in the plants captured light energy for photosynthesis. The amount of dissolved oxygen produced is an indication of the rate of photosynthesis and the amount of light energy absorbed. Blue light was absorbed more than orange light. Sunlight is a combination of all wavelengths, so when plants were exposed to sunlight, they absorbed both blue and orange wavelengths as well as some others. In the dark, the plants did not absorb any light energy for photosynthesis.

36. (B) Evolution and Diversity

Seashells were found in Sediment 3. This suggests that when Sediment 3 was deposited, the environment was marine.

37. (D) Evolution and Diversity

Rodents were the first mammals in the area shown in the picture, since of the three types of mammals (rodents, large herbivores, and big cats), rodents appeared in the lowest (earliest) sediment layer.

38. (E) Evolution and Diversity

The fossil is from the skull of a carnivore. One can gather a lot of information about an organism from the fossil that it leaves behind. Looking at a skull, you can tell how big the animal's brain was, how big its eyes were, whether it was a carnivore or herbivore, etc. This fossil has all sharp teeth, which indicates that the animal was a meat-eater, or carnivore.

39. (D)   Evolution and Diversity

Erosion can cause gaps in the fossil record, since this process eats away rock that contains fossils. Similarly, volcanic activity can disturb the fossil layer by shooting igneous rock up through sedimentary rock. This activity destroys fossils in the sedimentary rock and can cause layers of sedimentary rock to become disordered, therefore disordering the fossil record as well. Mass extinctions, however, will not affect the fossil record. What the record is recording will change when many species die out, as there will be fewer species to record. However, the record itself will not have any gaps in it, since the sedimentary layers will not be affected.

40. (D)   Genetics

The phase depicted is prophase I of meiosis. During this phase, chromosomes line up along the spindle in homologous pairs. Crossing-over (an exchange of corresponding pieces of DNA) also occurs during this phase. In contrast, prophase of mitosis does not involve crossing-over, and the double-stranded chromosomes line up individually along the spindle rather than in homologous pairs.

41. (D)   Genetics

The homologous chromosomes are engaged in crossing-over, which is the exchange of corresponding pieces of DNA between the homologues. In meiosis, the DNA in one diploid cell is duplicated and then divided twice to make four haploid daughter cells. Crossing-over is a very important process because it mixes the genetic material between the two homologous chromosomes before they are divided among the four haploid daughter cells. This increases the overall genetic variation between the gametes produced, which will all be genetically distinct.

42. (B)   Genetics

Crossing-over increases the number of genetic combinations in the gametes, producing offspring with greater variability of genotype and phenotype. Greater variability allows a population to more readily adapt to shifts in the environment.

43. (D)   Genetics

Mitosis and meiosis are similar because they both involve the replication of DNA during interphase. Mitosis produces two diploid cells that are genetically identical to one another. Meiosis involves independent assortment, crossing-over, and two cell divisions. Meiosis produces four genetically distinct haploid gametes.

44. (B)   Organismal Biology

Structure 2 is the esophagus. When food enters the esophagus, peristaltic contractions of smooth muscle move the food downward to the stomach.

45. **(D)**   Organismal Biology

The majority of digestion and absorption occurs in the small intestine, structure 6.

46. **(C)**   Organismal Biology

Bile is an emulsifier. Without chemically affecting the structure of fat, it breaks large fat globules into smaller globules. The greater surface area of smaller fat globules helps the enzymes that will eventually chemically digest the fats to work more quickly.

47. **(D)**   Organismal Biology

An ulcer is a hole or tear in the stomach lining caused by excessive acid production. Ulcers are often linked to stress.

48. **(B)**   Organismal Biology

Structure 1 is a salivary gland. Salivary glands secrete an enzyme called salivary amylase that breaks down carbohydrates.

49. **(D)**   Evolution and Diversity

Organism 1, a ladybug, is in the order Coleoptera. To arrive at the correct name, you had to follow the steps in the dichotomous key. The following key has the correct steps in bold print.

DICHOTOMOUS KEY		
1.	**Has 6 legs. . . . . go to 2**	
	Has more than 6 legs . . . . .go to 4	
2.	Hind legs are greatly enlarged. . . . . Orthoptera	
	All legs are approximately the same size. . . . . go to 3	
3.	**Has hard wings that are spotted . . . . Coleoptera**	
	Has soft wings that are striped . . . . Lepidoptera	
4.	Has 8 legs . . . . .Arachnida	
	Has more than 8 legs . . . . Chilopoda	

50. **(B)**   Evolution and Diversity

All of the organisms shown are in phylum Arthropoda. Animals in this phylum have jointed feet and a hard exoskeleton made of chitin. Members of phylum Arthropoda include insects, spiders, and crustaceans.

51. **(D)**   Evolution and Diversity

The lobster is a crustacean in phylum Arthropoda. The snail and clam are both in phylum Mollusca. The earthworm is in phylum Annelida. The jellyfish belongs to phylum Cnidaria.

52. **(E)**   Evolution and Diversity

The system that we use for classifying organisms is hierarchical. From most to least inclusive, the classification system is: kingdom, phylum, class, order, family, genus, species. If organisms are in the same phylum, then they are in the same kingdom but not necessarily in the same class, order, family, genus, or species.

53. **(C)**   Evolution and Diversity

Two individuals from separate species will never, ever share the same identical code, eliminating (A), (D), and (E) as possible answer choices. To decide between (B) and (C), you need to know that the definition of a species is a population of individuals that can breed and produce viable offspring (a viable offspring is an offspring that can itself produce offspring). According to this definition, individuals from two different species cannot interbreed and have viable offspring (if they could, they'd be in the same species!). So the answer is (C).

54. **(D)**   Genetics

A karyotype is a photo of chromosomes in which homologous chromosomes are grouped together and arranged by size.

55. **(E)**   Genetics

There are 47 chromosomes on this karyotype. There are 22 pairs of homologous autosomes and a pair of sex chromosomes (X and Y). Normally, a human cell has 46 chromosomes. This individual has an extra copy of chromosome 21.

56. **(B)**   Genetics

This individual has Down's syndrome, which results from trisomy of chromosome 21. Trisomy is a disorder caused by nondisjunction, an event in which a pair of chromosomes does not separate during meiosis. One of the daughter cells will have two copies of the chromosome, and the other daughter cell will have none. After fertilization, the embryo will have too many or too few chromosomes. If there is an extra chromosome, the disorder is called trisomy, and in most cases, the embryo cannot develop. If there is an absence of a chromosome, the disorder is called monosomy. Monosomy of the X-chromosome is the only monosomy that is compatible with life. Polyploidy occurs when there is an entire extra set of chromosomes. A human embryo with polyploidy will not develop. Polyploidy can result in viable embryos in fish and plants.

57. **(A)**   Genetics
This individual is male because he has a Y-chromosome as well as an X-chromosome (XY). Females have two X-chromosomes (XX). A mother can pass only an X-chromosome to her offspring. The father can pass either an X or a Y to his offspring. Therefore, the Y-chromosome had to have come from the father, and the X-chromosome came from the mother.

58. **(A)**   Organismal Biology
The number of rings on a tree is an indication of its age. This tree has 6 rings, so it is approximately 6 years old. Moving outward from the center, the rings are progressively older.

59. **(C)**   Organismal Biology
Drought restricts the growth of most plants. A tree ring formed during a drought will not be very thick. Ring 3 is the thinnest, indicating that precipitation was lowest during the year in which the ring was formed.

60. **(D)**   Organismal Biology
Tree rings are wood. Wood is xylem that can no longer conduct water and functions only to support the plant.

Biology E Solitary Multiple Choice

61. **(C)**   Evolution and Diversity
Evolution is defined as the change in gene frequency in a population over time.

62. **(D)**   Ecology
The living organisms in a habitat are called biotic factors. The non-living aspects, such as the weather, soil, and water, are called abiotic factors.

63. **(A)**   Organismal Biology
Clusters of neurons are called ganglia.

64. **(E)**   Evolution and Diversity
Fungi have cell walls made of chitin, not cellulose.

65. **(D)** Ecology

In a food chain or food web, energy transfer from one trophic level to the next is not very efficient. Only 10 % of the energy in a trophic level is captured by the subsequent level.

66. **(B)** Evolution and Diversity

Reptiles are the first vertebrate animals that evolved to be fully adapted to life on land. Dehydration is a major problem for animals that live away from water. Amphibians developed some adaptations for life on land, but these adaptations were not quite enough to support a fully terrestrial life. The adaptations included legs, lungs, and a heart that could deliver oxygen more efficiently. In addition to the adaptations found in amphibians, reptiles also developed an amniotic egg to protect the embryo from fluid loss and relatively impermeable skin to prevent dehydration.

Biology E Group Multiple Choice

67. **(D)** Organismal Biology

Conditioning or associative learning is when an animal learns to associate a stimulus with a set behavior. There are two types of conditioning. Classical conditioning involves the association of a novel stimulus with a stimulus that is recognized by instinct. Operant conditioning involves the development of a new behavior that is associated with a particular reward or punishment.

68. **(C)** Organismal Biology

Not all of the animals learned at the same rate. The first animal to press the lever for a treat was the ferret.

69. **(A)** Organismal Biology

Conditioning can be undone if the association between behavior and reward does not last. If the animals press the lever several times and no treat is given, they will cease to press the lever.

70. **(D)** Ecology

The seeds that had been scarified germinated most quickly.

71. **(B)** Ecology

By the end of the experiment, the group that had been exposed to heat had the highest percentage of germinated seeds.

72. **(E)**   Ecology

No manipulations were performed on the seeds left at ambient temperature. This was the control group.

73. **(E)**   Ecology

Of the hard-coated seeds that were scarified, 75% germinated. Of the soft-coated seeds that were scarified, only 4% germinated. Scarification probably helped to crack hard seed coats but damaged the material in the soft seed coats. Even if you were not immediately sure of this answer, you could have eliminated the other answer choices, which were not supported by the data.

74. **(A)**   Evolution and Diversity

From the data, you can see that the turtle derives its heat from its surroundings. As the environmental temperature goes up, so does the turtle's internal temperature, and vice versa. This fact eliminates all of the answer choices except for (A) and (B). To choose the right answer, you had to know that ectotherms are the animals whose body heat is dependent upon the environment.

75. **(C)**   Evolution and Diversity

The data shows that the rabbit maintains a body temperature of around 37°C regardless of the ambient temperature.

76. **(B)**   Evolution and Diversity

Fish, reptiles, and amphibians are ectothermic. Birds and mammals are endothermic.

77. **(C)**   Ecology

As the legend indicates, squares denote temperature, and circles denote precipitation. Find the square above the A (for April) and follow it horizontally to the y-axis on the left-hand side of the graph. The average temperature at Site 1 in April is 22°C.

78. **(C)**   Ecology

At Site 2, the precipitation line is always above the temperature line, indicating wet conditions.

79. **(E)** Ecology

At Site 1, precipitation is very low (less than 100 mm/year), and temperatures are above freezing during the winter and very hot during the summer. This climate is typical of deserts. At Site 2, the temperature is consistently between 27°C and 30°C. Because the temperatures are consistently so high, you would expect this biome to be near the equator. Precipitation is also very high (greater than 2000 mm/year) at Site 2. Consistently high temperature and precipitation is characteristic of tropical rainforests.

80. **(E)** Ecology

Tropical rainforests are generally found within 30° of the equator. Tropical rainforests are found in Central America, South America, Central Africa and Southeast Asia.

Biology M Solitary Multiple Choice

81. **(C)** The Cell

Exocytosis is the process by which molecules are secreted from a cell. A vesicle containing fluids or particles fuses with the cell membrane and releases its contents outside of the cell.

82. **(C)** Cell Processes

A set of three nucleotides in a DNA or mRNA molecule is called a codon. The anticodon is the complement of the codon and is found on tRNA. Each codon specifies a single amino acid.

83. **(C)** Evolution and Diversity

In evolutionary terms, the sponge is the most primitive of the animals listed. Sponges are the only animals that do not have at least two of the three embryonic tissues layers (endoderm, mesoderm, and ectoderm), and the cells are not organized into specific tissues and organs. Sponges, however, do have cell recognition and slightly complex cells for reproductive and digestive purposes.

84. **(C)** Genetics

If you want to determine whether an individual has a homozygous (BB) or a heterozygous (Bb) dominant genotype, you would mate the individual with another individual that is homozygous for the recessive trait. This is called a test cross or back cross. If the individual is homozygous (BB), all of the offspring will exhibit the dominant phenotype. If the individual is heterozygous (Bb), half of the offspring will show the dominant phenotype, and the other half will show the recessive phenotype.

85. (E)   The Cell

Prokaryotes do not have a nucleus. A prokaryotic cell is filled with cytoplasm in which circular DNA and ribosomes float. Prokaryotic cells maintain their shape with a cytoskeleton and a cell wall made of peptidoglycan.

86. (E)   Evolution and Diversity

A molecular clock is a gene or protein that has such a regular rate of change that the rate can be used to calculate the point at which two related species last shared a common ancestor.

Biology M Group Multiple Choice

87. (D)   Cell Processes

The process depicted is the electron transport chain (ETC). The ETC takes place on the inner membrane of the mitochondria and is the last step in aerobic respiration. The ETC uses the electrons from NADH and $FADH_2$ that were generated in the previous steps of respiration. The electrons are transferred to carrier molecules, one after another, and as they are transferred, they lose energy. The energy is used to pump H^+ out across the membrane, thereby establishing an electrochemical gradient.

88. (D)   Cell Processes

An electrochemical gradient was established by pumping H^+ across the membrane and out of the matrix. As the H^+ ions naturally flow back in across the membrane along their electrochemical gradient, they power the generation of ATP via oxidative phosphorylation.

89. (B)   Cell Processes

Oxygen is the final molecule in the ETC that accepts electrons. This is why oxygen is required for anaerobic respiration.

90. (A)   Cell Processes

Glycolysis takes place in the cytoplasm. Glycolysis occurs prior to the Krebs cycle and the electron transport chain. The Krebs cycle takes place in the matrix of the mitochondria. The electron transport chain takes place on the inner mitochondrial membrane.

91. (B)   Organismal Biology

Mr. Olsen's heart rate was the highest after walking, but Maria's increased the most (by 15 beats per minute) between sitting still and walking.

92. **(E)**   Organismal Biology

Some of the subjects reached their maximum breathing rate after jumping rope, while others' peaked after running. Exertion levels varied for the people engaging in these activities.

93. **(B)**   Organismal Biology

When pulse rate increases, breathing rate also increases. Activity in the heart and lungs is connected. When activity levels go up, the muscles of the body require more oxygen. The lungs must take in the oxygen, and the blood must deliver it.

94. **(A)**   Organismal Biology

The role of the lungs is to remove carbon dioxide and add oxygen to the blood. Blood transports these gases from and to all of the tissues in the body.

95. **(B)**   Organic and Biochemistry

From the image of the chromatography paper, you can see that the protein in Lane 1 contains the same amino acids that are in Lanes 2, 4, and 5. These amino acids are arginine, threonine, and valine.

96. **(C)**   Organic and Biochemistry

Nonpolar amino acids move farther up the chromatography paper than polar amino acids. The amino acid that moved furthest up the paper was threonine. Therefore, it must be the most nonpolar of the amino acids used in the experiment.

97. **(D)**   Organic and Biochemistry

Amino acids do not contain a nitrogenous base. Nitrogenous bases are found in nucleic acids, not amino acids. Attached to a central carbon atom, amino acids have a hydrogen atom, carboxyl group, amino group, and a variable R group.

98. **(B)**   Genetics

The dominant allele is the allele that controls the phenotype even when another allele is present. All of the offspring were tall; none were short. All of the offspring were green; none were yellow. Tall and green are the dominant alleles. Short and yellow are the recessive alleles.

99. **(B)**   Genetics

The genotype of the tall, green parent must be TTGG because all of the offspring were tall and green even though the other parent was homozygous recessive (ttgg). The genotypes of their offspring were all TtGg.

100. **(A)**   Genetics

A cross between individuals that are heterozygous for two traits will result in a phenotypic ratio of 9:3:3:1 in the offspring.

	TG	Tg	tG	tg
TG	TTGG	TTGg	TtGG	TtGg
Tg	TTGg	TTgg	TtGg	Ttgg
tG	TtGG	TtGg	ttGG	ttGg
tg	TtGg	Ttgg	ttGg	Ttgg

9/16 are tall, green.
3/16 are tall, yellow.
3/16 are short, green.
1/16 are short, yellow.

SAT II Biology
Practice Test 4

BIOLOGY TEST 4 ANSWER SHEET

1. Ⓐ Ⓑ Ⓒ Ⓓ Ⓔ	26. Ⓐ Ⓑ Ⓒ Ⓓ Ⓔ	51. Ⓐ Ⓑ Ⓒ Ⓓ Ⓔ	76. Ⓐ Ⓑ Ⓒ Ⓓ Ⓔ
2. Ⓐ Ⓑ Ⓒ Ⓓ Ⓔ	27. Ⓐ Ⓑ Ⓒ Ⓓ Ⓔ	52. Ⓐ Ⓑ Ⓒ Ⓓ Ⓔ	77. Ⓐ Ⓑ Ⓒ Ⓓ Ⓔ
3. Ⓐ Ⓑ Ⓒ Ⓓ Ⓔ	28. Ⓐ Ⓑ Ⓒ Ⓓ Ⓔ	53. Ⓐ Ⓑ Ⓒ Ⓓ Ⓔ	78. Ⓐ Ⓑ Ⓒ Ⓓ Ⓔ
4. Ⓐ Ⓑ Ⓒ Ⓓ Ⓔ	29. Ⓐ Ⓑ Ⓒ Ⓓ Ⓔ	54. Ⓐ Ⓑ Ⓒ Ⓓ Ⓔ	79. Ⓐ Ⓑ Ⓒ Ⓓ Ⓔ
5. Ⓐ Ⓑ Ⓒ Ⓓ Ⓔ	30. Ⓐ Ⓑ Ⓒ Ⓓ Ⓔ	55. Ⓐ Ⓑ Ⓒ Ⓓ Ⓔ	80. Ⓐ Ⓑ Ⓒ Ⓓ Ⓔ
6. Ⓐ Ⓑ Ⓒ Ⓓ Ⓔ	31. Ⓐ Ⓑ Ⓒ Ⓓ Ⓔ	56. Ⓐ Ⓑ Ⓒ Ⓓ Ⓔ	81. Ⓐ Ⓑ Ⓒ Ⓓ Ⓔ
7. Ⓐ Ⓑ Ⓒ Ⓓ Ⓔ	32. Ⓐ Ⓑ Ⓒ Ⓓ Ⓔ	57. Ⓐ Ⓑ Ⓒ Ⓓ Ⓔ	82. Ⓐ Ⓑ Ⓒ Ⓓ Ⓔ
8. Ⓐ Ⓑ Ⓒ Ⓓ Ⓔ	33. Ⓐ Ⓑ Ⓒ Ⓓ Ⓔ	58. Ⓐ Ⓑ Ⓒ Ⓓ Ⓔ	83. Ⓐ Ⓑ Ⓒ Ⓓ Ⓔ
9. Ⓐ Ⓑ Ⓒ Ⓓ Ⓔ	34. Ⓐ Ⓑ Ⓒ Ⓓ Ⓔ	59. Ⓐ Ⓑ Ⓒ Ⓓ Ⓔ	84. Ⓐ Ⓑ Ⓒ Ⓓ Ⓔ
10. Ⓐ Ⓑ Ⓒ Ⓓ Ⓔ	35. Ⓐ Ⓑ Ⓒ Ⓓ Ⓔ	60. Ⓐ Ⓑ Ⓒ Ⓓ Ⓔ	85. Ⓐ Ⓑ Ⓒ Ⓓ Ⓔ
11. Ⓐ Ⓑ Ⓒ Ⓓ Ⓔ	36. Ⓐ Ⓑ Ⓒ Ⓓ Ⓔ	61. Ⓐ Ⓑ Ⓒ Ⓓ Ⓔ	86. Ⓐ Ⓑ Ⓒ Ⓓ Ⓔ
12. Ⓐ Ⓑ Ⓒ Ⓓ Ⓔ	37. Ⓐ Ⓑ Ⓒ Ⓓ Ⓔ	62. Ⓐ Ⓑ Ⓒ Ⓓ Ⓔ	87. Ⓐ Ⓑ Ⓒ Ⓓ Ⓔ
13. Ⓐ Ⓑ Ⓒ Ⓓ Ⓔ	38. Ⓐ Ⓑ Ⓒ Ⓓ Ⓔ	63. Ⓐ Ⓑ Ⓒ Ⓓ Ⓔ	88. Ⓐ Ⓑ Ⓒ Ⓓ Ⓔ
14. Ⓐ Ⓑ Ⓒ Ⓓ Ⓔ	39. Ⓐ Ⓑ Ⓒ Ⓓ Ⓔ	64. Ⓐ Ⓑ Ⓒ Ⓓ Ⓔ	89. Ⓐ Ⓑ Ⓒ Ⓓ Ⓔ
15. Ⓐ Ⓑ Ⓒ Ⓓ Ⓔ	40. Ⓐ Ⓑ Ⓒ Ⓓ Ⓔ	65. Ⓐ Ⓑ Ⓒ Ⓓ Ⓔ	90. Ⓐ Ⓑ Ⓒ Ⓓ Ⓔ
16. Ⓐ Ⓑ Ⓒ Ⓓ Ⓔ	41. Ⓐ Ⓑ Ⓒ Ⓓ Ⓔ	66. Ⓐ Ⓑ Ⓒ Ⓓ Ⓔ	91. Ⓐ Ⓑ Ⓒ Ⓓ Ⓔ
17. Ⓐ Ⓑ Ⓒ Ⓓ Ⓔ	42. Ⓐ Ⓑ Ⓒ Ⓓ Ⓔ	67. Ⓐ Ⓑ Ⓒ Ⓓ Ⓔ	92. Ⓐ Ⓑ Ⓒ Ⓓ Ⓔ
18. Ⓐ Ⓑ Ⓒ Ⓓ Ⓔ	43. Ⓐ Ⓑ Ⓒ Ⓓ Ⓔ	68. Ⓐ Ⓑ Ⓒ Ⓓ Ⓔ	93. Ⓐ Ⓑ Ⓒ Ⓓ Ⓔ
19. Ⓐ Ⓑ Ⓒ Ⓓ Ⓔ	44. Ⓐ Ⓑ Ⓒ Ⓓ Ⓔ	69. Ⓐ Ⓑ Ⓒ Ⓓ Ⓔ	94. Ⓐ Ⓑ Ⓒ Ⓓ Ⓔ
20. Ⓐ Ⓑ Ⓒ Ⓓ Ⓔ	45. Ⓐ Ⓑ Ⓒ Ⓓ Ⓔ	70. Ⓐ Ⓑ Ⓒ Ⓓ Ⓔ	95. Ⓐ Ⓑ Ⓒ Ⓓ Ⓔ
21. Ⓐ Ⓑ Ⓒ Ⓓ Ⓔ	46. Ⓐ Ⓑ Ⓒ Ⓓ Ⓔ	71. Ⓐ Ⓑ Ⓒ Ⓓ Ⓔ	96. Ⓐ Ⓑ Ⓒ Ⓓ Ⓔ
22. Ⓐ Ⓑ Ⓒ Ⓓ Ⓔ	47. Ⓐ Ⓑ Ⓒ Ⓓ Ⓔ	72. Ⓐ Ⓑ Ⓒ Ⓓ Ⓔ	97. Ⓐ Ⓑ Ⓒ Ⓓ Ⓔ
23. Ⓐ Ⓑ Ⓒ Ⓓ Ⓔ	48. Ⓐ Ⓑ Ⓒ Ⓓ Ⓔ	73. Ⓐ Ⓑ Ⓒ Ⓓ Ⓔ	98. Ⓐ Ⓑ Ⓒ Ⓓ Ⓔ
24. Ⓐ Ⓑ Ⓒ Ⓓ Ⓔ	49. Ⓐ Ⓑ Ⓒ Ⓓ Ⓔ	74. Ⓐ Ⓑ Ⓒ Ⓓ Ⓔ	99. Ⓐ Ⓑ Ⓒ Ⓓ Ⓔ
25. Ⓐ Ⓑ Ⓒ Ⓓ Ⓔ	50. Ⓐ Ⓑ Ⓒ Ⓓ Ⓔ	75. Ⓐ Ⓑ Ⓒ Ⓓ Ⓔ	100. Ⓐ Ⓑ Ⓒ Ⓓ Ⓔ

BIOLOGY E/M TEST

FOR BOTH BIOLOGY-E AND BIOLOGY-M, ANSWER QUESTIONS 1–60

> Directions: Each set of lettered choices below refers to the numbered questions or statements immediately following it. Select the one lettered choice that best answers each question or best fits each statement, and then fill in the corresponding oval on the answer sheet. A choice may be used once, more than once, or not at all in each set.

Questions 1–3 refer to the following components of the circulatory system.

    (A) Plasma
    (B) Red blood cell
    (C) White blood cell
    (D) Hemoglobin
    (E) Platelet

1.   Iron-containing protein that can bind to oxygen molecules

2.   Biconcave disc with no nucleus and no major organelles

3.   Cell fragments that play a role in blood clotting

Questions 4–6 refer to the molecules of life.

    (A) Amino acid
    (B) Hydrocarbon chains
    (C) Nitrogenous base
    (D) Carbohydrates
    (E) Protein

4.   Contains carbon, hydrogen, and oxygen atoms in a ratio of about 1:2:1

5.   One of the building blocks of a nucleotide

6.   Found in lipids

Questions 7–9 refer to organisms of kingdom Animalia.

    (A) Phylum Mollusca
    (B) Phylum Cnidaria
    (C) Phylum Arthropoda
    (D) Phylum Annelida
    (E) Phylum Echinodermata

7.   Members have a foot, radula, and mantle

8.   Encompasses more species than all other animal phyla combined

9.   Includes sea urchins, sea cucumbers, and sea stars

Questions 10–12 refer to mitosis and meiosis.

    (A) Chromosome
    (B) Gamete
    (C) Spindle
    (D) Synapsis
    (E) Crossing-over

10. A haploid sperm or ovum

11. A long strand of DNA and its associated proteins

12. The process by which pairs of homologous chromosomes join together to form a tetrad

GO ON TO THE NEXT PAGE

<u>Directions:</u> Each of the questions or incomplete statements below is followed by five suggested answers or completions. Some questions pertain to a set that refers to a laboratory or experimental situation. For each question, select the best answer to the question and fill in the corresponding oval on the answer sheet.

13. A fungus is growing on a piece of cake that was left in the refrigerator. What set of terms best describes the fungus?

   (A) Autotroph, saprophyte
   (B) Heterotroph, decomposer
   (C) Heterotroph, primary producer
   (D) Autotroph, primary producer
   (E) Autotroph, decomposer

14. The wings of an eagle and the flippers of a penguin are examples of

   (A) acquired traits
   (B) convergent evolution
   (C) vestigial structures
   (D) analogous structures
   (E) homologous structures

15. Which of the following is part of the stamen of a flower?

   (A) Pistil
   (B) Anther
   (C) Stigma
   (D) Ovary
   (E) Style

16. A plant gets its carbon for photosynthesis by capturing

   (A) carbon monoxide from the atmosphere
   (B) elemental carbon from the soil
   (C) elemental carbon from the atmosphere
   (D) carbohydrates from the soil
   (E) carbon dioxide from the atmosphere

17. A population of mountain lions was almost completely eliminated by a forest fire 50 years ago. The lions that are currently in the area are genetically very similar to one another because they are all descendants of the few individuals that survived the fire. This is an example of

   (A) genetic drift
   (B) non-random mating
   (C) gene flow
   (D) natural selection
   (E) mutation

18. A blood vessel has thin walls and unidirectional valves. This blood vessel is

   I.   an artery
   II. returning blood to the heart
   III. carrying deoxygenated blood

   (A) I only
   (B) II only
   (C) I and III only
   (D) II and III only
   (E) I, II, and III

19. If a population's growth is not limited by predation, competition, disease, or any other factor, its growth pattern will be

   (A) density-dependent
   (B) logistic
   (C) s-shaped
   (D) exponential
   (E) linear

20. How many unique gametes can be produced by an individual with the genotype XXYyZz?

   (A) 2
   (B) 4
   (C) 6
   (D) 8
   (E) 12

21. Which of the following is NOT a type of connective tissue?

   (A) Cartilage
   (B) Bone
   (C) Blood
   (D) Skeletal muscle
   (E) Tendon

GO ON TO THE NEXT PAGE

22. The "tails" of the phospholipids in a phospholipid bilayer

    (A) are hydrophilic
    (B) are polar
    (C) face the cytoplasm of the cell
    (D) repel one another
    (E) are nonpolar

23. The cycling of a chemical substance between the non-living (air, water, soil) and the living components of an ecosystem is called the

    (A) Krebs cycle
    (B) biogeochemical cycle
    (C) geochemical cycle
    (D) citric acid cycle
    (E) molecular cycle

24. Each morning for a week, a man leads his dog to the newspaper, and after the dog has picked it up, the man gives the dog a treat. After the week of training, the dog brings the paper to the man every morning. This is an example of

    (A) habituation
    (B) conditioning
    (C) instinctual behavior
    (D) natural selection
    (E) imprinting

25. Elephants living in the savanna of Africa feed on trees and grasses. What is true regarding the position that the elephants occupy in the food chain?

    (A) The elephant is a top consumer because it is so large.
    (B) The elephant is a carnivore because it has large, sharp tusks.
    (C) The elephant is a primary producer because it converts carbon from the trees and grasses into organic molecules.
    (D) The elephant is a top predator because no other animal preys on it.
    (E) The elephant is a primary consumer because it eats plants.

26. Which of the following characteristics is not shared by ALL members of phylum Chordata?

    (A) A dorsal, hollow nerve cord
    (B) A notochord
    (C) A four-chambered heart
    (D) Gill slits present at least during embryonic development
    (E) Post-anal tail present at least during embryonic development

27. If brown is the dominant allele for eye color, and blue is the recessive allele, which of the following is not possible?

    (A) A brown-eyed man and a brown-eyed woman have a brown-eyed child.
    (B) A brown-eyed man and a brown-eyed woman have a blue-eyed child.
    (C) A brown-eyed man and a blue-eyed woman have a blue-eyed child.
    (D) A blue-eyed man and a blue-eyed woman have a brown-eyed child.
    (E) A blue-eyed man and a brown-eyed woman have a blue-eyed child.

GO ON TO THE NEXT PAGE

28. A person with a damaged larynx to would not be able to

    (A) chew food
    (B) inhale air
    (C) hear high pitches
    (D) move food from the mouth to the stomach
    (E) speak

29. The mitotic spindle begins to form and the nuclear membrane dissolves during

    (A) interphase
    (B) prophase
    (C) metaphase
    (D) anaphase
    (E) telophase

30. A fire destroys all the vegetation in a forest, leaving only bare rock. Over a long period of time, lichens begin to grow on the rocks, breaking them down into soil. Mosses and herbs displace the lichens and are displaced, in turn, by grasses, shrubs, poplar trees, and maple trees. As this process plays out from beginning to end, all of the following ecological changes occur EXCEPT

    (A) an increase in total biomass
    (B) an increase in total biodiversity
    (C) an increase in the loss of nutrients from the system
    (D) an increase in the average size of organisms
    (E) an increase in the average life span of organisms

GO ON TO THE NEXT PAGE

Questions 31–33 refer to the following figures, which depict the role of an enzyme in a chemical reaction.

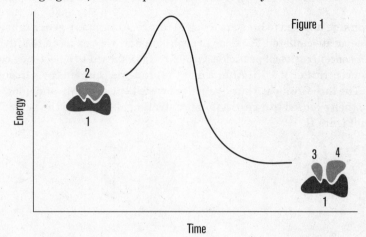

Figure 1

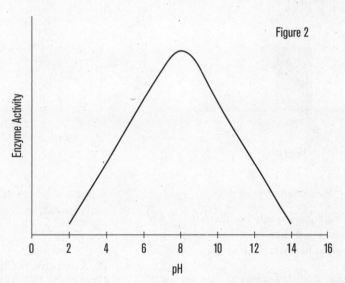

Figure 2

31. The structure labeled 1 is called a(n)

    (A) substrate
    (B) reactant
    (C) product
    (D) enzyme
    (E) cofactor

32. Which of the following is true regarding the chemical reaction depicted in Figure I?

    (A) The reactant contains more energy than the product.
    (B) The reactant contains less energy than the product.
    (C) The reaction is energy-absorbing.
    (D) The reaction cannot proceed because the activation energy is too high.
    (E) There are two reactants and one product.

33. According to Figure II, what is the optimal pH for this reaction?

    (A) 5
    (B) 6
    (C) 7
    (D) 8
    (E) 9

GO ON TO THE NEXT PAGE

<u>Questions 34–37</u> refer to experiments performed on a population of fleas.

Common fleas, *Siphonaptera,* were allowed to breed in a large culture. After many generations, students removed two groups of fleas and placed each into a separate canister. The fleas in each canister were exposed to different concentrations of pesticide. Group A was exposed to 0.3% concentration of pesticide, Group B was exposed to a pesticide concentration of 0.5% and Group C was exposed to a pesticide concentration of 0.7%. After a day, the students counted the percentage of surviving fleas in each group, as shown in Figure I. The three groups of surviving fleas were kept separate and allowed to produce offspring. The offspring in each group were then exposed to a pesticide concentration of 0.5% and the percentage of survivors in each group was determined, as shown in Figure II.

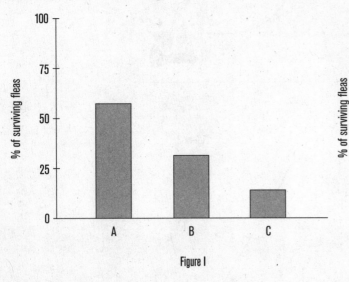

Figure I

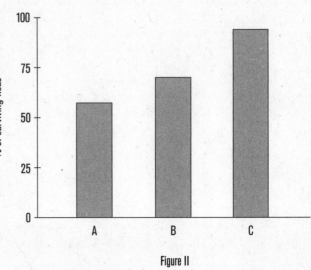

Figure II

34. From the data in Figure I, it can be inferred that

    (A) pesticides are becoming increasingly ineffective
    (B) pesticides must be used more than once over every twenty-four-hour period in order for it to be effective
    (C) temperature can affect pesticides' effectiveness
    (D) pesticides' effectiveness is indirectly proportional to the size of the flea population
    (E) pesticides' effectiveness is directly proportional to concentration

35. What is the best explanation for the results of the experiment, as depicted in Figure II?

    (A) Mutation
    (B) Selection
    (C) Adaptive radiation
    (D) Hardy-Weinberg equilibrium
    (E) Habituation

GO ON TO THE NEXT PAGE

36. Scientists perform a series of crosses and discover that resistance to the pesticide in the fleas is a recessive trait. What would happen if a population of fleas that were resistant to the pesticide were bred over a series of generations, along with a population of fleas that were not resistant?

    (A) All of the offspring would be resistant to the pesticide.
    (B) The offspring would develop fatal mutations.
    (C) The majority of offspring would be resistant, while a minority would not be resistant.
    (D) The majority of offspring would not be resistant, while a minority would be resistant.
    (E) Even though the trait is recessive, the offspring would become increasingly resistant since only the resistant fleas would survive to produce offspring.

37. The fleas in Group C are treated with higher and higher concentrations of pesticide during each successive generation of offspring. After a year, the fleas are completely resistant to the pesticide, regardless of its concentration. The fleas are then returned to the original culture of fleas, and scientists notice that the completely resistant fleas can only produce viable offspring with each other. The process that occurred during the year of the experiment is called

    (A) genetic drift
    (B) succession
    (C) speciation
    (D) convergent evolution
    (E) stabilizing selection

GO ON TO THE NEXT PAGE

Questions 38–41 relate to the following graph of temperature and atmospheric carbon dioxide concentrations from 1850 to 1990.

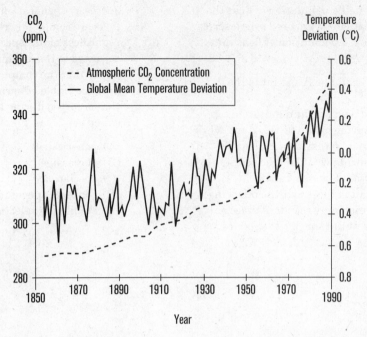

38. Based on the graph, what statement can you make?

    (A) Temperature has increased and CO_2 has decreased since 1850.
    (B) Temperature and CO_2 both have increased since 1850.
    (C) The increase in CO_2 has caused the increase in temperature.
    (D) The increase in temperature has caused the decrease in CO_2.
    (E) CO_2 will drop over the next 50 years.

39. By approximately how much did atmospheric CO_2 concentrations increase between 1850 and 1990?

    (A) 20 ppm
    (B) 30 ppm
    (C) 50 ppm
    (D) 60 ppm
    (E) 70 ppm

40. Chemicals in the air such as CO_2, sulfur, methane, and nitrous oxide can prevent heat from escaping from the atmosphere. This phenomenon is known as

    (A) global cooling
    (B) the carbon cycle
    (C) the heat cycle
    (D) the greenhouse effect
    (E) heat magnification

41. Which of the following describes the path that carbon might take in the carbon cycle?

    (A) Carbon in the soil is converted into organic plant compounds by carbon-fixing bacteria, ingested by animals, and given back to the environment through respiration of carbon dioxide.
    (B) Plants and animals take in carbon dioxide during respiration and return carbon dioxide to the air through decaying waste and, after death, decaying organic matter.
    (C) Plants take in carbon dioxide during respiration; animals ingest the carbon compounds and return carbon dioxide to the air through decaying waste and, after death, decaying organic matter.
    (D) Inert carbon in the atmosphere is taken in by plants during photosynthesis and returned to the soil as carbonate compounds when the plant dies.
    (E) Plants take in carbon dioxide during photosynthesis; animals ingest the plant carbon compounds and return carbon dioxide to the air through respiration and as decaying waste.

GO ON TO THE NEXT PAGE

Questions 42–45 refer to a genetic disease.

A man and woman are both heterozygous for a disease called phenylketonuria (PKU), which affects a person's ability metabolize an amino acid called phenylalanine. The man and woman are both phenotypically normal and do not have any symptoms of the disease. Men and woman are equally likely to have the disease.

42. This disease is

    (A) autosomal recessive
    (B) autosomal dominant
    (C) sex-linked recessive
    (D) sex-linked dominant
    (E) X-linked

43. The man and woman are both carriers of PKU. Therefore:

    I.   The man and woman could pass the disease on to their offspring.
    II. The man and woman will die from the disease.
    III. At least one of the man's parents was a carrier of the disease.
    (A) I only
    (B) II only
    (C) I and II only
    (D) I and III only
    (E) II and III only

44. What is the probability that a child born to the couple will be a heterozygous carrier of the disease?

    (A) 0%
    (B) 25%
    (C) 50%
    (D) 75%
    (E) 100%

45. The couple has had three phenotypically normal children. What is the probability that their fourth child will have the disease?

    (A) 0%
    (B) 25%
    (C) 50%
    (D) 75%
    (E) 100%

GO ON TO THE NEXT PAGE

Questions 46–50 refer to the following macromolecules.

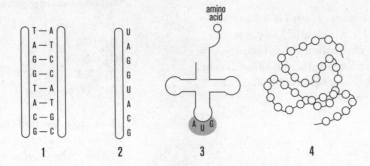

46. What is the relationship between the above macromolecules?

   (A) Structure 1 is made from Structure 2 during a process called transcription. Structure 1 then travels to the cytoplasm and bonds to a ribosome. During translation, Structure 3 brings amino acids to the ribosomes in a sequence defined by Structure 1. The amino acids are linked together to form Structure 4.
   (B) Structure 2 is made from Structure 1 during a process called transcription. Structure 2 then travels to the cytoplasm and bonds to a ribosome. During translation, Structure 3 brings amino acids to the ribosomes in a sequence defined by the Structure 2. The amino acids are linked together to form Structure 4.
   (C) Structure 3 is made from Structure 1 during a process called transcription. Structure 3 then travels to the cytoplasm and bonds to a ribosome. During translation, Structure 4 brings amino acids to the ribosomes in a sequence defined by Structure 3. The amino acids are linked together to form Structure 2.
   (D) Structure 2 chain is made from Structure 3 during a process called transcription. Structure 2 then travels to the cytoplasm and bonds to a ribosome. During translation, Structure 4 brings amino acids to the ribosomes in a sequence defined by Structure 2. The amino acids are linked together to form Structure 1.
   (E) Structure 2 chain is made from Structure 1 during a process called transcription. Structure 2 then travels to the cytoplasm and bonds to a ribosome. During translation, free-floating amino acids bump into Structure 2 and are linked together to form Structure 4.

47. Which of the following is NOT correct?

   (A) Uracil is found in DNA but not in RNA.
   (B) Transcription occurs before translation.
   (C) A codon is a three-base sequence.
   (D) Proteins are synthesized on ribosomes.
   (E) The tRNA contains the anticodon.

48. What DNA triplet would specify the tRNA anticodon GUA?

   (A) GTA
   (B) CAT
   (C) CAU
   (D) GUA
   (E) AUG

49. Where is DNA found?

   (A) Ribosomes
   (B) Cytoplasm
   (C) Nucleus
   (D) Endoplasmic reticulum
   (E) Golgi apparatus

50. Which of the following is NOT a component of Structure 4?

   (A) Carboxyl group
   (B) Nitrogenous base
   (C) Central carbon
   (D) Amino group
   (E) Variable R group

GO ON TO THE NEXT PAGE

Questions 51–53 refer to observations of changes in populations over time.

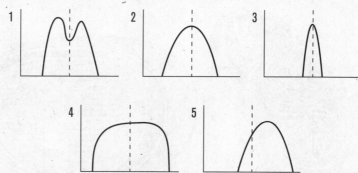

51. Male longhorn beetles compete for entrance into the burrows of potential female mates. Large males always outcompete medium-sized males in physical battle. Small males are able to trick their competitors because they are mistaken for females and allowed into the burrows. The large males and the small males are able to mate with more females than the medium-sized males. Which drawing best depicts the evolution of male size in longhorn beetles?

    (A) 1
    (B) 2
    (C) 3
    (D) 4
    (E) 5

52. In a particular grassland, short grasses are selected against because they cannot compete well for light. Tall grasses are selected against because they cannot withstand high winds. Which drawing best depicts the evolution of height in the grasses?

    (A) 1
    (B) 2
    (C) 3
    (D) 4
    (E) 5

53. The mode of evolution in the case of the grasses is called

    (A) mutation
    (B) migration
    (C) non-random mating
    (D) natural selection
    (E) gene flow

GO ON TO THE NEXT PAGE

Questions 54–56 refer to cellular organelles.

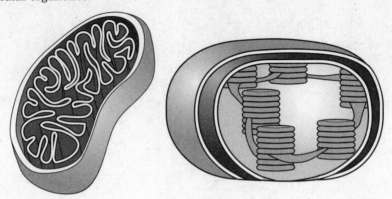

54. The two organelles pictured are found in

    (A) monerans
    (B) bacteria
    (C) prokaryotes
    (D) plants
    (E) viruses

55. Structure 2 is required for

    (A) glycolysis
    (B) photosynthesis
    (C) DNA replication
    (D) aerobic respiration
    (E) protein synthesis

56. What do these structures have in common?

    (A) Both contain chlorophyll.
    (B) Both are thought to have originated from
        endosymbiotic bacteria.
    (C) Both are found in animal cells.
    (D) Both have only one membrane.
    (E) Both contain DNA housed in a nucleus.

GO ON TO THE NEXT PAGE

Questions 57–60 refer to the following nutrition-related experiment.

A dietician prepares four different lunch menus for forty students. The students are divided into four groups of ten, and each group eats a different meal at noon. The students have their blood sugar levels monitored throughout the day.

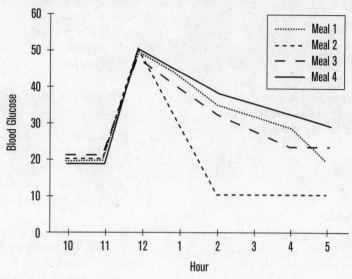

57. What chemical is released directly after the meals are eaten?

    (A) Prolactin
    (B) Glucagon
    (C) Oxytocin
    (D) Insulin
    (E) Creatine

58. From highest to lowest, rank the meals according to the blood glucose levels of the students at 3:00p.m.

    (A) 2, 3, 1, 4
    (B) 4, 3, 2, 1
    (C) 4, 1, 3, 2
    (D) 1, 2, 3, 4
    (E) 4, 2, 3, 1

59. Which meal probably contains the highest simple sugar-to-protein ratio?

    (A) 1
    (B) 2
    (C) 3
    (D) 4
    (E) It cannot be determined from the data.

60. A person suffering from diabetes mellitus

    (A) will never have high blood glucose levels
    (B) must eat a diet that is high in simple sugars
    (C) will have blood sugar patterns similar to those of the students in this experiment
    (D) has an inadequate number of glucagon receptors
    (E) either cannot make enough insulin or has an inadequate number of insulin receptors

GO ON TO THE NEXT PAGE

61. The Weddell seal (*Leptonychotes weddelli*) is a mammal that can stay under water for 20 minutes or more. You might infer that the seal has a very efficient

    (A) endocrine system
    (B) digestive system
    (C) respiratory system
    (D) immune system
    (E) reproductive system

62. A boy goes to visit his grandparents. As he drives along, he sees many birch, oak, and maple trees that are losing their leaves. What biome type is the boy visiting?

    (A) Tropical rainforest
    (B) Desert
    (C) Taiga
    (D) Temperate deciduous forest
    (E) Savanna

63. Which of the following is more advanced, in evolutionary terms, than an amphibian but more primitive than a bird?

    (A) Frog
    (B) Polar bear
    (C) Hagfish
    (D) Lizard
    (E) Chicken

64. Marmots, bears, and huskies are animals that live in cold climates. Which of the following is NOT a mechanism by which an animal might deal with cold?

    (A) Secretion of epinephrine to increase metabolism
    (B) Hibernation
    (C) Vasoconstriction
    (D) Shivering
    (E) Panting

65. Which of the following is the best example of a population?

    (A) All of the bears on Kodiak Island
    (B) All of the alligators in the world
    (C) All of the organisms that live in the rainforest
    (D) A tapeworm and its human host
    (E) Lions and hyenas living together in the Serengeti

66. Carbon-14 dating is a method used to approximate the age of fossils. It takes 5,600 years for carbon-14 to decay to carbon-12. If the ratio of carbon-14 to carbon-12 in a sample is X, how much carbon-14 will the sample contain in 16,800 years?

    (A) X
    (B) X/2
    (C) X/3
    (D) X/4
    (E) X/8

Questions 67–70 refer to the respiratory system.

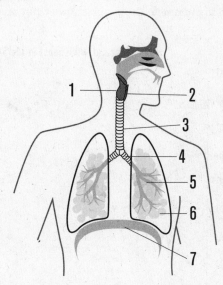

67. Structure 3 is called the

    (A) esophagus
    (B) trachea
    (C) bronchus
    (D) lung
    (E) diaphragm

68. When oxygenated blood leaves the lungs, it goes to the

    (A) right atrium
    (B) left atrium
    (C) right ventricle
    (D) inferior vena cava
    (E) superior vena cava

69. What causes a person to feel out of breath?

    (A) There is too much oxygen in the blood.
    (B) The blood pH is too high.
    (C) There is not enough oxygen in the blood.
    (D) There is too much carbon dioxide in the blood, causing the pH to be low.
    (E) There is not enough carbon dioxide in the blood.

70. Exposure to carbon monoxide is extremely dangerous for aerobic organisms, because

    (A) carbon monoxide destroys hemoglobin in red blood cells
    (B) carbon monoxide causes the lungs to secrete too much mucous
    (C) carbon monoxide displaces oxygen molecules on hemoglobin, and the body becomes oxygen deprived
    (D) carbon monoxide combines with carbon dioxide to create a poisonous chemical
    (E) carbon monoxide paralyzes the diaphragm

GO ON TO THE NEXT PAGE

Questions 71–73 refer to a population of wildebeests in the Serengeti. In around 1960, the wildebeests contracted a disease called Rinderpest, causing the population to plummet. The graph shows what occurred after the population recovered from Rinderpest.

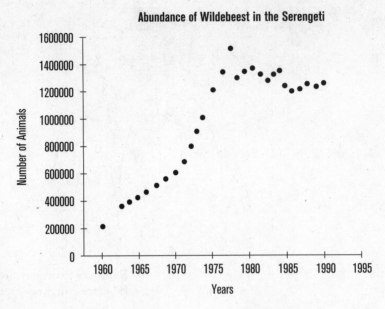

71. The period during which the wildebeest population increased at the greatest rate is

(A) 1965–1970
(B) 1970–1975
(C) 1975–1980
(D) 1980–1990
(E) 1985–1990

72. When Rinderpest is not present, the carrying capacity of this environment for wildebeests is

(A) greater than 160,000
(B) less than 60,000
(C) approximately 20,000
(D) approximately 80,000
(E) approximately 120,000

73. What other occurrences would have an affect on the population that is similar to that of Rinderpest?

I. A drought that reduces the amount of grass in the area
II. Vaccination of the population against Rinderpest
III. An increase in the number of poachers in the area
IV. Supplemental feeding of the wildebeests
V. The introduction of more lions that prey on wildebeests

(A) I, II, and III only
(B) I, III, and V only
(C) II, III, IV, V only
(D) II and IV only
(E) I, III, IV, V only

GO ON TO THE NEXT PAGE

Questions 74–76 refer to taxonomy and classification.

Phylum	Traits					
	Endoderm & Ectoderm	Gut With at Least 1 Opening	Gut with 2 Openings	Heart	Deuterostome Development	Notochord
A	Yes	Yes	Yes	Yes	Yes	Yes
B	Yes	Yes	No	No	No	No
C	No	No	No	No	No	No
D	Yes	Yes	Yes	No	No	No
E	Yes	Yes	Yes	Yes	No	No

74. Of the choices below, which two phyla are most closely related?

    (A) A and C
    (B) A and D
    (C) C and E
    (D) B and D
    (E) A and B

75. Phylum A is which of the following?

    (A) Porifera
    (B) Chordata
    (C) Arthropoda
    (D) Nematoda
    (E) Mollusca

76. According to the information in the table, which drawing shows the proper evolutionary tree of phyla A, B, C, D, and E?

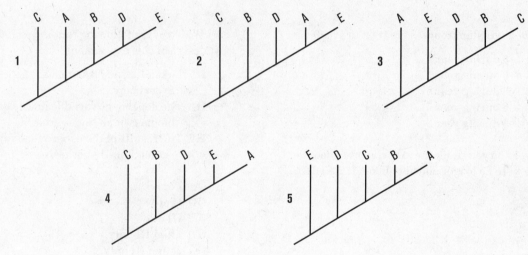

    (A) 1
    (B) 2
    (C) 3
    (D) 4
    (E) 5

GO ON TO THE NEXT PAGE

<u>Questions 77–80</u> refer to the following experiment in which nutrients were added to six lakes.

Each year, nutrients were added to three of the lakes (lakes 1, 2, and 3), and the remaining three lakes were left unaltered. Each summer, scientists measured the biomass of photosynthetic phytoplankton in each lake. The researchers hypothesized that adding nutrients would more than double the biomass of the phytoplankton.

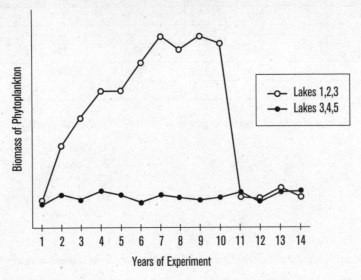

77. Biomass of phytoplankton was greatest in

    (A) lakes 1–3 during year 1
    (B) lakes 4–6 during year 1
    (C) lakes 1–3 during year 5
    (D) lakes 4–6 during year 5
    (E) lakes 1–3 during year 9

78. In what year do you think the experiment ended (i.e., nutrients were no longer added to lakes 1, 2, and 3)?

    (A) Year 3
    (B) Year 5
    (C) Year 8
    (D) Year 10
    (E) Year 14

79. In a food chain, phytoplankton would be considered

    (A) primary consumers
    (B) primary producers
    (C) secondary consumers
    (D) detritivores
    (E) secondary producers

80. Which of the following can be concluded based on the design of this experiment?

    I.   Lakes 1, 2, and 3 served as the "controls" for the experiment.
    II. The dependent variable in this experiment is the biomass of phytoplankton.
    III. The results of the experiment support the researchers' hypothesis.

    (A) I only
    (B) II only
    (C) III only
    (D) I and III only
    (E) II and III only

GO ON TO THE NEXT PAGE

BIOLOGY-M SECTION

**If you are taking the Biology-M test, continue with questions 81–100.
Be sure to start this section of the test by filling in oval 81 on your answer sheet.**

<u>Directions:</u> Each of the questions or incomplete statements below is followed by five suggested answers or completions. Some questions pertain to a set that refers to a laboratory or experimental situation. For each question, select the one choice that is the best answer to the question and then fill in the corresponding oval on the answer sheet.

81. If you wanted to look at a three-dimensional image of a sperm cell that is magnified 10,000x, you would use a(n)

    (A) light microscope
    (B) compound light microscope
    (C) electron microscope
    (D) magnifying glass
    (E) proton laser microscope

82. Which of the following is an example of a vestigial structure?

    (A) Ostrich wing
    (B) Wasp wing
    (C) Human gall bladder
    (D) Giraffe neck
    (E) Alligator leg

83. A girl puts five drops of red food coloring into a test tube of water and then shakes the tube. The liquid in the tube becomes pink. The process by which food coloring and water molecules mixed is called

    (A) diffusion
    (B) active transport
    (C) osmosis
    (D) hyperfusion
    (E) ion transport

84. A human zygote

    (A) is haploid
    (B) has 23 chromosomes
    (C) has 44 autosomes and 2 sex chromosomes
    (D) has genetic material from 2 sperm and 1 egg
    (E) is a germ cell

85. An asteroid lands on Earth, and a scientist studying the asteroid finds a cell. The cell has circular DNA and a cell wall; it can replicate itself, and it moves using a threadlike propeller. This alien cell most resembles a(n)

    (A) plant cell
    (B) animal cell
    (C) virus
    (D) bacteria
    (E) eukaryote

86. Scientists who study evolution consider cytochrome c to be an excellent molecular clock because

    (A) scientists have determined when cytochrome c was first evolved by an organism
    (B) changes or mutations in cytochrome c occur at regular intervals over time
    (C) cytochrome c has a known half-life that can be used to date the time when an organism lived
    (D) cytochrome c exists in far greater quantities on asteroids than on Earth; large deposits of cytochrome c in the fossil record indicate asteroid impact
    (E) cytochrome c is the molecule in bones that hardens and leaves fossils after death

GO ON TO THE NEXT PAGE

Questions 87–89 refer to the following data set.

Students are monitoring the water chemistry and biota of a stream near their school. They collect data on the pH of the water, the concentration of dissolved oxygen, and the insects present.

Month of Sampling	pH of Stream Water	Concentration of Dissolved Oxygen
November	7.0	8.5 mg/L
December	7.5	9.0 mg/L
January	8.0	9.0 mg/L
March	7.6	8.0 mg/L
May	7.7	7.5 mg/L

87. Rank the samples from highest to lowest hydrogen ion concentration.

(A) January, November, December, March, May
(B) January, May, March, December, November
(C) November, December, March, May, January
(D) May, March, December, November, January
(E) March, May, November, December, January

88. A type of algae found in the stream thrives in a neutral environment but is extremely sensitive to minor changes in pH. From November to May, the population size of algae in the stream

(A) began at a high point in November and fell over the next four months
(B) rose in November and December to a high point in January, then fell in March and May
(C) remained constant, since stream water moves quickly and will remove any excess hydrogen ions
(D) spiked to its highest point in December, fell quickly in January and more slowly in March and May
(E) had high points in December and March and low points in November and January

89. Which of the following is the best prediction of what would happen if the dissolved oxygen concentration of the water were to drop to very low levels?

(A) Fish populations would grow exponentially.
(B) Heterotrophic vertebrates would not have enough oxygen for photosynthesis and would all die.
(C) The water would be toxic to the animals that drink it.
(D) The water would get colder.
(E) Heterotrophic animals would not have enough oxygen for respiration, and their population sizes might decrease.

GO ON TO THE NEXT PAGE

Questions 90–92 refer to fermentation.

A vineyard owner is making wine by fermenting yeast in grape juice. The following graph represents the rise in ethanol during the fermentation process.

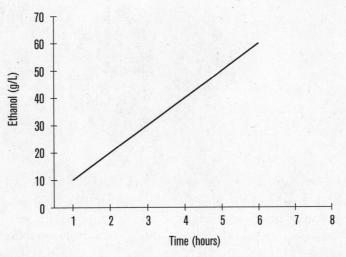

90. Which of the following best represents the fermentation reaction that is taking place?

(A) Pyruvate + NADH $\rightarrow$ lactic acid + NAD$^+$
(B) $6CO_2 + 6H_2O \rightarrow$ light $\rightarrow$ $C_6H_{12}O_6 + 6O_2$
(C) Pyruvate + NADH $\rightarrow$ ethanol + NAD$^+$ + CO_2
(D) $6O_2 + C_6H_{12}O_6 \rightarrow 6CO_2 + 6H_2O$ + ATP energy
(E) $6CO_2 + 6H_2O \rightarrow$ light $\rightarrow$ ethanol + NAD$^+$ + CO_2

91. What is the rate of ethanol accumulation during the fermentation process?

(A) 10 g/L/hour
(B) 60 g /L/hour
(C) 20 g/L/hour
(D) 5 g/L/hour
(E) 10 mg/L/hour

92. Why does fermentation stop when the ethanol concentration reaches about 12 %?

(A) The yeast have run out of carbon dioxide from the grapes.
(B) The yeast have run out of oxygen and can no longer generate ATP.
(C) Ethanol is toxic, and 12 % is about the upper limit of tolerance of yeast for ethanol.
(D) The lactic acid build-up kills the yeast.
(E) The oxygen bubbles that are produced get in the way of the yeast that are searching for glucose molecules.

GO ON TO THE NEXT PAGE

Questions 93–96 refer to the following experiment on brain activity.

A neuroscientist is studying the human brain. He hooks several subjects up to monitors that allow him to see what part of the brain is most active at any one time. He then has the subjects perform different tasks while he watches their brain activity.

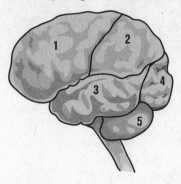

93. From the data that the scientist gathered, you might infer that the part of the brain that controls hearing is

    (A) 1
    (B) 2
    (C) 3
    (D) 4
    (E) 5

94. The part of the brain that is labeled 5 is called the

    (A) cerebrum
    (B) cerebellum
    (C) spinal cord
    (D) occipital lobe
    (E) frontal lobe

95. If the subject were handed a piece of paper and asked to read the words on it aloud, what section(s) of the brain do you think would be most active?

    (A) 2 only
    (B) 3 only
    (C) 3 and 4
    (D) 1 and 4
    (E) 2 and 5

96. Which of the following statements is false?

    (A) The brain is part of the peripheral nervous system.
    (B) The subjects raised their right hand, so the left side of their brain showed activity.
    (C) A person with damage to Section 5 would have difficulty with balance and coordination.
    (D) Members of phylum Porifera (sponges) do not have a brain.
    (E) The spinal cord is part of the central nervous system.

GO ON TO THE NEXT PAGE

Questions 97–100 refer to the pedigree for albinism.

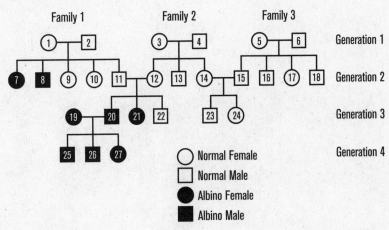

97. The inheritance pattern for this disorder is

    (A) simple recessive
    (B) simple dominant
    (C) sex-linked recessive
    (D) sex-linked dominant
    (E) simple sex-linked

98. Which of the following statements is false?

    (A) Both Individuals 1 and 2 must be carriers of the disorder.
    (B) Both Individuals 3 and 4 must be carriers of the disorder.
    (C) Individual 11 does not have albinism.
    (D) Neither Individual 5 nor Individual 6 could be a carrier of the disorder.
    (E) Individual 8 received a recessive allele from each parent.

99. If Individual 21 were to have a child with a person who is genotypically normal for this trait, what is the probability that their child would have albinism?

    (A) 0%
    (B) 25%
    (C) 50%
    (D) 75%
    (E) 100%

100. Which of the following individuals could be incorrectly matched with his or her genotype? ("A" is dominant; "a" recessive.)

    (A) 3 – Aa
    (B) 7 – aa
    (C) 12 – AA
    (D) 14 – Aa
    (E) 22 – AA

S T O P

IF YOU FINISH BEFORE TIME IS CALLED, YOU MAY CHECK YOUR WORK ON THIS TEST ONLY.
DO NOT TURN TO ANY OTHER TEST IN THIS BOOK.

SAT II Biology Test 4
Explanations

Answers to SAT II Biology Practice Test 4

Question Number	Correct Answer	Right	Wrong	Question Number	Correct Answer	Right	Wrong	Question Number	Correct Answer	Right	Wrong
1.	D			34.	E			67.	B		
2.	B			35.	B			68.	B		
3.	E			36.	D			69.	D		
4.	D			37.	C			70.	C		
5.	C			38.	B			71.	B		
6.	B			39.	E			72.	E		
7.	A			40.	D			73.	B		
8.	C			41.	E			74.	D		
9.	E			42.	A			75.	B		
10.	B			43.	D			76.	D		
11.	A			44.	C			77.	E		
12.	D			45.	B			78.	D		
13.	B			46.	B			79.	B		
14.	E			47.	A			80.	E		
15.	B			48.	A			81.	C		
16.	D			49.	C			82.	A		
17.	A			50.	B			83.	A		
18.	B			51.	A			84.	C		
19.	D			52.	C			85.	D		
20.	B			53.	D			86.	B		
21.	D			54.	D			87.	C		
22.	E			55.	B			88.	A		
23.	B			56.	B			89.	E		
24.	B			57.	D			90.	C		
25.	E			58.	C			91.	A		
26.	C			59.	B			92.	C		
27.	D			60.	E			93.	C		
28.	E			61.	C			94.	B		
29.	B			62.	D			95.	D		
30.	C			63.	D			96.	A		
31.	D			64.	E			97.	A		
32.	A			65.	A			98.	D		
33.	D			66.	E			99.	A		
								100.	C		

Your raw score for the SAT II Biology test is calculated from the number of questions you answer correctly and incorrectly. Once you have determined your composite score, use the conversion table on page **21** of this book to calculate your scaled score. To calculate your raw score, count the number of questions you answered correctly: _____

A

Count the number of questions you answered incorrectly, and multiply that number by $\frac{1}{4}$:

$$\underline{\hspace{2cm}}_{B} \times \frac{1}{4} = \underline{\hspace{2cm}}_{C} .$$

Subtract the value in field C from value in field A: _____

D

Round the number in field D to the nearest whole number. This is your raw score: _____

E

Biology E/M Classification Questions

1. **(D)**   Organismal Biology
Hemoglobin is an iron-containing protein that can bind to oxygen. The question is a little tricky because red blood cells contain hemoglobin, and students are often taught that red blood cells carry oxygen. The key is that the question asks for a protein, and a red blood cell has many more types of organic molecules than just a single protein.

2. **(B)**   Organismal Biology
Red blood cells have no nucleus or major organelles and, as a result, have a biconcave shape. Red blood cells are the most abundant cell type in blood, are packed with hemoglobin, and are produced by specialized cells in the bone marrow.

3. **(E)**   Organismal Biology
Platelets are not really cells but rather are fragments of cytoplasm. Platelets circulate in the blood. When they encounter a wound in a blood vessel, they secrete a protein that causes red blood cells to clot and close the wound.

4. **(D)**   Organic and Biochemistry
Carbohydrates are molecules that contain carbon, hydrogen, and oxygen in a ratio of about 1:2:1. Glucose is an example of a carbohydrate.

5. **(C)**   Organic and Biochemistry
A nitrogenous base is a nitrogen-containing compound found in the nucleotides of DNA and RNA. In addition to a nitrogenous base, each nucleotide also has a sugar and a phosphate group. The nitrogenous bases are adenine, guanine, thymine, cytosine, and uracil. Adenine, guanine, and cytosine are found in both DNA and RNA. Thymine is found in DNA but not in RNA. Uracil is found in RNA but not in DNA.

6. **(B)**   Organic and Biochemistry
Lipids are distinguished from other macromolecules because they contain hydrocarbon chains—strings of carbon with hydrogens attached to them. These hydrocarbon chains are nonpolar and make lipids hydrophobic.

7. **(A)**   Evolution and Diversity
Members of phylum Mollusca include snails, slugs, squid, octopuses, clams, and oysters. Members of this phylum typically have a muscular "foot" for movement, a rasping tongue for eating, and a mantle that secretes a hard shell for protection.

8. **(C)** Evolution and Diversity

Phylum Arthropoda contains the majority of the animal species on Earth—more than all of the other animal phyla combined. Within phylum Arthropoda, the largest class is Insecta.

9. **(E)** Evolution and Diversity

Phylum Echinodermata includes sea urchins, sea cucumbers, and sea stars. Members of this phylum may look primitive, but their embryonic development suggests that they are more closely related to the chordates than to the other animal phyla.

10. **(B)** Cell Processes

Gametes are haploid sex cells. The male gamete is the sperm, and the female gamete is the ovum. During fertilization, the sperm and ovum fuse to form a single diploid zygote that can develop into an individual.

11. **(A)** Cell Processes

A chromosome is a long strand of DNA and its associated proteins. Within this long strand are shorter segments, called genes, that code for particular traits. Chromosomes also have "junk DNA," or segments that do not code for specific proteins and are not expressed.

12. **(D)** Cell Processes

Synapsis is the process by which a pair of homologous chromosomes join together and intertwine to form a tetrad (four chromatids, two from each homologous pair). Synapsis happens just before crossing-over. Crossing-over is the process by which the chromatids in the tetrads exchange corresponding pieces of DNA.

Biology E/M Solitary Multiple Choice

13. **(B)** Organismal Biology

Members of the kingdom Fungi are heterotrophic and obtain their energy by breaking down non-living organic matter and absorbing the nutrients. Therefore, fungi are decomposers. The terms "decomposer" and "saprophyte" are often used synonymously.

14. **(E)** Evolution and Diversity

Eagles and penguins live in very different environments, and eagles use their wings to fly while penguins use their flippers to help propel them through water. Nonetheless, the two organisms are both birds and both share a common ancestor. Their wings (and flippers) therefore share a common structure and are homologous.

15. **(B)** Organic and Biochemistry

The male reproductive parts of a flower are the anther and filament—collectively called the stamen. The female reproductive parts of a flower are the stigma, style, and ovary—collectively called the pistil.

16. **(E)** Cell Processes

Photosynthesis is the process by which plants use energy from the sun to synthesize glucose from CO_2 and water. The carbon comes from atmospheric CO_2. CO_2 diffuses into the plant through the stomata in the leaves. The chemical equation for photosynthesis is

$$6CO_2 + 6H_2O + \text{light} \rightarrow C_6H_{12}O_6 + 6O_2$$

17. **(A)** Evolution and Diversity

Genetic drift is a mechanism of evolution that occurs in small populations. In small populations, a chance event such as a fire or flood can reduce a population to only a few survivors. If a particular allele were found in only a few individuals, a chance event that killed those individuals would eliminate that allele from the gene pool.

18. **(B)** Organismal Biology

A blood vessel with thin walls and unidirectional valves is a vein. All veins return blood to the heart, but while most veins carry deoxygenated blood, the pulmonary vein carries oxygen-rich blood. Arteries are thicker than blood vessels because the heart pumps blood out to the body with great force, and the arteries must be able to withstand that force. There is less pressure in the veins, so they do not need to be as thick as arteries. Muscles around the veins contract and move blood by squeezing the veins.

19. **(D)** Ecology

An exponential growth curve shows a population with a constant rate of growth and an exponential increase in size. The curve is J-shaped. A population grows exponentially if there are unlimited resources, no predation, and no disease. Exponential population growth rarely happens in nature.

20. **(B)** Genetics

There are four gametes that could be created by a person with the genotype XXYyZz. The gametes are XYZ, XYz, XyZ, and Xyz.

21. (D) Organismal Biology

There are four kinds of tissues in the body: nervous tissue, epithelial tissue, muscle tissue, and connective tissue. Connective tissue provides support, insulation, and protection. Cartilage, bone, tendons, blood, and fat are all connective tissues. Skeletal muscle is muscle tissue.

22. (E) The Cell

The phospholipid bilayer is made of two sheets of phospholipids. The heads of the phospholipids are polar and thus hydrophilic. They face the watery regions on the inside and outside of the cell. The long hydrocarbon chains (tails) of the phospholipids are nonpolar and hydrophobic. They are attracted to one another and repelled by the water on the inside and outside of the cell. The hydrocarbon chains are in the interior of the bilayer.

23. (B) Ecology

Biogeochemistry is the study of the cycling of chemicals between living organisms and the non-living components of the earth (atmosphere, soil, water). The nitrogen, water, and carbon cycles are all biogeochemical cycles.

24. (B) Organismal Biology

Conditioning is the learning of a new, non-instinctual behavior because of an association between the behavior and a particular reward or punishment. The dog was able to learn to retrieve the paper and was given a treat as a reward.

25. (E) Ecology

The elephant eats plants, which signifies that it is a primary consumer. The size of an animal is not necessarily related to its role in the food chain.

26. (C) Evolution and Diversity

Not all chordates have a four-chambered heart. Only chordates that evolved after birds have a four-chambered heart. However, all members of phylum Chordata possess a dorsal, hollow nerve cord, a notochord, gill slits present at least during embryonic development, and a post-anal tail present at least during embryonic development.

27. (D) Genetics

Let's say that the allele for brown eyes is "B," and the allele for blue eyes is "b." For a person to have brown eyes, they must have the phenotype "BB" or "Bb." For a person to have blue eyes, they must have the phenotype "bb." If the father and the mother both have blue eyes, their genotypes must both be "bb." It is not possible for any of their biological children to have brown eyes because they have no "B" allele to pass on to their offspring.

28. **(E)**   Organismal Biology

The larynx is a structure composed of cartilage that contains the vocal chords. The larynx is sometimes called the "voice box." If the larynx were sufficiently damaged, a person would lose the ability to speak.

29. **(B)**   Cell Processes

In prophase of mitosis, the double-chromatid chromosomes have formed and are visible under a microscope, the centrioles move to opposite poles of the cell, the mitotic spindle begins to form, and the nuclear membrane disintegrates.

30. **(C)**   Ecology

As an ecological community goes through ecological succession from pioneer organisms to climax community, the biomass of the community will increase, as will the biodiversity, size of organisms, and life span of organisms. The system will also become *more* adept at maintaining nutrients, the opposite of what is stated in choice (C).

Biology E/M Group Multiple Choice

31. **(D)**   Organic and Biochemistry

Structure 1 is an enzyme. Enzymes are proteins that increase the speed of chemical reactions by lowering their activation energy (the energy needed to start a chemical reaction).

32. **(A)**   Organic and Biochemistry

In the reaction depicted, the reactant, or substrate, is at a higher energetic state than the products. This is an energy-releasing reaction.

33. **(D)**   Organic and Biochemistry

The enzyme activity is highest at a pH of 8. Most enzymes have an optimal range of pH values. A pH outside this range may alter the three-dimensional structure of the enzyme and render it less effective.

34. **(E)**   Evolution and Diversity

In the experiment depicted in Figure I, Group A is exposed to the lowest concentration of pesticide, Group B to a middle concentration, and Group C to the highest concentration. In the experiment, the most individual fleas died in Group C, with a moderate number dying in Group B and the fewest dying in Group A. This data indicates that as the pesticide increases in concentration, it becomes increasingly effective at killing fleas.

35. (B)   Evolution and Diversity

The first experiment exposed the various groups of fleas to different concentrations of pesticide. The low concentration killed few fleas, while the higher concentration killed many fleas. However, another way to look at it is that the high concentration of pesticides selected the hardiest fleas for survival, while the lower concentration let less hardy fleas sneak through. When the offspring of the fleas were then exposed to a moderate level of pesticide concentration, a greater percentage of the offspring in Group C (the offspring of the hardiest fleas) survived. This is natural selection in action.

36. (D)   Genetics

When recessive and dominant individuals have offspring, genetics states that the majority of offspring will be phenotypically dominant. The question states that resistance to pesticide in fleas is recessive, so if resistant fleas and non-resistant fleas produce offspring, the majority will *not* be resistant. Choice (E) is tricky because it assumes that the breeding fleas are *always* living in the presence of pesticide, which is not stated in the problem. In the absence of pesticide, there is no competitive edge to being resistant to pesticide.

37. (C)   Evolution and Diversity

The scientific definition of species is "a discrete group of organisms that can only breed within its own confines." When the resistant fleas became unable to mate and produce viable offspring with the fleas from the original culture, the resistant fleas became a new species.

38. (B)   Ecology

Global averages of temperature and CO_2 have been increasing since 1850. You cannot infer that the increase in CO_2 has caused the increase in temperature, or vice versa. Correlation between two trends does not mean that one caused the other—correlation does not imply causation.

39. (E)   Ecology

Between 1850 and 1990, CO_2 concentrations increased by approximately 70 parts per million.

40. **(D)**   Ecology

The greenhouse effect results in the warming of the earth's atmosphere. Solar radiation enters the atmosphere and warms the earth. Greenhouse gases such as water vapor, carbon dioxide, methane, and nitrous oxide keep heat from escaping from the atmosphere. Just like in a greenhouse, heat is trapped.

41. **(E)**   Ecology

Only answer (E) describes a path that carbon might take through the carbon cycle. (A) is incorrect because carbon-fixing bacteria do not exist; (B) and (C) are incorrect because carbon dioxide is taken in by plants through photosynthesis, not respiration; (D) is wrong because plants take in carbon dioxide during photosynthesis, not elemental carbon.

42. **(A)**   Genetics

PKU is an autosomal recessive disease. You can infer that the disease is recessive because heterozygous individuals do not manifest the disease, even if they are carriers. The disease is not sex-linked because males and females are equally likely to have the disease.

43. **(D)**   Genetics

Because the parents are carriers of the disease, they can pass the disease to their offspring. Any carrier of the disease most likely received the recessive allele from a parent. The man and woman are genetic carriers of the disease, but they do not have the disease and therefore cannot die from it.

44. **(C)**   Genetics

Each of the couple's children will have a 50% chance of being a heterozygous carrier of the disease, a 25% chance of being homozygous for the disease, and a 25% chance of being homozygous for the normal phenotype.

	P	p
P	PP	Pp
p	Pp	pp

45. **(B)**   Genetics

Punnett squares are often misunderstood. Students may think that if the couple has four children, then three of them will be phenotypically normal, and one of them will have the disease. That is not true. Each child that is conceived will have a 25% chance of being homozygous for the disease, a 50% chance of being a heterozygous carrier of the disease, and a 25% chance of being genotypically normal / free of the disease.

46. **(B)** Cell Processes

All of the macromolecules depicted play a role in protein synthesis. The DNA is housed in the nucleus. A complementary strand of mRNA is made from the DNA. The mRNA leaves the nucleus and enters the cytoplasm, where it bonds to a ribosome. The mRNA contains triplets of bases (codons) that code for specific amino acids. The tRNA brings amino acids to the ribosomes according to the code specified by the mRNA. At the ribosomes, the amino acids are linked together to form a protein.

47. **(A)** Cell Processes

Uracil is found in RNA but not in DNA. In DNA, cytosine pairs with guanine and adenine pairs with thymine. In RNA, thymine is replaced with uracil.

48. **(A)** Cell Processes

The sequence of the base pairs in a codon of mRNA is the exact opposite of the sequence of base pairs in the anticodon of tRNA. So, if the tRNA anticodon is GUA, then the mRNA codon must be CAU. The mRNA codon is a complement of a DNA triplet. So, if the mRNA codon is CAU, then the DNA triplet must be GTA.

49. **(C)** Cell Processes

DNA is found in the nucleus.

50. **(B)** Cell Processes

Structure 4 is a protein. Proteins are made of amino acids that are joined together by peptide bonds. Each amino acid contains a central carbon to which an amino group, a variable R group, a hydrogen, and a carboxyl group are attached. Amino acids do not contain nitrogenous bases. DNA and RNA contain nitrogenous bases.

51. **(A)** Evolution and Diversity

In this population of longhorn beetles, the two extremes of body size are favored over the intermediate, so the distribution will have two peaks rather than one. This is called disruptional selection.

52. **(C)** Evolution and Diversity

In this population of grasses, selection is eliminating both extremes of height, so the distribution would become narrower. This is called stabilizing selection. The other two types of selection are disruptional selection (seen in question #51) and directional selection. In directional selection, one extreme is eliminated, and the frequency of the trait moves in one direction.

53. (D)   Evolution and Diversity

The mechanism of evolution in the example grasses is called natural selection. In natural selection, some alleles confer a survival advantage over other alleles. The alleles that confer the advantage will increase in frequency, and the alleles that do not will decrease in frequency. Other mechanisms of evolution include mutation, gene flow, non-random mating, and genetic drift.

54. (D)   The Cell

The organelles are a mitochondrion and a chloroplast. Both of these organelles would be found in a eukaryotic cell, which is more complex and evolutionarily advanced than a prokaryotic cell. The only eukaryotic organism on the list is the plant. Bacteria are prokaryotes and are members of phylum Monera. Bacteria would not have either mitochondria or chloroplasts. Viruses are not as complex as eukaryotes and do not possess these organelles. Animal cells are eukaryotic. Animal cells have mitochondria, but they cannot photosynthesize and would not have chloroplasts.

55. (B)   The Cell

Structure 2 is a chloroplast. Photosynthesis occurs in chloroplasts.

56. (B)   The Cell

Both chloroplasts and mitochondria are thought to have originated from endosymbiotic bacteria. The organelles are similar to bacteria because of their size and the fact that they contain their own circular DNA and ribosomes. Only chloroplasts contain chlorophyll. The chloroplast is not found in animal cells. Both mitochondria and chloroplasts have double membranes. Both contain circular DNA that is not housed in a nucleus.

57. (D)   Organismal Biology

Directly after a meal is eaten, the blood sugar levels rise, which prompts the release of insulin. The role of insulin is to lower blood sugar levels by promoting the accumulation of glycogen by the liver and by stimulating the uptake of glucose by muscles. Glucagon is a hormone that has the opposite effect of insulin. Glucagon prompts the liver to release sugar into the bloodstream.

58. (C)   Organismal Biology

At 3:00p.m., the students who ate meal #4 had the highest blood glucose levels, and the students who ate meal #2 had the lowest blood glucose levels. Students who ate meals #1 and #3 had intermediate blood glucose levels.

59. (B)   Organismal Biology
Subjects who ate meal #2 had the earliest drop in blood sugar levels and the lowest blood sugar levels in the afternoon. This is the meal that probably has the highest simple sugar-to-protein ratio. Simple sugars are more quickly digested than proteins or complex carbohydrates. For this reason, eating simple sugars does not promote a steady and moderate blood sugar level.

60. (E)   Organismal Biology
A person with diabetes mellitus has trouble obtaining glucose molecules from the blood because their bodies do not make enough insulin or they do not have enough insulin receptors. Remember that insulin is the hormone that lowers blood sugar levels by promoting the uptake of glucose out of the blood by the cells of the liver and muscles.

Biology E Solitary Multiple Choice

61. (C)   Organismal Biology
All mammals acquire oxygen by breathing air into their lungs. An animal that can hold its breath for 20 minutes must have a very efficient respiratory system.

62. (D)   Ecology
A temperate deciduous forest has trees that drop their leaves during a period of winter dormancy. This biome has distinct summer and winter seasons and supports animals such as deer, squirrels, raccoons, foxes, and owls.

63. (D)   Evolution and Diversity
A lizard is a reptile. Reptiles evolved after fish and amphibians but before birds and mammals.

64. (E)   Organismal Biology
Panting is not a mechanism used to deal with cold temperatures but rather a behavior that lowers body heat by evaporative cooling. Therefore, panting is something that animals do when they are hot, not cold.

65. (A)   Ecology
A population is a group of organisms of the same species that inhabit a specific area. Only (A) describes a group of organisms within a limited area.

66. **(E)** Evolution and Diversity

Radioactive isotopes are used to determine the age of fossils. Radioactive isotopes decay at a regular rate called a half-life. The half-life is the amount of time that the isotope takes to decay into another atom. 16,800 years is three half-lives of carbon-14, so the sample would contain one-eighth the original amount of carbon-14.

Biology E Group Multiple Choice

67. **(B)** Organismal Biology

Structure 3 is the trachea. The trachea is a hollow tube through which air passes into the bronchi of the lungs.

68. **(B)** Organismal Biology

The respiratory and cardiovascular systems are closely linked. The respiratory system removes carbon dioxide from red blood cells and adds oxygen to them. Deoxygenated blood leaves the right ventricle of the heart and travels to the lungs through the pulmonary artery. Oxygenated blood returns from the lungs to the left atrium of the heart.

69. **(D)** Organismal Biology

A person feels out of breath because the presence of too much carbon dioxide in the blood lowers the pH of blood. The medulla oblongata receives information about blood pH from receptors in the carotid artery. If the pH is too low, the person feels out of breath, and the breathing rate is adjusted.

70. **(C)** Organismal Biology

Carbon monoxide is dangerous because it displaces oxygen molecules carried by hemoglobin. Without oxygen, the cells of the body must undergo anaerobic respiration, which does not produce enough ATP to keep the body's systems running.

71. **(B)** Ecology

Rinderpest was a disease that kept the population very low. When the disease was eliminated, the population was not resource-limited and could grow exponentially. The greatest rate of growth was between 1970 and 1975.

72. **(E)** Ecology

The carrying capacity of the population is the number of individuals that can be supported by an environment, or the point at which birth and death rates are equal. The carrying capacity usually fluctuates around a number because resources, predators, and disease rates vary from year to year. In the case of the wildebeest, after the population recovered from Rinderpest, it grew and stabilized at around 120,000 animals.

73. (B)   Ecology

Rinderpest decreased the carrying capacity of the environment. A population-carrying capacity can be lowered by a decrease in food supply, an increase in predation or poaching, or disease.

74. (D)   Evolution and Diversity

To determine which of the phyla are most closely related, you have to see which phyla share the most common traits. Checking over the chart, it becomes apparent that phyla B and D share all but one trait, making them the most closely related.

75. (B)   Evolution and Diversity

Of the phyla in the chart, phylum A is the only one that contains organisms with notochords. Similarly, Chordata is the only phylum among the answer choices to have notochords.

76. (D)   Evolution and Diversity

An evolutionary tree shows the relative evolutionary closeness between organisms, or, in the case of this question, phyla. The phylum with the fewest traits in the chart will be the least evolutionarily advanced, and therefore, the first to appear in the tree. In the chart, phylum C has none of the traits, so it should appear first on the tree. You can eliminate answers (C) and (E) as possibilities. Only phylum C has all of the traits listed on the chart, so it should appear last on the tree, giving you the correct answer, (D).

77. (E)   Ecology

The greatest biomass of phytoplankton was observed in years 7 and 9 in lakes 1, 2, and 3.

78. (D)   Ecology

After year 10, the biomass of phytoplankton decreased to the levels observed prior to the addition of nutrients in the lakes. Year 10 was the last year of the experiment.

79. (B)   Ecology

Phytoplankton can produce carbohydrates through the use of carbon dioxide, water, and energy from the sun. They are primary producers.

80. **(E)**   Ecology

Lakes 4, 5, and 6 served as the controls for this experiment. The dependent variable is the biomass of phytoplankton. The hypothesis of the researchers was that an increase in nutrients would more than double the biomass of phytoplankton. This hypothesis was supported by the data.

Biology M Solitary Multiple Choice

81. **(C)**   The Cell

There are two major types of microscopes used to look at cells—the light microscope and the electron microscope. Light microscopes magnify their subjects using light and lenses. The light microscopes typically found in high schools can magnify an object up to 430x. Electron microscopes use beams of electrons rather than light to magnify their subjects. An electron microscope can offer a much higher resolution than a light microscope and can magnify objects 10,000x or more.

82. **(A)**   Evolution and Diversity

Vestigial structures are bodily structures that developed in the past but that no longer serve their function. Ostriches have wings but cannot use them to fly. All of the other structures still fulfill their various functions.

83. **(A)**   Cell Processes

Diffusion is the movement of molecules from an area of higher concentration to an area of lower concentration. Diffusion tends to distribute molecules uniformly. The red food coloring was concentrated in one area when it first was dropped into the water. Shaking the test tube allowed the food coloring and water to diffuse and mix uniformly. Diffusion resulted in a pink liquid rather than a liquid with a red phase and a clear phase.

84. **(C)**   Genetics

A zygote is formed from the fusion of one egg cell and one sperm cell. The zygote is diploid and contains 44 autosomal chromosomes and two sex chromosomes (XX or XY). The total number of chromosomes in a normal human zygote is 46.

85. **(D)**   The Cell

This cell most resembles a bacteria, or prokaryote. Prokaryotes have circular DNA, a cell wall, and can self-replicate. Prokaryotes often also have whiplike flagella to propel themselves in liquid. Plant and animal cells are eukaryotes and are more advanced than bacteria. Viruses cannot self-replicate.

86. **(B)**   Evolution and Diversity
Molecular clocks are genes or proteins that change at a constant rate over time. Scientists can use the rate of change in the gene or protein to calculate the point at which two species last shared a common ancestor.

Biology M Group Multiple Choice

87. **(C)**   Organic and Biochemistry
The pH is the negative log of the hydrogen ion concentration. A low pH indicates a high hydrogen ion concentration. A high pH indicates a low hydrogen ion concentration. The pH scale goes from 1 to 14, with one being the most acidic and 14 being the most basic. A pH of 7 is neutral. The ranking of the samples from highest to lowest hydrogen ion concentration would be: $7.0 > 7.5 > 7.6 > 7.7 > 8.0$.

88. **(A)**   Organic and Biochemistry
pH is neutral at 7. Therefore, the algae population would be at its peak in November, when the pH of the water was 7, and would fall in all of the following months, when the pH was non-neutral.

89. **(E)**   Organic and Biochemistry
Heterotrophs are animals that cannot synthesize their own food. They eat other organisms to get glucose and other nutrients. Cellular respiration is the process by which cells break down glucose to generate energy. Heterotrophs (and autotrophs too) require oxygen for cellular respiration. Low dissolved oxygen concentrations in the water mean that organisms may not have enough oxygen for cellular respiration, and their populations would decline.

90. **(C)**   Cell Processes
Alcoholic fermentation is a type of anaerobic respiration. Glycolysis converts glucose to pyruvate. During fermentation, the pyruvate is reduced to ethanol, NAD^+ is regenerated and CO_2 is formed. The overall equation is: Pyruvate $+ NADH \rightarrow$ ethanol $+ NAD^+ + CO_2$.

91. **(A)**   Cell Processes
Each hour, the amount of glucose increases by 10 g/L. Therefore, the rate of accumulation is 10 grams per liter per hour, or 10 g/L/h.

92. **(C)** Cell Processes

Neither carbon dioxide nor oxygen molecules are needed for alcoholic fermentation, so choices (A) and (B) are wrong. Neither lactic acid nor oxygen molecules are products of alcoholic fermentation, so choices (D) and (E) are wrong. The only answer that could be correct is (C). Ethanol is toxic to yeasts when it reaches a concentration of around 12%. That is why wine and beer generally have an alcohol content of around 12% or less.

93. **(C)** Organismal Biology

When the subjects were asked to listen to words, Section 3 of the brain (the temporal lobe) was most active. You can infer that this is the section of the brain that controls hearing.

94. **(B)** Organismal Biology

The part of the brain labeled 5 is the cerebellum. The cerebellum regulates balance, posture, and coordination.

95. **(D)** Organismal Biology

When a person reads aloud, he or she must see the words on the page and then speak them. The parts of the brain that control vision and speech are 4 (occipital lobe) and 1 (frontal lobe), respectively. If you didn't know what each part of the brain does, you could infer from the data that Section 4 controls vision, and Section 1 controls speech.

96. **(A)** Organismal Biology

The brain and spinal cord are components of the central nervous system. The peripheral nervous system includes sensory neurons and motor neurons.

97. **(A)** Genetics

The inheritance pattern for albinism is simple recessive. In simple recessive disorders, not everyone who manifests the disease has a parent who also manifests the disease. If two parents have the disease, all of their children will have the disease. The trait is not sex-linked because males and females have an equal chance of getting the disease.

98. **(D)** Genetics

None of the offspring of Individuals 5 and 6 display albinism, and none of their offspring's offspring do, either. But, since albinism is a recessive disorder, it is necessary for both parents to carry and pass on the recessive gene in order for their offspring to be an albino. In other words, nothing in this pedigree proves that Individuals 5 and 6 are not carriers. It is quite possible that one of them is a carrier. In fact, it's possible that both are carriers but that they just did not both pass on the recessive gene to the same children.

99. **(A)** Genetics

If an albino woman were to have children with a man who does not carry the allele for albinism, then none of their children would manifest the trait because none of them would be homozygous recessive for albinism.

	a	a
A	Aa	Aa
A	Aa	Aa

100. **(C)** Genetics

Some of the offspring of Individual 12 are albino, which means that Individual 12 cannot possibly have the genotype AA. A person who only has two dominant alleles cannot pass the recessive albino allele on to his or her children.

SAT II Biology
Practice Test 5

BIOLOGY TEST 5 ANSWER SHEET

1. Ⓐ Ⓑ Ⓒ Ⓓ Ⓔ	26. Ⓐ Ⓑ Ⓒ Ⓓ Ⓔ	51. Ⓐ Ⓑ Ⓒ Ⓓ Ⓔ	76. Ⓐ Ⓑ Ⓒ Ⓓ Ⓔ
2. Ⓐ Ⓑ Ⓒ Ⓓ Ⓔ	27. Ⓐ Ⓑ Ⓒ Ⓓ Ⓔ	52. Ⓐ Ⓑ Ⓒ Ⓓ Ⓔ	77. Ⓐ Ⓑ Ⓒ Ⓓ Ⓔ
3. Ⓐ Ⓑ Ⓒ Ⓓ Ⓔ	28. Ⓐ Ⓑ Ⓒ Ⓓ Ⓔ	53. Ⓐ Ⓑ Ⓒ Ⓓ Ⓔ	78. Ⓐ Ⓑ Ⓒ Ⓓ Ⓔ
4. Ⓐ Ⓑ Ⓒ Ⓓ Ⓔ	29. Ⓐ Ⓑ Ⓒ Ⓓ Ⓔ	54. Ⓐ Ⓑ Ⓒ Ⓓ Ⓔ	79. Ⓐ Ⓑ Ⓒ Ⓓ Ⓔ
5. Ⓐ Ⓑ Ⓒ Ⓓ Ⓔ	30. Ⓐ Ⓑ Ⓒ Ⓓ Ⓔ	55. Ⓐ Ⓑ Ⓒ Ⓓ Ⓔ	80. Ⓐ Ⓑ Ⓒ Ⓓ Ⓔ
6. Ⓐ Ⓑ Ⓒ Ⓓ Ⓔ	31. Ⓐ Ⓑ Ⓒ Ⓓ Ⓔ	56. Ⓐ Ⓑ Ⓒ Ⓓ Ⓔ	81. Ⓐ Ⓑ Ⓒ Ⓓ Ⓔ
7. Ⓐ Ⓑ Ⓒ Ⓓ Ⓔ	32. Ⓐ Ⓑ Ⓒ Ⓓ Ⓔ	57. Ⓐ Ⓑ Ⓒ Ⓓ Ⓔ	82. Ⓐ Ⓑ Ⓒ Ⓓ Ⓔ
8. Ⓐ Ⓑ Ⓒ Ⓓ Ⓔ	33. Ⓐ Ⓑ Ⓒ Ⓓ Ⓔ	58. Ⓐ Ⓑ Ⓒ Ⓓ Ⓔ	83. Ⓐ Ⓑ Ⓒ Ⓓ Ⓔ
9. Ⓐ Ⓑ Ⓒ Ⓓ Ⓔ	34. Ⓐ Ⓑ Ⓒ Ⓓ Ⓔ	59. Ⓐ Ⓑ Ⓒ Ⓓ Ⓔ	84. Ⓐ Ⓑ Ⓒ Ⓓ Ⓔ
10. Ⓐ Ⓑ Ⓒ Ⓓ Ⓔ	35. Ⓐ Ⓑ Ⓒ Ⓓ Ⓔ	60. Ⓐ Ⓑ Ⓒ Ⓓ Ⓔ	85. Ⓐ Ⓑ Ⓒ Ⓓ Ⓔ
11. Ⓐ Ⓑ Ⓒ Ⓓ Ⓔ	36. Ⓐ Ⓑ Ⓒ Ⓓ Ⓔ	61. Ⓐ Ⓑ Ⓒ Ⓓ Ⓔ	86. Ⓐ Ⓑ Ⓒ Ⓓ Ⓔ
12. Ⓐ Ⓑ Ⓒ Ⓓ Ⓔ	37. Ⓐ Ⓑ Ⓒ Ⓓ Ⓔ	62. Ⓐ Ⓑ Ⓒ Ⓓ Ⓔ	87. Ⓐ Ⓑ Ⓒ Ⓓ Ⓔ
13. Ⓐ Ⓑ Ⓒ Ⓓ Ⓔ	38. Ⓐ Ⓑ Ⓒ Ⓓ Ⓔ	63. Ⓐ Ⓑ Ⓒ Ⓓ Ⓔ	88. Ⓐ Ⓑ Ⓒ Ⓓ Ⓔ
14. Ⓐ Ⓑ Ⓒ Ⓓ Ⓔ	39. Ⓐ Ⓑ Ⓒ Ⓓ Ⓔ	64. Ⓐ Ⓑ Ⓒ Ⓓ Ⓔ	89. Ⓐ Ⓑ Ⓒ Ⓓ Ⓔ
15. Ⓐ Ⓑ Ⓒ Ⓓ Ⓔ	40. Ⓐ Ⓑ Ⓒ Ⓓ Ⓔ	65. Ⓐ Ⓑ Ⓒ Ⓓ Ⓔ	90. Ⓐ Ⓑ Ⓒ Ⓓ Ⓔ
16. Ⓐ Ⓑ Ⓒ Ⓓ Ⓔ	41. Ⓐ Ⓑ Ⓒ Ⓓ Ⓔ	66. Ⓐ Ⓑ Ⓒ Ⓓ Ⓔ	91. Ⓐ Ⓑ Ⓒ Ⓓ Ⓔ
17. Ⓐ Ⓑ Ⓒ Ⓓ Ⓔ	42. Ⓐ Ⓑ Ⓒ Ⓓ Ⓔ	67. Ⓐ Ⓑ Ⓒ Ⓓ Ⓔ	92. Ⓐ Ⓑ Ⓒ Ⓓ Ⓔ
18. Ⓐ Ⓑ Ⓒ Ⓓ Ⓔ	43. Ⓐ Ⓑ Ⓒ Ⓓ Ⓔ	68. Ⓐ Ⓑ Ⓒ Ⓓ Ⓔ	93. Ⓐ Ⓑ Ⓒ Ⓓ Ⓔ
19. Ⓐ Ⓑ Ⓒ Ⓓ Ⓔ	44. Ⓐ Ⓑ Ⓒ Ⓓ Ⓔ	69. Ⓐ Ⓑ Ⓒ Ⓓ Ⓔ	94. Ⓐ Ⓑ Ⓒ Ⓓ Ⓔ
20. Ⓐ Ⓑ Ⓒ Ⓓ Ⓔ	45. Ⓐ Ⓑ Ⓒ Ⓓ Ⓔ	70. Ⓐ Ⓑ Ⓒ Ⓓ Ⓔ	95. Ⓐ Ⓑ Ⓒ Ⓓ Ⓔ
21. Ⓐ Ⓑ Ⓒ Ⓓ Ⓔ	46. Ⓐ Ⓑ Ⓒ Ⓓ Ⓔ	71. Ⓐ Ⓑ Ⓒ Ⓓ Ⓔ	96. Ⓐ Ⓑ Ⓒ Ⓓ Ⓔ
22. Ⓐ Ⓑ Ⓒ Ⓓ Ⓔ	47. Ⓐ Ⓑ Ⓒ Ⓓ Ⓔ	72. Ⓐ Ⓑ Ⓒ Ⓓ Ⓔ	97. Ⓐ Ⓑ Ⓒ Ⓓ Ⓔ
23. Ⓐ Ⓑ Ⓒ Ⓓ Ⓔ	48. Ⓐ Ⓑ Ⓒ Ⓓ Ⓔ	73. Ⓐ Ⓑ Ⓒ Ⓓ Ⓔ	98. Ⓐ Ⓑ Ⓒ Ⓓ Ⓔ
24. Ⓐ Ⓑ Ⓒ Ⓓ Ⓔ	49. Ⓐ Ⓑ Ⓒ Ⓓ Ⓔ	74. Ⓐ Ⓑ Ⓒ Ⓓ Ⓔ	99. Ⓐ Ⓑ Ⓒ Ⓓ Ⓔ
25. Ⓐ Ⓑ Ⓒ Ⓓ Ⓔ	50. Ⓐ Ⓑ Ⓒ Ⓓ Ⓔ	75. Ⓐ Ⓑ Ⓒ Ⓓ Ⓔ	100. Ⓐ Ⓑ Ⓒ Ⓓ Ⓔ

BIOLOGY E/M TEST

FOR BOTH BIOLOGY-E AND BIOLOGY-M, ANSWER QUESTIONS 1–60

Directions: Each set of lettered choices below refers to the numbered questions or statements immediately following it. Select the one lettered choice that best answers each question or best fits each statement, and then fill in the corresponding oval on the answer sheet. A choice may be used once, more than once, or not at all in each set.

Questions 1–3 refer to the movement of substances across the cell membrane.

(A) Exocytosis
(B) Endocytosis
(C) Osmosis
(D) Facilitated diffusion
(E) Active transport

1. Requires ATP

2. Process by which water crosses a cell membrane

3. Occurs when a vesicle fuses with the cell membrane and releases its contents into the outside

Questions 4–6 refer to structures found in plants.

(A) Stigma
(B) Ovary
(C) Anther
(D) Tuber
(E) Bulb

4. Can develop into fruit

5. Part of the stamen

6. Fleshy underground storage structures that are enlarged parts of the stem

Questions 7–9 refer to concepts used in community ecology.

(A) Mutualism
(B) Biome
(C) Community
(D) Commensalism
(E) Niche

7. The functional role of a species in an ecosystem

8. A type of symbiosis in which one species benefits and the other remains unaffected

9. Refers to all of the populations that interact with each other in a given environment and geographical area

Questions 10–12 refer to evidence of evolution.

(A) Analogous structures
(B) Vestigial structures
(C) Fossils
(D) Comparative embryology
(E) Molecular clocks

10. Mineralized remains or traces of prehistoric life

11. Bodily structures that evolved in the past but that no longer serve an apparent function

12. Certain genes or proteins in organisms that change at a constant rate over time

GO ON TO THE NEXT PAGE

Directions: Each of the questions or incomplete statements below is followed by five suggested answers or completions. Some questions pertain to a set that refers to a laboratory or experimental situation. For each question, select the best answer to the question and fill in the corresponding oval on the answer sheet.

13. The exoskeleton of an arthropod is made of

    (A) cellulose
    (B) keratin
    (C) peptidoglycan
    (D) chitin
    (E) hair

14. Rank the following in order from most inclusive to least inclusive:

    (A) Biome, biosphere, ecosystem, community, population
    (B) Biosphere, biome, ecosystem, community, population
    (C) Population, community, ecosystem, biosphere, biome
    (D) Population, community, biome, ecosystem, biosphere
    (E) Biosphere, ecosystem, biome, community, population

15. Movement first evolved in which phylum of kingdom Animalia?

    (A) Porifera
    (B) Mollusca
    (C) Cnidaria
    (D) Arthropoda
    (E) Annelida

16. During which phase of mitosis is DNA replicated?

    (A) Prophase
    (B) Metaphase
    (C) Telophase
    (D) Interphase
    (E) Anaphase

17. A culture of animal cells and a culture of plant cells are pulverized and analyzed for the presence of certain molecules. Which of the following is most likely?

    (A) The plant and animal cells will contain identical molecules in identical proportions.
    (B) The plant and animal cells will contain identical molecules in different proportions.
    (C) The animal cells will contain adenosine triphosphate, while the plant cells will not.
    (D) The plant cells will contain glucose, while the animal cells will not.
    (E) The plant cells will contain chlorophyll, while the animal cells will not.

18. Which of the following is true regarding the genotype of an individual organism?

    I.   The genotype depends on the phenotype.
    II. The genotype is acquired during an individual's lifetime.
    III. The genotype can be homozygous or heterozygous.
    IV. The genotype determines the phenotype.

    (A) I only
    (B) I and II only
    (C) III and IV only
    (D) II, III, IV only
    (E) I and III only

19. Stomach fluid has a pH of 2. The fluid in the stomach

    (A) is basic
    (B) has a low hydrogen ion concentration
    (C) has a high hydrogen ion concentration
    (D) has the same pH as water
    (E) is neutral

20. Lions and hyenas both live in Serengeti National Park. Why are they both able to live in the same community?

    (A) They are both predators.
    (B) They occupy different niches.
    (C) They are both in Hardy-Weinberg equilibrium.
    (D) They cannot. They will compete until one population eliminates the other.
    (E) They are in the same genus.

GO ON TO THE NEXT PAGE

21. Which of the following is the correct listing of kingdom Plantae from least to most evolutionarily advanced?

    (A) Gymnosperms, angiosperms, seedless vascular plants, bryophytes
    (B) Bryophytes, seedless vascular plants, gymnosperms, angiosperms
    (C) Bryophytes, seedless vascular plants, angiosperms, gymnosperms
    (D) Seedless vascular plants, bryophytes, gymnosperms, angiosperms
    (E) Angiosperms, gymnosperms, seedless vascular plants, bryophytes

22. A scientist isolates a single strand of DNA that had bonded with an mRNA strand and analyzes the proportions of nitrogenous bases in the bonded string. Which of the following could be the proportions discovered by the scientist?

    (A) 20% adenine, 30% cytosine, 30% guanine, 20% thymine
    (B) 20% adenine, 30% cytosine, 30% guanine, 20% uracil
    (C) 20% adenine, 20% cytosine, 20% guanine, 20% thymine, 20% uracil
    (D) 20% adenine, 30% cytosine, 30% guanine, 10% thymine, 10% uracil
    (E) 40% adenine, 20% cytosine, 10% guanine, 15% thymine, 15% uracil

23. Two diploid plants are crossed, and the resulting offspring are tetraploid. The type of nondisjunction event that occurred is called

    (A) polyploidy
    (B) monosomy
    (C) trisomy
    (D) matrimony
    (E) parthenogenesis

24. All of the following characteristics differentiate between monocots and dicots EXCEPT for

    (A) the number of petals on the flowers
    (B) whether or not the plant has vascular tissue
    (C) the venation pattern of the leaves
    (D) the arrangement of the vascular bundles
    (E) the number of cotyledons that the plant has during embryonic development

25. In glycolysis, the net gain of ATP per molecule of glucose is

    (A) 2
    (B) 4
    (C) 6
    (D) 18
    (E) 36

26. Which of the following is NOT found in the nucleus?

    (A) Messenger RNA
    (B) Lysosomes
    (C) Nucleolus
    (D) Chromosomes
    (E) DNA

27. The person who discovered the Law of Dominance, the Law of Segregation, and the Law of Independent Assortment was

    (A) Liam Hooke
    (B) Charles Darwin
    (C) Alfred Russell Wallace
    (D) Gregor Mendel
    (E) Rosalind Franklin

28. What is the purpose of the myelin sheath?

    (A) To receive information from other cells
    (B) To insulate the axon and make the impulse go faster
    (C) To stop the nerve impulse
    (D) To reverse the direction of the nerve impulse
    (E) To regulate temperature

29. A still pond contains many strings of jelly-coated eggs. These eggs could have been laid by a member of

    (A) class Mammalia
    (B) class Aves
    (C) phylum Reptilia
    (D) class Reptilia
    (E) class Amphibia

30. A tree growing on the top of a mountain is exposed to very high winds from the north. The trunk of the tree is thicker on the side that faces the wind. This is an example of

    (A) phototropism
    (B) thigmotropism
    (C) gravitropism
    (D) aquatropism
    (E) photoperiodism

GO ON TO THE NEXT PAGE

Questions 31–34 refer to the following drawing of the female anatomy.

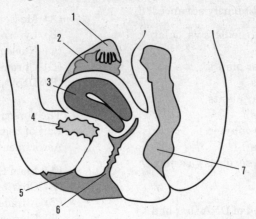

31. Which two systems are best represented in this drawing?

    (A) Reproductive and respiratory systems
    (B) Skeletal and endocrine systems
    (C) Nervous and excretory systems
    (D) Reproductive and excretory systems
    (E) Respiratory and digestive systems

32. In what structure are the egg cells produced?

    (A) 1
    (B) 2
    (C) 3
    (D) 4
    (E) 5

33. Which of the following is a function of Structure 3?

    (A) Produce progesterone
    (B) Connect the uterus with the ovaries
    (C) Store urine
    (D) House the placenta and developing fetus
    (E) Produce milk

34. In what structure is estrogen produced?

    (A) 1
    (B) 2
    (C) 3
    (D) 4
    (E) 5

GO ON TO THE NEXT PAGE

Questions 35–38 refer to the following two-part experiment.

In Part 1, populations of two different species were grown separately under constant conditions, and each population was given the same amount of food each day. In Part 2, the two species were cultured together under constant conditions and given the same amount of food each day.

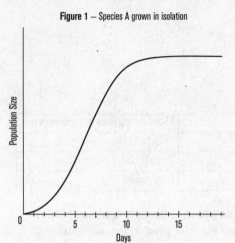

Figure 1 – Species A grown in isolation

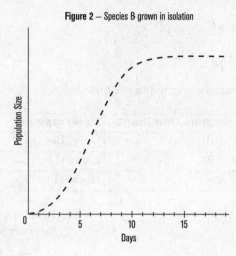

Figure 2 – Species B grown in isolation

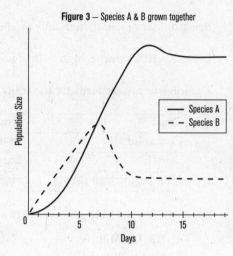

Figure 3 – Species A & B grown together

35. In Figure 1, the point on the curve at which the population growth levels off is called the

 (A) carrying capacity
 (B) niche
 (C) high point
 (D) displacement point
 (E) birth rate

36. When grown separately, what is the factor that likely limits the growth of each population?

 (A) Predation
 (B) Parasitism
 (C) Disease
 (D) Competition among individuals of different species
 (E) Competition among individuals of the same species

37. Which of the following statements is supported by the data in Figure 3?

 (A) When grown together, Species A has the larger population size on Day 2.
 (B) When grown together, Species B outcompetes Species A.
 (C) When cultured separately, Species A and Species B both have similar growth patterns.
 (D) When grown together, Species B has the larger population size on Day 12.
 (E) When cultured separately, Species A and B both reach their maximum population size on Day 8.

38. Of the following, which might be hypothesized from the data recorded when Species A and Species B were cultured together?

 (A) Species B is a stronger competitor than Species A.
 (B) When resources were abundant, there was little need for competition between Species A and B.
 (C) Species A will soon eliminate all individuals in Species B.
 (D) Species A and B are mutualistic.
 (E) If the population of Species A were to suddenly die off, while the rest of the environment in the culture remained the same, the population of Species B would also diminish.

GO ON TO THE NEXT PAGE

Questions 39–42 relate to the genetics of goats on a farm.

A farmer has three breeds of goat.

Breed X – White, large, low milk production

Breed Y – Gray, small, high milk production

Breed Z – Black, large, high milk production

The inheritance patterns for the traits are summarized in the table below.

Trait	Homozygous Dominant	Heterozygous	Homozygous Recessive
Coat color (B)	Black (BB)	Gray (Bb)	White (bb)
Size (L)	Large (LL)	Large (Ll)	Small (ll)
Milk production (M)	High (MM)	High (Mm)	Low (mm)

39. What is a possible genotype of Breed X?

   (A) BB, LL, MM
   (B) bb, LL, mm
   (C) bb, ll, mm
   (D) BB, ll, Mm
   (E) Bb, Ll, MM

40. The alleles for coat color exhibit

   (A) incomplete dominance
   (B) codominance
   (C) simple dominance
   (D) crossing-over
   (E) mutation

41. To determine whether Breed Y is homozygous or heterozygous for milk production, one could

   (A) cross Breed Y with Breed Z and observe the number of offspring that have low milk production
   (B) cross Breed Y with Breed Z and observe the number of offspring that have high milk production
   (C) mutate the gene with radioactive isotopes
   (D) cross Breed Y with Breed X and observe the number of offspring that have high milk production
   (E) perform a Punnett square test

42. Assume that Breed X and Breed Z are both homozygous for all traits. If you were to cross Breed X with Breed Z, what would be the phenotype of their offspring?

   (A) Gray, large, high milk production
   (B) Gray, small, high milk production
   (C) White, large, high milk production
   (D) Black, large, low milk production
   (E) Black, small, low milk production

GO ON TO THE NEXT PAGE

<u>Questions 43–45</u> refer to evolution in a population of turtles.

A species of turtle was observed by scientists on a small, isolated island in the Caribbean. Scientists counted the number of turtles and measured the size of each turtle.

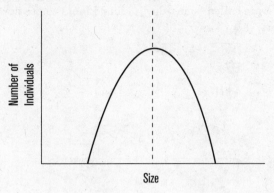

Fig. 1 Turtle Size in 1940

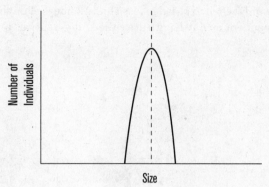

Fig. 2 Turtle Size in 1990

Fifty years later, a second team of scientists came to observe the turtles. They counted the number of turtles and again measured the size of each turtle.

43. What happened to the population over time?

   (A) Evolution
   (B) Stabilizing selection
   (C) Disruptive selection
   (D) Directional selection
   (E) Hardy-Weinberg equilibrium

44. A large turtle can better withstand extreme high winds than a small turtle. What do you think would happen to turtle size on the island if the island became subject to regular and repeated high winds for a decade or more?

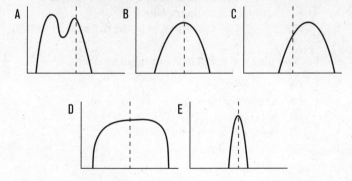

45. The population of turtles on the island grew from a few turtles that came to the island from a nearby continent. In a breeding experiment, scientists discovered that the turtles from the island can no longer breed with turtles from the continent. What has happened?

   (A) Convergent evolution
   (B) Hardy-Weinberg equilibrium
   (C) Mutation
   (D) Allopatric speciation
   (E) Extinction

GO ON TO THE NEXT PAGE

<u>Questions 46–49</u> refer to the following experiment in which plant species A and B were exposed to dark and light environments for various lengths of time. The shaded areas represent "night" and the unshaded areas represent "day".

In this experiment, plants that flower only when exposed to 12 or more hours of daylight are called "long-day" plants. Plants that flower only when exposed to less than 12 hours of daylight are called "short-day" plants. Plants whose flowering patterns are not dependent on day length are called "day-neutral" plants.

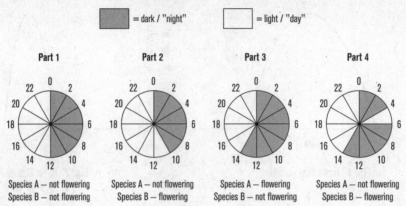

46. The dependence of flowering on the duration of light and dark periods is called

    (A) gravitropism
    (B) thigmoperiodism
    (C) phototropism
    (D) photoperiodism
    (E) thigmotropism

47. Which of the following statements is correct?

    (A) Plant A is a long-day plant.
    (B) Plant B is a short-day plant.
    (C) Plant A is a day-neutral plant.
    (D) Plant A is a short-day plant.

(E) Plant B is a day-neutral plant.

48. Which of the following statements is NOT supported by the data?

    (A) Plant A flowers when exposed to 14 hours of darkness.
    (B) Neither plant will flower when exposed to 12 hours of light and 12 hours of darkness.
    (C) Plant A will not flower if there is an interruption of exposure to darkness, even if the total hours of darkness in a full day is greater than 12 hours.
    (D) Plant B will not flower if there is an interruption of exposure to darkness that causes "night" to be less than 14 hours long.
    (E) Plant B flowers when exposed to 14 hours of light.

49. The plants used in this experiment are all

    (A) gymnosperms
    (B) angiosperms
    (C) bryophytes
    (D) tricots
    (E) non-vascular

GO ON TO THE NEXT PAGE

Questions 50–52 refer to evolutionary relationships between members of Subphylum Vertebrata.

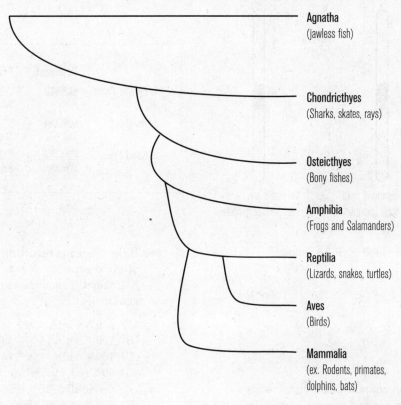

Agnatha
(jawless fish)

Chondricthyes
(Sharks, skates, rays)

Osteicthyes
(Bony fishes)

Amphibia
(Frogs and Salamanders)

Reptilia
(Lizards, snakes, turtles)

Aves
(Birds)

Mammalia
(ex. Rodents, primates,
dolphins, bats)

50. The above diagram is called a

(A) Punnett diagram
(B) phylogram
(C) karyotype
(D) diversity chain
(E) phylogenetic tree

51. Sharks and dolphins both have a dorsal fin. In this instance, the dorsal fin is an example of a(n)

(A) vestigial structure
(B) analogous structure
(C) homologous trait
(D) molecular clock
(E) defense structure

52. Of the following choices, which pair is most closely related?

(A) Agnatha and Mammalia
(B) Reptilia and Osteicthyes
(C) Agnatha and Osteicthyes
(D) Amphibia and Chondricthyes
(E) Reptilia and Aves

GO ON TO THE NEXT PAGE

Questions 53–56 refer to the chromosomes depicted below.

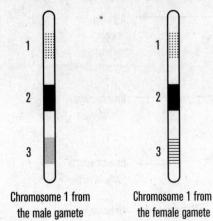

Chromosome 1 from
the male gamete

Chromosome 1 from
the female gamete

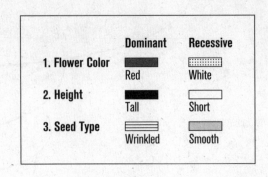

53. How many traits are coded for in the above chromosomes?

   (A) 1
   (B) 2
   (C) 3
   (D) 6
   (E) 7

54. The two gametes that contain these chromosomes unite during fertilization and become part of the same zygote. What would be the individual's phenotype?

   (A) Red flower, tall, smooth seeds
   (B) Red flower, short, smooth seeds
   (C) White flower, short, wrinkled seeds
   (D) Red flower, tall, wrinkled seeds
   (E) White flower, tall, wrinkled seeds

55. If the offspring resulting from the union of these original gametes were to be self-crossed, what is the likelihood of each trait appearing in this second generation?

   (A) 100% white, 100% tall, 75% wrinkled, 25% smooth
   (B) 100% white, 100% tall, 50% wrinkled, 50% smooth
   (C) 100% white, 100% tall, 25% wrinkled, 75% smooth
   (D) 50% red, 50% white, 50% tall, 50% short, 75% wrinkled, 25% smooth
   (E) 50% red, 50% white, 50% tall, 50% short, 75% wrinkled, 25% smooth

56. What is the process by which these gametes were formed?

   (A) Mitosis
   (B) Synapsis
   (C) Meiosis
   (D) Fertilization
   (E) Genesis

GO ON TO THE NEXT PAGE

<u>Questions 57–60</u> refer to the following description of kangaroo rats.

Kangaroo rats are adapted to life in hot, dry climates and have very efficient kidneys to conserve water. The following table compares kangaroo rats to humans with respect to their gain and loss of water. (Data from Schmidt-Nielsen, K. 1990. *Animal Physiology: Adaptation and Environment,* 4th ed. Cambridge University Press, Cambridge.)

57. Most of the water lost by humans is a result of

    (A) drinking
    (B) evaporation
    (C) excretion of solid wastes
    (D) urination
    (E) metabolism

58. What might be the explanation for the low percentage of water that the kangaroo rat loses through urine?

    (A) Because the kangaroo rat does not often drink or eat, it does not produce much urine.
    (B) Urine might allow a predator to track and kill a kangaroo rat.
    (C) Most of the water that is lost through urine is reabsorbed by the kangaroo rat's kidneys.
    (D) Water lost by evaporation is less vital to the survival of the organism.
    (E) Urine in the bladder might freeze during extremely cold temperatures and kill the organism.

59. The kangaroo rat is a mammal. What might be some of the adaptations that help it to conserve water?

    I.   Nocturnal lifestyle
    II. Exceptionally long loops of Henle in the kidney
    III. A waxy exoskeleton
    IV. An amniotic egg

    (A) I and II only
    (B) III and IV only
    (C) I, II, III only
    (D) I, II, IV only
    (E) I, II, III, and IV

60. In what biome would you expect the kangaroo rat to live?

    (A) Tropical rainforest
    (B) Temperate deciduous forest
    (C) Marine
    (D) Desert
    (E) Arctic tundra

GO ON TO THE NEXT PAGE

BIOLOGY-E SECTION

If you are taking the Biology-E test, continue with questions 61–80.
If you are taking the Biology-M test, go to question 81 now.

<u>Directions:</u> Each of the questions or incomplete statements below is followed by five suggested answers or completions. Some questions pertain to a set that refers to a laboratory or experimental situation. For each question, select the one choice that is the best answer to the question and then fill in the corresponding oval on the answer sheet.

61. A population is in Hardy-Weinberg equilibrium. The frequency of the dominant allele in the population is p = 0.6. What is the frequency of the recessive allele?

    (A) 36%
    (B) 0.4
    (C) 16%
    (D) 0.6
    (E) 48%

62. A deer has a tapeworm residing in its digestive system. The tapeworm feeds on the food that the deer ingests. This is an example of

    (A) coevolution
    (B) commensalism
    (C) mutualism
    (D) parasitism
    (E) positive symbiosis

63. A baby bird hatches from an egg and first sees a human girl. The bird then treats the girl as its mother. This is an example of

    (A) conditioning
    (B) habituation
    (C) imprinting
    (D) associative learning
    (E) unlearning

64. The smallest unit in which evolution can occur is a(n)

    (A) population
    (B) gene
    (C) cell
    (D) community
    (E) individual

65. The components of the blood that control clotting are

    (A) white blood cells
    (B) hemoglobin molecules
    (C) platelets
    (D) plasma
    (E) red blood cells

66. Carbon dioxide is released into the atmosphere by all of the following processes EXCEPT

    (A) animal respiration
    (B) combustion of fossil fuels
    (C) decomposition of dead material by microbes
    (D) photosynthesis
    (E) burning of forests

GO ON TO THE NEXT PAGE

Questions 67–70 refer to the following drawings of members of kingdom Animalia.

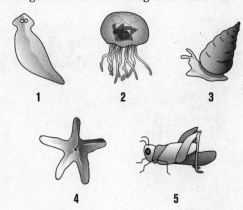

67. Which of the pictured organisms exhibit radial symmetry?

  (A) 1, 3, 4
  (B) 1, 2, 3
  (C) 2, 3
  (D) 2, 4
  (E) 3, 4, 5

68. Organism 1 is a member of phylum

  (A) Nematoda
  (B) Cnidaria
  (C) Arthropoda
  (D) Mollusca
  (E) Platyhelminthes

69. Which of the above organisms has a foot, radula, and mantle?

  (A) 1
  (B) 2
  (C) 3
  (D) 4
  (E) 5

70. Which of the above organisms is most closely related to phylum Chordata?

  (A) 1
  (B) 2
  (C) 3
  (D) 4
  (E) 5

GO ON TO THE NEXT PAGE

Questions 71–73 refer to the effects of temperature and precipitation on the placement and productivity of biomes.

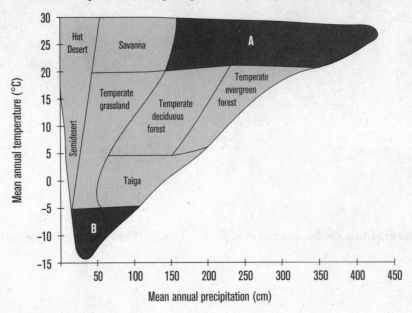

71. A region in South America has a mean annual precipitation of 50 cm and a mean annual temperature of 10°C. The area is likely a

    (A) desert
    (B) taiga
    (C) temperate deciduous forest
    (D) tundra
    (E) temperate grassland

72. In which biome would you find prairie dogs, bison, and antelope?

    (A) Desert
    (B) Taiga
    (C) Temperate deciduous forest
    (D) Tundra
    (E) Temperate grassland

73. Two of the biomes in Figure 1 are labeled A and B, respectively. What are these biomes?

    (A) A is tropical rainforest; B is desert.
    (B) A is savanna; B is tropical rainforest.
    (C) A is tundra; B is tropical rainforest.
    (D) A is tropical rainforest; B is tundra.
    (E) A is desert; B is tundra.

GO ON TO THE NEXT PAGE

Questions 74–76 refer to the life cycle of a plant.

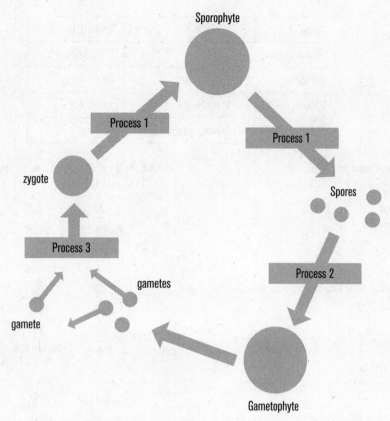

74. What is the name of the process labeled 3?

    (A) Meiosis
    (B) Mitosis
    (C) Fertilization
    (D) Asexual reproduction
    (E) Duplication

75. Which of the following elements of the plant life cycle is incorrectly matched with a description of its chromosomes?

    (A) Spores – diploid
    (B) Gametophyte – haploid
    (C) Zygote – diploid
    (D) Gametes – haploid
    (E) Sporophyte – diploid

76. The type of life cycle depicted is common in plants and is called

    (A) alternation of generations
    (B) parthenogenesis
    (C) budding
    (D) pedogenesis
    (E) dominance of the diploid

GO ON TO THE NEXT PAGE

Questions 77–80 refer to a food web involving grasses, rabbits, foxes, and mountain lions.

Organism	Diet	Total Biomass
Grasses	—	150,000 kg
Rabbits	Grasses	48,000 kg
Foxes	Rabbits	5,000 kg
Mountain Lions	Rabbits/Foxes	600 kg

77. In this food web, the grasses are

(A) primary consumers
(B) primary producers
(C) secondary consumers
(D) top carnivore
(E) secondary producer

78. What is the original source of the energy in this food web?

(A) Soil
(B) Carbon and nitrogen
(C) Sun
(D) Water
(E) Atmosphere

79. Which of the following organisms are carnivores?

(A) Foxes and rabbits only
(B) Foxes only
(C) Mountain lions only
(D) Foxes, rabbits, and mountain lions only
(E) Foxes and mountain lions only

80. Which diagram best represents the food web described in the table?

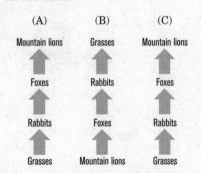

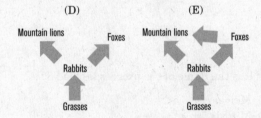

GO ON TO THE NEXT PAGE

BIOLOGY-M SECTION

If you are taking the Biology-M test, continue with questions 81–100.
Be sure to start this section of the test by filling in oval 81 on your answer sheet.

<u>Directions:</u> Each of the questions or incomplete statements below is followed by five suggested answers or completions. Some questions pertain to a set that refers to a laboratory or experimental situation. For each question, select the one choice that is the best answer to the question and then fill in the corresponding oval on the answer sheet.

81. Which of the following statements is NOT correct?

Cell Organelles	Cell A	Cell B
Vacuole	Yes	No
Cell wall	Yes	Yes
Nucleus	Yes	No
Flagella	No	Yes
Golgi complex	Yes	No
Chloroplasts	Yes	No

(A) Cell A is a eukaryote.
(B) Cell B is a prokaryote.
(C) Cell A is a plant.
(D) Cell B is evolutionarily less advanced than Cell A.
(E) Cell B would have mitochondria, and Cell A would not.

82. An enzyme-aided reaction occurs in a solution. If the solution is already saturated with substrates, what could be done to speed the reaction's progress?

(A) Reduce the temperature of the solution to 0°C.
(B) Add more substrate to the solution.
(C) Increase the temperature of the solution to 120°C.
(D) Add an allosteric inhibitor to the solution.
(E) Add more enzymes to the solution.

83. Which of the following occurs in both aerobic and anaerobic respiration?

(A) Fermentation
(B) The Krebs cycle
(C) Glycolysis
(D) The Electron transport chain
(E) Transcription

84. A volcanic eruption separates one population of birds into two isolated populations. Many generations pass. Two individuals, one from each of the two isolated populations, are brought together in the hope that they will mate with one another. What would NOT be considered evidence that the two populations had evolved into different species?

(A) The individuals mate, and the offspring are deformed and die soon after birth.
(B) The individuals mate, and the offspring are sterile.
(C) The female does not recognize the male's courtship song and will not mate with him.
(D) The individuals produce fertile offspring, and the offspring do not resemble either parent.
(E) The individuals try to mate but are not physically compatible.

85. A tall plant is bred with another tall plant, and all 50 of the resulting offspring are tall. A short plant is then bred with another short plant, and all 50 of the offspring are short. The tall offspring are bred together, and all of the offspring are again tall. The short offspring are also crossbred, and all of the offspring are short. If one of the tall plants is then bred with one of the short plants, and the resulting offspring are all short, this demonstrates

(A) that the tall plants were heterozygous for tallness
(B) that the short plants were heterozygous for shortness
(C) the Law of Segregation
(D) that the allele for tallness is recessive in this plant
(E) codominance

86. The procedure of injecting healthy DNA into a person with a genetic problem is called

(A) recombination
(B) DNA fingerprinting
(C) gene therapy
(D) vaccination
(E) electrophoresis

GO ON TO THE NEXT PAGE

Questions 87–90 refer to the early development of a human fetus.

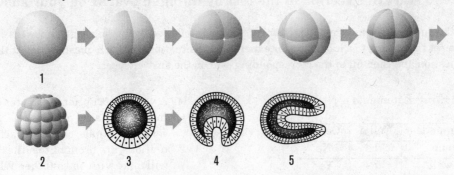

87. Structure 1 is

    (A) haploid
    (B) diploid
    (C) a gamete
    (D) a blastula
    (E) an unfertilized egg

88. Which structure is the morula?

    (A) 1
    (B) 2
    (C) 3
    (D) 4
    (E) 5

89. Cells in a developing zygote increase in number through

    (A) respiration
    (B) meiosis
    (C) mitosis
    (D) gametogenesis
    (E) translation

90. Which embryonic tissue layers does Structure 5 possess?

    (A) Endoderm only
    (B) Endoderm and mesoderm only
    (C) Endoderm and ectoderm only
    (D) Mesoderm and ectoderm only
    (E) Endoderm, mesoderm, and ectoderm

GO ON TO THE NEXT PAGE

Questions 91–94 refer to the genetic disease called hemophilia, which affects the blood's ability to clot.

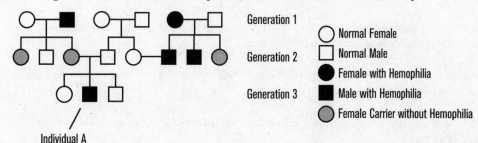

91. The inheritance pattern for this disease is

(A) simple dominant
(B) sex-linked dominant
(C) sex-linked recessive
(D) simple recessive
(E) none of the above

92. On which chromosome is this disease carried?

(A) The Y-chromosome
(B) The X-chromosome
(C) An autosome
(D) Chromosome 21
(E) Indeterminable

93. Which of the following statements is NOT true?

(A) If the father has hemophilia, all of his children have the disease or are carriers of the disease.
(B) If the mother has hemophilia, all of her children have the disease or are carriers.
(C) Males cannot carry an allele of the disease and still be phenotypically normal.
(D) Females who carry one allele for the disease are phenotypically normal.
(E) If both parents are phenotypically and genotypically normal, none of their children have hemophilia.

94. If Individual A has a daughter with a woman who does not have or carry hemophilia, what is the probability that their daughter will be a carrier of hemophilia?

(A) 0%
(B) 25%
(C) 50%
(D) 75%
(E) 100%

GO ON TO THE NEXT PAGE

Questions 95–97 refer to a dialysis experiment, as discussed below.

Dialysis tubing is a semi-permeable membrane across which water and monosaccharides such as glucose and fructose can cross but across which disaccharides such as sucrose cannot cross.

Experiment 1: A section of dialysis tubing is filled with water and tied at the end to make a bag. The bag is submersed into a beaker containing a solution of 0.4 M fructose.

Experiment 2: A section of dialysis tubing is filled with a 0.5 M solution of sucrose and tied at the end to make a bag. The bag is submersed in beaker of water.

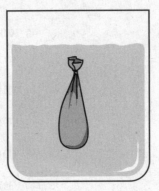

95. In Experiment 1, which molecules will cross the membrane?

   (A) Glucose will diffuse into the bag.
   (B) Fructose will diffuse into the bag.
   (C) Sucrose will diffuse into the bag.
   (D) Complex sugars will diffuse into the bag.
   (E) Disaccharides will diffuse out of the bag.

96. The movement of fructose across the dialysis tubing membrane

   (A) requires energy
   (B) is an example of active transport
   (C) is an example of facilitated diffusion
   (D) requires exocytosis
   (E) is an example of passive diffusion

97. Which of the following is true regarding Experiment 2?

   (A) The bag is hypertonic relative to the water in the beaker.
   (B) The bag is isotonic relative to the water in the beaker.
   (C) The bag will lose fluid.
   (D) Sucrose will diffuse out of the bag.
   (E) The water in the beaker is hypertonic relative to the bag.

GO ON TO THE NEXT PAGE

Questions 98–100 refer to different types of bonds between molecules.

$$H^{\bullet} + Y^{\bullet} = X^{+} \ :Y$$

2

$$H^{\bullet} + Y^{\bullet} = X:Y$$

4

98. Bond 1 is called a(n)

(A) dehydration bond
(B) phosphodiester bond
(C) covalent bond
(D) ionic bond
(E) hydrogen bond

99. Bond 3 is commonly found in

(A) proteins
(B) carbohydrates
(C) nucleotides
(D) water
(E) fats

100. Which of the bonds are ionic?

(A) 1 only
(B) 2 only
(C) 1 and 2 only
(D) 3 only
(E) 4 only

S T O P

IF YOU FINISH BEFORE TIME IS CALLED, YOU MAY CHECK YOUR WORK ON THIS TEST ONLY.
DO NOT TURN TO ANY OTHER TEST IN THIS BOOK.

SAT II Biology Test 5
Explanations

Answers to SAT II Biology Practice Test 5

Question Number	Correct Answer	Right	Wrong	Question Number	Correct Answer	Right	Wrong	Question Number	Correct Answer	Right	Wrong
1.	E			34.	B			67.	D		
2.	C			35.	A			68.	E		
3.	A			36.	E			69.	C		
4.	B			37.	C			70.	D		
5.	C			38.	B			71.	E		
6.	D			39.	B			72.	E		
7.	E			40.	A			73.	D		
8.	D			41.	D			74.	C		
9.	C			42.	A			75.	A		
10.	C			43.	B			76.	A		
11.	B			44.	C			77.	B		
12.	E			45.	D			78.	C		
13.	D			46.	D			79.	E		
14.	B			47.	D			80.	E		
15.	C			48.	C			81.	E		
16.	D			49.	B			82.	E		
17.	E			50.	E			83.	C		
18.	C			51.	B			84.	D		
19.	C			52.	E			85.	D		
20.	B			53.	C			86.	C		
21.	B			54.	E			87.	B		
22.	D			55.	A			88.	B		
23.	A			56.	C			89.	C		
24.	B			57.	D			90.	E		
25.	A			58.	C			91.	C		
26.	B			59.	A			92.	B		
27.	C			60.	D			93.	A		
28.	B			61.	B			94.	E		
29.	E			62.	D			95.	B		
30.	C			63.	C			96.	E		
31.	D			64.	A			97.	A		
32.	B			65.	C			98.	E		
33.	D			66.	D			99.	A		
								100.	B		

Your raw score for the SAT II Biology test is calculated from the number of questions you answer correctly and incorrectly. Once you have determined your composite score, use the conversion table on page **21** of this book to calculate your scaled score. To calculate your raw score, count the number of questions you answered correctly: _____
                                                                          A

Count the number of questions you answered incorrectly, and multiply that number by $\frac{1}{4}$:

$$\underset{B}{\underline{\hspace{2cm}}} \times \frac{1}{4} = \underset{C}{\underline{\hspace{2cm}}}$$

Subtract the value in field C from value in field A: _____
                                                    D

Round the number in field D to the nearest whole number. This is your raw score: _____
                                                                                  E

Biology E/M Classification Questions

1. (E)   The Cell

Active transport is the movement of molecules across a cell membrane from an area of low solute concentration to an area of high solute concentration. Because active transport moves molecules against their concentration gradient, the process requires the input of energy. ATP is the form of energy.

2. (C)   The Cell

Osmosis is the passive diffusion of water across a membrane.

3. (A)   The Cell

Exocytosis is the process by which materials are secreted from a cell. Vesicles containing materials for export fuse with the cell membrane and the contents are released to the outside of the cell.

4. (B)   Organismal Biology

The ovary is a female reproductive part of a plant. It houses the egg-containing ovules. The ovary can develop into fruit, and the fertilized ovules develop into seeds.

5. (C)   Organismal Biology

The stamen is the male reproductive part of the flower, comprised of the anther and the filament.

6. (D)   Organismal Biology

Tubers are fleshy underground storage structures that are enlarged parts of the stem. An example of a tuber is the potato.

7. (E)   Ecology

A niche is the role that a particular species plays in an ecosystem. A niche is often described in terms of how an organism utilizes space, what and how it eats, its optimal temperature, its moisture requirements, its mating habits, and so on. An organism's niche is more than simply the role it plays in the food chain.

8. (D)   Ecology

Commensalism is a type of symbiosis in which one species benefits while the other is neither helped nor harmed. In contrast, parasitism is when one species benefits and the other is harmed. Mutualism is when both species benefit.

9. **(C)**   Ecology

A community is a group of organisms that interact with each other in a given environment and geographic area.

10. **(C)**   Evolution and Diversity

A fossil is a preserved remnant or impression of an organism that lived in the past. The fossil record gives scientists an idea of the types of organisms that have lived on earth and their relative ages.

11. **(B)**   Evolution and Diversity

Vestigial structures are bodily structures that evolved in the past but that no longer serve an apparent function. The human appendix is an example of a vestigial structure.

12. **(E)**   Evolution and Diversity

Certain genes or proteins are so constant in their rate of change that they can be useful in comparing the molecular evolution of different species. These genes and proteins are called molecular clocks.

Biology E/M Solitary Multiple Choice

13. **(D)**   Organismal Biology

Arthropods are unique among animals because they have a hard exoskeleton made of chitin. The exoskeleton provides support and protection for the organism. In order for the organism to grow, the exoskeleton has to be shed and regrown periodically.

14. **(B)**   Ecology

Ecology takes individuals and puts them in increasingly larger contexts. A population is a group of same-species organisms that exist in a specific geographic location and are interbreeding. A community is a group of populations of different species that interact with each other in a given environment and geographical area. An ecosystem is a community of organisms and their abiotic environment. A biome is a group of ecosystems with similar climates and characteristic plant and animal life. The biosphere is the entire portion of the earth that is inhabited by life.

15. **(C)**   Evolution and Diversity

Movement first evolved in phylum Cnidaria, which includes jellyfish, hydras, sea anemones and coral. The only animal phylum more primitive than phylum Cnidaria is phylum Porifera, which includes sponges. Sponges are not capable of movement.

16. **(D)**   Cell Processes

DNA replication occurs during interphase of mitosis. The subsequent phases of mitosis are prophase, metaphase, anaphase, and telophase. During prophase, the nuclear envelope dissolves, and the chromosomes attach to the spindle at their centromeres. During metaphase, the chromosomes are aligned along the middle of the cell. During anaphase, the pairs of chromosomes split and begin to move toward opposite poles of the cell. During telophase, the chromosomes reach opposite poles, the spindle falls apart, and a nuclear envelope forms around each set of chromosomes.

17. **(E)**   The Cell

Animal cells do not perform photosynthesis, so they do not contain chlorophyll. Plant cells do perform photosynthesis and therefore contain chlorophyll.

18. **(C)**   Genetics

The genotype is the genetic composition of an organism. The genotype can be heterozygous or homozygous and determines the phenotype. If the alleles for eye color are B = brown and b = blue, then an individual's genotype for eye color could be BB, Bb, or bb. Their phenotype could either be brown or blue.

19. **(C)**   Organic and Biochemistry

Stomach fluid is acidic, which means it has a high hydrogen ion concentration. The pH scale ranges from 1 to 14, 1 being the most acidic and 14 being the most basic. Solutions that are acidic have a high concentration of hydrogen ions. In fact, pH is defined as the negative log of the hydrogen ion concentration, $pH = -\log(H^+)$.

20. **(B)**   Ecology

Two species can coexist in the same community because they occupy different niches. A niche is the specific role that an organism plays in a community. The more two species' niches differ from each other, the less the species will compete with each other for space, food, and other resources.

21. **(B)**   Evolution and Diversity

Ranked from least to most evolutionarily advanced, the members of kingdom Plantae are: bryophytes, seedless vascular plants, gymnosperms, and angiosperms. Bryophytes have no vascular tissue and must distribute water and nutrients via absorption and diffusion. Seedless vascular plants have xylem and phloem, but, like bryophytes, reproduce using spores. Gymnosperms have vascular tissue and reproduce using seeds. The pollen and seeds of gymnosperms are distributed by wind and water. Angiosperms also have vascular tissue and reproduce using seeds. Instead of depending on wind and water for pollen and seed dispersal, Angiosperms have flowers and fruit to attract animals and provide protection. The flowers and fruit attract animals that help pollinate the plants and spread seeds.

22.   (D)   Organismal Biology

A single strand of DNA contains the nitrogenous bases adenine, cytosine, guanine, and thymine, while a strand of mRNA contains adenine, cytosine, guanine, and uracil. When a strand of DNA pairs with a strand of mRNA, the two strands together must contain adenine, cytosine, guanine, thymine, *and* uracil. Therefore, answer choices (A) and (B) can be eliminated. Of the remaining answers, you may have been tempted to choose (C) because nitrogenous bases pair complementarily. However, this question is a little tricky because while the adenine in DNA pairs with uracil in the mRNA, the adesine in mRNA pairs with thymine in the DNA. Therefore, when mRNA bonds with DNA, there is twice as much adesine as uracil or thymine in the strand. Only answer (D) provides the proper proportions.

23.   (A)   Genetics

Polyploidy occurs during the formation of gametes. In polyploidy, the number of chromosomes is not reduced by half during meiosis, so when the gametes from the parents fuse, the resulting offspring have more chromosomes than the parents. In this case, the parents are 2N, and the offspring are 4N.

24.   (B)   Organismal Biology

Angiosperms are divided into two groups—monocots and dicots. All angiosperms have vascular tissue, xylem and phloem, so that is not a characteristic that could be used to distinguish between monocots and dicots. Monocots and dicots can be distinguished on the basis of the number of cotyledons they have, the venation pattern of their leaves, the arrangement of the vascular bundles in their stems, the types of roots they have, and whether the flower parts are in groups of 3, 4, or 5. Monocots have one cotyledon (seed leaf) during embryonic development, while dicots have two cotyledons. Monocots have leaves with parallel veins, and dicots have leaves with a net-like venation. The vascular bundles of monocots are scattered throughout the stem, while the vascular bundles of dicots are arranged in rings. Monocots tend to have fibrous roots, and dicots can have a long taproot. Monocots have flower parts in multiples of three. Dicots have flower parts in multiples of four or five.

25.   (A)   Cell Processes

During glycolysis, a cell must invest 2 ATP to produce 4 ATP. This results in a net gain of 2 ATP.

26. **(B)**   The Cell

The nucleus contains chromosomes composed of DNA. DNA is the genetic material that directs most of the cell's functions. The nucleolus is a region within the nucleus that helps manufacture ribosomes. Messenger RNA is created in the nucleus, using DNA as a template. Lysosomes are organelles located outside the nucleus. Lysosomes digest the cell's waste.

27. **(C)**   Genetics

The reappearance in the third generation of traits from the first generation that had disappeared in the second generation was the crucial evidence that helped Gregor Mendel surmise the Law of Segregation, which held that each individual held two alleles for each trait, one from each parent.

28. **(B)**   Organismal Biology

The myelin sheath is a fatty layer that surrounds the axons. The myelin sheath insulates the axon and causes the impulse to move faster.

29. **(E)**   Evolution and Diversity

Of the choices given, the only group that lays soft eggs is class Amphibia.

30. **(C)**   Organismal Biology

Thigmotropism is the tendency of parts of the plant to thicken or coil as they touch or are touched by environmental entities. Phototropism is the tendency of a plant to move toward light. Gravitropism is a plant's tendency to grow toward or against gravity. Aquatropism is the tendency of plants to grow toward water. Photoperiodism refers to the time of day during which a plant will flower.

Biology E/M Group Multiple Choice

31. **(D)**   Organismal Biology

This diagram best represents the reproductive and excretory systems.

32. **(B)**   Organismal Biology

The eggs are produced in the ovaries (Structure 2).

33. **(D)**   Organismal Biology

Structure 3 is the uterus. The uterus houses the placenta and the developing fetus. The ovaries produce progesterone. The fallopian tubes connect the uterus with the ovaries. Urine is stored in the bladder. The mammary glands produce milk.

34. **(B)** Organismal Biology

Estrogen is produced in the ovaries.

35. **(A)** Ecology

In Figure 1, the point on the curve at which the population growth levels off is called the carrying capacity. The carrying capacity is the maximum number of individuals within a population that can be sustained in a given environment.

36. **(E)** Ecology

Factors that can limit population growth include shortage of resources, predation, and disease. In the trials in which the species were grown separately and in isolated conditions, there was no occurrence of predation or disease. The population growth was limited because there was a finite amount of food. Because there was only one species being cultured, competition for the food was between individuals of the same species.

37. **(C)** Ecology

When cultured separately, Species A and Species B both have similar growth patterns. When cultured together, the two species compete with one another and have different growth patterns. Species A is the better competitor, and the population of Species A grows to a larger size than does the population of Species B.

38. **(B)** Ecology

The graph in Figure 3 shows that the populations of Species A and B both initially increased, but as the populations both grew, Population A continued to increase and level off, while Population B plummeted before leveling off. This data clearly indicates that Species A has outcompeted Species B and gives no evidence to support the idea that the two species are mutualistic. Since both populations leveled off, though, there is also no reason to believe that Species A will eventually eliminate all of the individuals in Species B. Since Species B thrived in the culture environment when it was alone, it is much more likely that if Species A were to suddenly die off, Species B would begin to thrive rather than decline. Of the answer choices, the only one that the data supports is (B). Because both populations originally grew at fairly normal rates, it is easy to hypothesize that there was little competition between the two populations when resources were relatively abundant. Only as the populations grew in size and had to compete for food did it become clear that Species A was more dominant.

39. **(B)** Genetics

Breed X is white, large, and has low milk production. A white coat color is recessive and would result from a homozygous recessive genotype (bb). Large size is dominant and could result from a homozygous dominant genotype (LL) or a heterozygous genotype (Ll). Low milk production is recessive and would result from a homozygous recessive genotype (mm). The genotype of Breed X could either be bbLLmm or bbLlmm.

40. (A) Genetics

The alleles for coat color exhibit incomplete dominance, which occurs when two alleles of the same gene are both partially expressed in a heterozygote. The resulting phenotype is intermediate between the homozygous phenotypes of the two alleles. The animals that are heterozygous for coat color are not black or white; they are gray.

41. (D) Genetics

A test cross is the means by which you can determine whether an individual with a dominant phenotype has a homozygous dominant (MM) or heterozygous (Mm) genotype. The test cross involves mating the individual with the dominant phenotype to an individual with the recessive phenotype genotype (mm). In order to determine whether Breed Y has a homozygous dominant or a heterozygous genotype for milk production, you would breed the individual with an organism that is known to be homozygous recessive for the trait. Breed X is homozygous recessive (mm) for milk production. If all of the resulting offspring show the dominant trait, you would know that Breed Y is homozygous for the trait. If 50 % of the offspring showed the recessive trait, then you would know that Breed Y is heterozygous for the trait.

	m	m
M	Mm	Mm
M	Mm	Mm

	m	m
M	Mm	Mm
m	Mm	mm

42. (A) Genetics

If you were to cross Breed X (bbLLmm) with Breed Z (BBLLMM), their offspring would all be gray, large, and have high milk production. You can arrive at this answer by doing a Punnett square for each trait. Cross bb with BB. Cross LL with LL. Cross mm with MM.

Cross for Coat Color

	B	b
B	Bb	Bb
B	Bb	Bb

100% Gray

Cross for Size

	L	L
L	LL	LL
L	LL	LL

100% Large

Cross for Milk Production

	m	m
M	Mm	Mm
M	Mm	Mm

100% High Milk Production

43. **(B)** Evolution and Diversity

What occurred over 50 years was stabilizing selection. Stabilizing selection is when selection pressures favor the average form of a trait. The distribution of turtle sizes deviated less from the median in 1990 than it did in 1940.

44. **(C)** Evolution and Diversity

Because large turtles can withstand high winds better than smaller turtles, you would expect an increase in the proportion of large turtles and a decrease in the proportion of small turtles. Directional selection would occur in favor of large individuals and against small individuals.

45. **(D)** Evolution and Diversity

Allopatric speciation occurs when populations of a species are isolated from one another and evolve along different paths until they become so different that they can no longer interbreed and are considered different species. The turtles on the island were separated from the turtles on the mainland, and after many generations of evolution, the two populations could no longer be considered the same species because they could not interbreed.

46. **(D)** Organismal Biology

Photoperiodism is an organism's response to the length of day and night during a 24-hour period. The relative lengths of day and night are often the factors that determine the point at which a plant will flower.

47. **(D)** Organismal Biology

Plant A is a short-day plant because it flowers when the lengths of the days are short (< 12 hours per day).

48. **(C)** Organismal Biology

Part 4 of the experiment shows that Plant A will not flower if there is an interruption in its exposure to darkness, even if the total duration of darkness in a day is 14 hours.

49. **(B)** Organismal Biology or Evolution and Diversity

The plants used in this experiment are flowering plants. Angiosperms are all flowering plants. No other division of plants is capable of producing flowers.

50. **(E)** Evolution and Diversity

The diagram is a phylogenetic tree. A phylogenetic tree is a branching diagram that illustrates the evolutionary relationships between organisms.

51. **(B)**   Evolution and Diversity

In order to answer this question, you must look at the chart to determine the relation between sharks and dolphins, and you also must have a good grasp of the classes *between* Chondricthyes (the sharks' class) and class Mammalia (the dolphins' class). The chart clearly shows that at some point in the very distant past, Chondricthyes and Mammalia shared a common ancestor, so you might think that the dorsal fin of the shark and dolphin are homologous. However, if you look at the classes between Chondricthyes and Mammalia, you will see that the shark dorsal fin has no corollary on many of the intermediate classes, such as Amphibia and Reptilia. Therefore, the dolphin dorsal fin was a much later evolutionary development that is similar to the shark dorsal fin because both perform the same function but arose as a result of separate ancestral lines.

52. **(E)**   Evolution and Diversity

For each pair of choices, look at the distance separating the species on the phylogenetic tree. Classes that are closely related will be located near one another on the phylogenetic tree. Of the choices, classes Reptilia and Aves have the shortest distance between them.

53. **(C)**   Evolution and Diversity

There are three traits coded for in the chromosomes depicted. The traits are flower color, height, and seed type.

54. **(E)**   Genetics

If the gametes fused, the resulting diploid individual would have a white flower, would be tall, and would have wrinkled seeds.

55. **(A)**   Genetics

The offspring resulting from the union of the original gametes have the following genotype: they are homozygous recessive for flower color (white phenotype), homozygous dominant for height (tall), and heterozygous for seed type (so the phenotype manifests the dominant allele: wrinkled). If two of these offspring were to unite during fertilization, *their* offspring would still have to be homozygous recessive for flower color and homozygous dominant for height. In other words, their offspring would have to be 100% white and 100% tall. Choices (D) and (E) can therefore be quickly eliminated. Now all you have to do is make a Punnett square for seed type, the heterozygous trait.

	W	w
W	WW	Ww
w	Ww	ww

The second-generation offspring will be 25% homozygous dominant, 50% heterozygous, and 25% homozygous recessive. In terms of phenotype, this means that 75% of the second-generation offspring will have wrinkled seeds, and 25% will have smooth seeds.

56. (C) Genetics

Meiosis is the process by which gametes form. In meiosis, a cell's genetic material is replicated and divided between two gametes. If the original cell has 2N chromosomes, each gamete will have 1N chromosomes. When the male and female gametes fuse, their resulting offspring will be 2N.

57. (D) Organismal Biology

Most of the water lost by humans is through urination, as shown in the second table.

58. (C) Organismal Biology

Urine is filtered through the kidneys, and the amount of urine excreted depends largely upon the amount of water that is reabsorbed during kidney filtration. Kangaroo rats have very efficient kidneys that reabsorb much of the water that has either been ingested or created during metabolism.

59. (A) Organismal Biology

All of the adaptations listed could be found in animals that are proficient at conserving water. A nocturnal lifestyle keeps the animal out of the heat; exceptionally long loops of Henle in the kidney help with the reabsorption of water; a waxy exoskeleton would limit evaporation; and an amniotic egg decreases water loss as offspring develop. However, the kangaroo rat is a mammal and would not have an exoskeleton or an amniotic egg. Mammals have an internal skeleton and give birth to live young.

60. (D) Organismal Biology or Ecology

Adaptations to conserve water would be most helpful in a hot, dry environment. The desert is a biome with a low mean annual precipitation and a high mean annual temperature.

Biology E Solitary Multiple Choice

61. (B) Evolution and Diversity

The Hardy-Weinberg principle states that, when added together, the frequency of the dominant allele (p) and the frequency of the recessive allele (q) must equal 1, i.e., $p + q = 1$. If $p = 0.6$, then $q = 0.4$.

62. **(D)**   Ecology

The tapeworm receives nutrients at the expense of its host. Of the answer choices, parasitism is the only type of symbiosis in which one species benefits and the other is harmed.

63. **(C)**   Organismal Biology

Imprinting is an instinctual behavior in which social bonds are formed during early development.

64. **(A)**   Evolution and Diversity

Evolution is defined as the change in the gene frequency in a population over time. Individuals and cells do not evolve because their genetic make-up stays constant over their lifetime. Communities can change over time, but the change has nothing to do with genetics. Change in communities over time is called succession. The smallest unit in which evolution can occur is the population.

65. **(C)**   Ecology

The components in the blood that control clotting are called platelets. Red blood cells carry the oxygen- and carbon dioxide-containing hemoglobin around the body. White blood cells are important in defense against pathogens. Plasma is the liquid matrix in which the blood cells are suspended.

66. **(D)**   Evolution and Diversity

Photosynthesis does not release carbon dioxide to the atmosphere. In fact, photosynthesis consumes carbon dioxide from the atmosphere and produces oxygen.

Biology E Group Multiple Choice

67. **(D)**   Evolution and Diversity

Jellyfish (2) and starfish (4) exhibit radial symmetry. An organism with radial symmetry has a circular body plan with similar structures that are arranged like spokes on a wheel. Radial symmetry is present in cnidarians and echinoderms. Sometimes, it is hard to see how a jellyfish has radial symmetry, but if you look at the animal from above rather than from the side, you can see that the shape is regular and can be divided like spokes on a wheel.

68. **(E)**   Evolution and Diversity

Platyhelminthes is the phylum to which Organism 1 belongs. Platyhelminthes are flatworms such as *Planaria*, tapeworms, and flukes.

69. **(C)**   Evolution and Diversity

Members of phylum Mollusca have a foot, radula, and mantle. Phylum Mollusca includes snails, squid, octopuses, clams, and oysters. Organism 3 is a snail.

70. **(D)**   Evolution and Diversity

The starfish (4) is in phylum Echinodermata, which is most closely related to phylum Chordata. Both phyla have deuterostome development.

71. **(E)**   Ecology

To answer this question, you would locate 50 cm on the x-axis (mean annual precipitation) and 10°C on the y-axis (mean annual temperature) and note that these values intersect in the area labeled temperate grassland.

72. **(E)**   Ecology

Prairie dogs, bison, and antelope are animals that would be found in temperate grasslands.

73. **(D)**   Ecology

The biome labeled A has both high temperature and precipitation. Biome A is a tropical rainforest. Biome B has the lowest temperature of all of the biomes. The coldest biome is the tundra.

74. **(C)**   Organismal Biology

In the image of the life cycle of a plant, two gametes fuse to form a zygote. The name of the process in which this occurs is fertilization.

75. **(A)**   Organismal Biology

The spores are haploid, not diploid. The spores are created when the diploid sporophyte undergoes meiosis.

76. **(A)**   Organismal Biology

Alternation of generations is common in plants and is a life cycle in which a multicellular haploid generation alternates with a multicellular diploid generation. The cycle begins when the male and female gametes fuse to form a diploid zygote. The diploid zygote develops into a diploid sporophyte via mitosis. The sporophyte undergoes

meiosis to create haploid spores. The haploid spores develop into the haploid gameto-
phytes via mitosis. The gametes are formed from the gametophyte via mitosis.

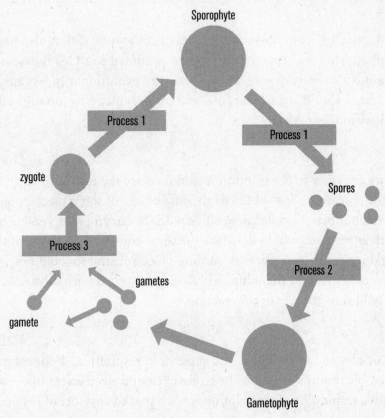

77. (B)   Ecology

Grasses are primary producers. Primary producers are autotrophs that harness the
sun's energy to create carbohydrates. Primary producers are at the bottom of the food
chain and are eaten by primary consumers.

78. (C)   Ecology

The sun is the ultimate source of energy in every food web.

79. (E)   Ecology

Carnivores are animals that eat other animals. In this food web, the foxes and the
mountain lions both get their energy from eating other animals.

80. (E)   Ecology

Food Web E best represents the food web, since only it shows that mountain lions
prey on both foxes and rabbits.

Biology M Solitary Multiple Choice

81. (E)   The Cell

Cell A has organelles, which indicates that it is a eukaryote. Cell A also has a cell wall and chloroplasts, so it is a plant cell rather than an animal cell. Cell B has no organelles and is consequently a prokaryote. Prokaryotes are evolutionarily less advanced than eukaryotes. Since Cell B is a prokaryote, and prokaryotes have no organelles, Cell B would not have mitochondria.

82. (E)   Organic and Biochemistry

Adding more enzymes to the solution would increase the rate of product formation. Lowering the temperature would slow the movement of the molecules and decrease the rate at which substrate molecules collide with the enzymes. Increasing the temperature to such an extreme would denature the three-dimensional shape of the enzyme (protein) and render it less effective. Adding more substrate would not increase the rate of the reaction because the solution is already saturated with substrate. Adding an inhibitor would slow the rate of the reaction.

83. (C)   Cell Processes

Glycolysis occurs in both aerobic and anaerobic respiration. Fermentation occurs only in anaerobic respiration, while the Krebs cycle and electron transport chain occur only in aerobic respiration. Transcription is not a part of any sort of respiration; it is a part of protein synthesis.

84. (D)   Evolution and Diversity

The definition of a species is a group of organisms that can mate and produce viable offspring with each other and no other type organism. Choices (A), (B), (C), and (E) all fail to live up to this definition, since the two individuals are either unable to produce any offspring or produce sterile offspring or offspring that soon die. Choice (D), however, describes a situation in which the two individuals do produce viable offspring. Therefore, scenario (D) would not be considered evidence that the two populations had evolved into different species.

85. (D)   Genetics

When the tall plants were bred and crossbred, the offspring were all tall. The original tall plants must therefore have been homozygous for tallness, as must their offspring. When the short plants were bred and crossbred, the offspring were all short. The original short plants must therefore have been homozygous for shortness, as must their offspring. If a plant that is homozygous for tallness is bred with a plant that is homozygous for shortness, and resulting offspring are all short, the allele for shortness must be dominant, and the allele for tallness must be recessive.

86. **(C)** Genetics

Gene therapy is the procedure of inserting a healthy portion of DNA into a person with a defective gene. The inserted DNA will replace or supplement the defective gene.

Biology M Group Multiple Choice

87. **(B)** Organismal Biology

Structure 1 is a fertilized egg, or zygote. It was formed when the haploid gametes (sperm and egg) fused to form a diploid zygote.

88. **(B)** Organismal Biology

Structure 2 is the morula. Within 24 hours of fertilization, the single-celled zygote begins to divide into more and more cells until a solid ball of cells known as the morula is formed.

89. **(C)** Organismal Biology or Cell Processes

Mitosis is the process by which the single-celled zygote transforms into a multiple-celled embryo. In mitosis, a cell divides into two genetically identical daughter cells.

90. **(E)** Organismal Biology

Structure 5 is a late-stage gastrula. The late-stage gastrula has all three embryonic tissue layers, endoderm, mesoderm, and ectoderm. Structures 3 (blastula) and 4 (early stage gastrula) have only two embryonic tissue layers—ectoderm and endoderm.

91. **(C)** Genetics

The inheritance pattern of this disease is sex-linked recessive. You can determine that the disease is recessive because not all of the individuals who carry the allele for hemophilia will have hemophilia. You can determine that the disease is sex-linked because it does not occur equally in males and females.

92. **(B)** Genetics

The trait of hemophilia is sex-linked recessive. The fact that it is sex-linked tells you that it will be carried on a sex chromosome. This disease is carried on the X-chromosome. Males have only one X-chromosome, so if their X-chromosome has the trait, then they will have the disease. Notice that there are no male carriers of the disease, only males that have the disease. Women have two X-chromosomes, so if their genotype is X'X, they will be carriers of the disease, but they will not be hemophiliacs because the disease is recessive. If a woman's genotype is X'X', she will have hemophilia because she is homozygous recessive for the trait.

93. (A) Genetics

If a father has hemophilia, not all of his children will necessarily be carriers or have the disease. The father's genotype is X'Y. If he has children with a normal woman who has the genotype XX, none of their sons will be carriers or have the disease because they will get a normal X-chromosome from their mother and a normal Y-chromosome from their father. All of the daughters will be carriers of the disease (X'X) because even though they will get a normal X-chromosome from their mother, the X-chromosome that they get from their father will have the trait.

94. (E) Genetics

Individual A is a man with hemophilia, so his genotype is X'Y. The woman with whom he has children is both phenotypically and genotypically normal, so her genotype is XX. If the couple has a daughter, she has a 100% chance of being a carrier of hemophilia but will not manifest the disease. She will get a copy of one of her mother's normal X-chromosomes and a copy of her father's abnormal X-chromosome. This means that her genotype will be X'X.

95. (B) The Cell

Fructose, sucrose, and water are the molecules used in Experiment 1. Sucrose is too large to cross the membrane. Fructose is a simple sugar and can cross the membrane. Because molecules tend to diffuse from an area of high concentration to an area of low concentration, fructose will diffuse into the bag.

96. (E) The Cell

Fructose is a simple sugar and can cross the membrane. It will passively diffuse from an area of low concentration to an area of high concentration. When a molecule moves along its concentration gradient, the transport does not require energy.

97. (A) The Cell

The terms "hypertonic," "hypotonic," and "isotonic" are relative terms. A hypertonic solution has a higher concentration of solutes than the solution to which it is being compared. A hypotonic solution has a lower concentration of solutes than the solution to which it is being compared. Isotonic solutions have equal concentrations of solutes. The bag is hypertonic because it has a higher concentration of solutes than the water in the beaker.

98. **(E)**   Organic and Biochemistry
Bond 1 is a hydrogen bond. Hydrogen bonds are weak bonds between the hydrogen in water and an electronegative element in another molecule (e.g., oxygen in water). Hydrogen bonds are a type of dipole-dipole interaction.

99. **(A)**   Organic and Biochemistry
Bond 3 is a phosphodiester bond that links amino acids together to form a protein.

100. **(B)**   Organic and Biochemistry
Bond 2 is an ionic bond. In ionic bonds, an electron from one molecule is transferred completely to another molecule, and the two bonded atoms are oppositely charged.

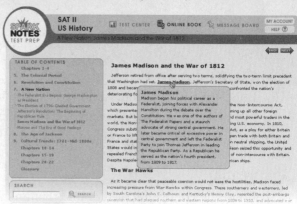
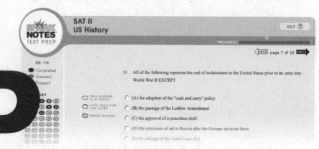

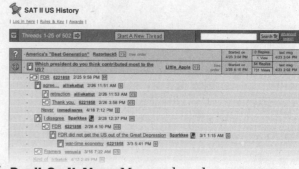